Past P

*A History of Chislehurst
and Sidcup Grammar School*

By
Charles Wells
&
John Hazelgrove

CHISLEHURST AND SIDCUP
GRAMMAR SCHOOL

First edition published 2002
FOR CATHERINE

Second edition published 2011
For Carole and Sam and for Alex, Izzy, Edward, Joe and Aiden

ISBN 978-0-9569063-0-4

Published by
Chislehurst and Sidcup Grammar School
Hurst Road, Sidcup, Kent DA15 9AG

Cover illustration by Quentin Blake

Design and layout Bill McClean

Printed and bound in Great Britain by
Cox & Wyman Limited, Reading, Berkshire

The paper used in this edition is a natural, recyclable product
made from wood grown in sustainable forests. The manufacturing
processes conform to the environmental regulations of the country
of origin

The authors have made every endeavour to ensure the accuracy of the
text herein. Any errors or omissions notified to the above address
will be rectified at the first available opportunity.

Contents

	Acknowledgements First Edition	iv
	Acknowledgements Second Edition	v
1	Foundation	1
2	Doctor Mac	9
3	27 Station Road	21
4	Into the Glasshouse	38
5	War	49
6	Moving On	70
7	Hurst Road: the Pedley Years	93
8	The Embattled Years of Michael Brown	117
9	The Arrival of the Girls	146
10	Sennett Centre Stage	159
11	All Change	183
12	Rouncefield and Renewal	217
13	The Interregnum	242
14	The Second Doctor	252
15	Walker Steps In	267
	Index of Names	277

Acknowledgements First Edition

IN WRITING THIS HISTORY I am indebted to many people who have helped me in a wide variety of ways. I owe a particular debt of gratitude to Brian Burgess, Bill Bray and Joyce Crust, who have been generous with their time and expertise. Roger McGregor Williams and his sister, Norah Sedgwick, gave me much valuable information about their father. Important archive material and wise advice were provided by, among others, Michael Brown, John Sennett, Bob Buxton, Derrick Aughterlony, Brian Coulson and Don Murray. I was favoured with interviews by – in addition to those already mentioned – Quentin Blake, Will Hutton, Enid Palmer, Jack Watkins, Douglas Flindall, Alastair Wilson, Martyn Berry, Pauline Matkins, Kate Trodd, Sheila Ford, Graham Lightwood and Steve Gooden. A number of the above read and commented upon sections of the text as a result of which many errors were put right. I entered into a great deal of correspondence and three people in particular – Michael Carreck, Roger Dracup and Edgar Martin – cast illumination upon a number of murky corners. Jenny Breen gave me a pleasant and informative conducted tour of 27 Station Road.

I am extremely grateful to the ever helpful staffs of the Imperial War Museum, the Kent County Archive in Maidstone and the Bexley Local History Archive in the Central Reference Library at Bexleyheath, to which I made frequent recourse. I would also like to thank Brenda Allen for her inexhaustible patience and for the ready help she provided as far as the School's own extensive archive was concerned.

On the technical side I am grateful for advice and assistance from Richard Wells, from Howard Carter and others at the printers, Cox and Wyman / Mackays, and, especially, from graphic designer Roger Walker whose input has been extensive. I am very much indebted to Phil Paddock for his generous help with photography.

My wife, Mary, was a tower of strength throughout the two year writing process and her critical input has been invaluable at every stage.

Lastly, I would like to thank, most sincerely, Jim Rouncefield without whose enthusiastic support and encouragement this project would never have seen the light of day.

Charles Wells
August 2002

Acknowledgements Second Edition

LIKE THE AUTHOR OF THE FIRST EDITION, I wish to acknowledge my debt to a number of people without whose help the writing of the Second Edition would have been almost impossible. Charles Wells was the most important of this splendid group. Charles guided me with understanding, expertise, gentle humour and acute intelligence throughout the whole process. The support and quiet professionalism of Bill McClean, who happily took on the responsibility for photography, graphic design and format, has been invaluable. I am also grateful for the informed advice readily given by Howard Carter of Cox and Wyman. I also wish to thank Nigel Walker who was very keen to promote a second edition of this history and made time and facilities available to me and approved my editorial and authorial decisions.

I am extremely grateful to Quentin Blake. Quentin, an old boy of the school, made time to discuss the design of the cover with Charles Wells and myself. Even though he is one of the country's most prestigious, talented and busy illustrators, he was very keen to support his school by producing a quite wonderful picture for this second edition.

A particular debt of gratitude is owed to all those who willingly gave up their time to be interviewed. Richard Wallbridge, Mike Rushton, Cecilia Connor, Brian Simber, Joanne King, Jim Rouncefield, Parm Thind, Graham Lightwood and Dr. Vitagliano were all extremely helpful in this regard. Nicola Sayell in the School Office has been particularly supportive and, although she is extremely busy with her secretarial duties, Nicola has always made time to give me administrative assistance. I would like to extend this thanks to Lisa Dytch and Karen Maynard who treated my random visits and urgent requests with very good humour.

The onerous and often thankless task of proof reading has fallen to Jean Hitchcock, Charles Wells, Samuel Hazelgrove and Carole Hazelgrove. All have given their time with grace and, unlike the author, have kept to deadlines most religiously.

Not only has my wife, Carole, helped edit this history, she has supported me from start to finish and has been the person I have turned to whenever calm judgement has been required.

John Hazelgrove
June 2011

The first School building, 1931.

CHAPTER ONE

Foundation

"ENJOY LIFE AT ITS best in the garden town of the Garden of England. When you ask anybody if they have been there and the answer is in the affirmative the person answering will always add: "and it's a very pretty place." There is no place so near London with which it can be compared. Its splendid rural surroundings and its stately streets make it a place to be reckoned with. The inhabitants quietly follow their callings, undismayed by the quarrellings of the perturbed world."

Those not recognising this idyllic spot may be surprised to learn that the subject of the extravagant eulogy is Sidcup, Kent, as described in a prospectus published by New Ideal Homesteads Ltd and issued to sell "The 1931 Super Home".

As late as the nineteen twenties Sidcup had been not so much a village as some 3,000 acres of agricultural land but the coming of the Southern Railway's new electric trains in 1926 brought young married couples to the area in their thousands and rapidly turned it into the quintessential dormitory suburb.

The earliest known reference to Sidcup is to be found in a document of 1254 in the reign of Henry III. The word "sikecoppe", as it was originally spelt, is believed to signify a sheep-fold on a "copp" or hill-top. When Henry VI was crowned in 1429 the estate was owned by Thomas Sidcopp, from which variant form it is a minor leap to its modern spelling. For centuries Sidcup was little more than a hamlet on the London-Maidstone road, consisting of an inn, a forge and a few scattered houses and cottages within the parish boundaries of Foots Cray to the north and Chislehurst to the south.

Sidcup Station, on the South Eastern Railway's new Dartford Loop Line, opened in 1866 and the surrounding area started to attract professional people anxious to move out of previously fashionable inner suburbs such as Camberwell and New Cross which had begun to decline socially. Those unable to afford to join the gentry in Chislehurst built sizeable houses on the cheaper land further north and commuted (as we would now say) to the City and the West End. Nevertheless the area remained predominantly rural until electrification of the line greatly improved the reliability and frequency of trains up to town.

Now the speculative builders arrived in strength, buying up great swathes of farm land at rock bottom prices as a result of the slump in agriculture following the First World War. The expanding middle class poured into the new housing estates and by the end of the twenties Sidcup was well on the way to becoming the south eastern mirror image, so to speak, of "Betjemanland" on the Metropolitan Line to London's north west. Now, in truth, an outer suburb in all but name, its population approached 12,000 by 1930 and was set to treble over the next two decades.

New, mass-production building techniques were used, some of them involving prefabricated manufacturing methods. Bricks were imported cheaply from Belgium and ready-made window frames brought in from as far afield as Czechoslovakia, being shipped along the Thames and offloaded at Erith. The economic slump made piece-rate labour cheap and readily available. It is said that a house could be completed within a fortnight of digging the foundations. A two-bedroom semi was yours for £695 freehold on the upmarket Marlborough Park Estate while, down the road at Penhill Park, a three bedroom terrace property might set you back a mere £395. Such prices, coupled with the advantageous mortgage deals offered by the building firms themselves, certainly placed the latter, at least, within reach of young married couples whose parents would never have dreamed of house ownership.

Not surprisingly the strain upon local schooling soon became intolerable, a problem compounded by the government's recently stated intention of raising the leaving age as a way of lowering the unemployment figures. The Lamorbey district of Sidcup was expanding with particular rapidity and it soon became clear that a secondary school for boys would be needed in this area. Currently the area was being served by schools as far away as Dartford and Erith.

After persistent prompting by both the Bexley and the Sidcup Urban District Councils – and, later, by the Bromley Rural and Chislehurst District Education Committee under the chairmanship of Colonel

Francis Edlmann – the attention of Maidstone was eventually drawn to the urgency of the situation. The fact that, as was pointed out, potential sites for a new school were being bought up for more housing developments and would soon be unavailable if further delay took place concentrated minds at County Hall.

Accordingly, on the 8th of April 1930, the Secondary and University Education Sub-Committee of the Kent County Council recorded in its minutes that arrangements had been provisionally made "to take possession of a fifteen acre site in Watery Lane" for a new secondary school for boys. In the meantime, the proposal went, the school, to be known as the Sidcup County School for Boys, would be opened in the buildings of the County School for Girls, which had opened in 1925 and was shortly to be moving to its newly completed buildings in Beaverwood Road. The Watery Lane site would be available as playing fields during the building process. Since the Beaverwood site was expected to be ready for occupation at the start of the Autumn Term, 1931, it was proposed that the Boys' School should open at the same time in the vacated premises at 27 Station Road.

These proposals were formally ratified by the full Kent County Council meeting on Monday April 28th 1930 at the Sessions House in Maidstone. At the foot of the minutes for this meeting, now stored deep in the County Archives, can be seen, in bright blue ink, the signature of the Chairman, Sir Mark Collet. With that flamboyant stroke of the pen the new School was born.

It was the month in which Amy Johnson completed her famous solo flight from England to Australia and, more ominously, the month in which the number of unemployed reached the staggering total of two million. The Great Depression was deepening and even "the garden town of the garden of England" would not be immune from its contagion.

Sir Mark's blue ink was scarcely dry on the page before work began to alter the red-brick, virginia creeper-covered building with its Ionic columns and elegant green cupola on the corner of Station and Victoria Roads, about 750 yards from Sidcup Station and its gleaming new electric line. Built around 1900, it had begun life as the Sidcup High School for Girls and Kindergarten Ltd., run by the three Misses Chadbourne.

The girls of the County School still being in occupation did not prevent workmen from moving onto the site. Additional office space was installed and, mysteriously, it was deemed necessary to make improvements to the cloakroom ventilation, according to the meticulous minutes that have preserved such trifles for posterity. Perhaps it was felt that boys were the smellier sex! S.W.Gibson and Co. supplied a superior heating system at a cost of £2,635 7s 6d and improved boundary fencing and gates were erected by W.H.Allen and Co. at a cost of £276 11s 4d. Surely a mass escape attempt was not anticipated?

While this work was underway in Station Road things were moving apace at Watery Lane, Crittall's Corner. Agreement was reached with the tenant, Mr Vinson, who accepted the sum of £35 in full settlement of his claim regarding the destruction of his crops. He was allowed to continue farming there on a pro tem basis, for an annual rent of £45 per acre. The cost of "conditioning the site", as the Kent Finance and General Purposes Committee rather quaintly put it in its minutes of 21st July 1930, was pre-

Francis Edlmann, first
Chairman of Governors
(1931–1950).

dicted to be £624, while further alterations at the Girls' School were costed at a slightly lower figure.

That same month the Secondary Education Sub-Committee decided to appoint the new headmaster by the following Easter and that a staff of four or five assistant masters should be engaged to take up their duties when the School opened for the Autumn Term,1931.

The Kentish Times noted that this would be the first boys' secondary school in the Sidcup area and declared that it was long overdue if the district were to compete with similar localities elsewhere in the county. Much of the credit, the article continued, was due to the hard work of Colonel Edlmann, chairman of the district education committee, and to Mr Thomas Beeton its secretary. Both men had "done much to oil the bearings and ensure success in the development of these school services." Appropriately, Colonel Edlmann was chosen to be the first Chairman of Governors of the new school.

Advertisements were placed and, in the Spring of 1931, it was announced that the first headmaster of the County Secondary School for

Boys, Sidcup, would be Dr. C.R. McGregor Williams, M.A., Docteur de l'Université de Paris and formerly headmaster of Uckfield Grammar School in Sussex. Even bearing in mind the bleak economic climate of the day and the mass unemployment this entailed, it comes as a shock to discover that there were in excess of four hundred applications for each of the four assistant master posts. Not surprisingly the successful candidates were all men of very high calibre, as the succeeding years would show.

Mr A.E.Parsons, B.Sc. (London) was appointed to be Senior Assistant Master on a starting salary of £416 per annum. His colleagues were Mr J.R.Banfield, B.Sc. (Manchester), Mr E.T.Palmer B.A. (Cambridge) and Mr G.W.Cook B.A. (London) all three of whom were paid, at the outset, a salary of £249 per annum or a little less than £5 per week before stoppages.

The new establishment, the public learnt, would "adhere to the usual secondary school subjects" and was "designed to provide a sound education on modern lines, calculated to fit boys for either industrial or professional occupations."

All that remained was to recruit the boys themselves. The number was set at 62 of whom 52 would be fee-paying. Eight were to have free-place scholarships and the remaining two would be "junior exhibitioners". The fees were set at £4 per term for those resident in the counties of Kent or London, a sum which represented approximately one third of the average cost of educating a secondary pupil. "Outsiders" were charged £10 per term. Announcements appeared in the local press and applications flooded in.

Pride of place must go to Michael Carreck whose father put his name down for admission within minutes of the notice appearing. Now in his eighties and living in Portugal, Mr Carreck still has memories of his interview. He recalls gazing through the Head's window at a donkey clip-clopping up the still rustic Station Road pulling a rag-and-bone man's cart. "How do you spell 'cauliflower'?" Despite giving a wrong answer, the nervous young Carreck was accepted and became, therefore, in a manner of speaking, "pupil number one" at the new school, a distinction of which he is still very proud. A decade or so later he was to win the far greater distinction of a D.F.C. for his service in Bomber Command.

Hot on his heels came Peter Ost whose father bumped into Carreck senior on his way out of the education office in Hatherley Road. Sixty more

Part of the first School photograph, 1932. (Staff, L to R : E.T.Palmer,
A.E.Parsons, C.R.McGregor Williams, J.R.Banfield, G.W.Cook. To R. of
Mr Cook are N. Barber and A.Murray. To L. of Mr Palmer are P. Ost
and J.Whitbread).

names were added to the list. Leonard Cade, Henry Cruttenden, Peter
Hall, Geoffrey Martin, Robert Palmer, Arthur Stanyon, John Whitbread
and Francis Whitehorn won free-place scholarships and the first two
junior exhibitioners were Cyril Owen and Kenneth Stuart. Exactly half of
the pioneering 62 lived in Sidcup itself, the remainder coming in from
such districts as Chislehurst, Petts Wood, Orpington, Foots Cray and New
Eltham. For reasons that remain unclear, one enterprising young student
travelled in all the way from Buxted in Sussex.

At nine in the morning on Thursday September 17th 1931 the big
brass bell clanged and the sixty-two, resplendent in their grey uniforms
with purple trim, were shepherded into the small assembly-hall-cum-gym
by Mr Parsons and surveyed by the watchful eyes of Messrs Banfield,
Palmer and Cook.

Onto the stage strode the short, stocky but commanding figure of the
Headmaster in a black gown with the red, white and blue, fur-trimmed,
stole of his Paris doctorate flung back over his left shoulder. He broke the

tense silence by introducing himself as Dr McGregor Williams and telling the assembled boys in no uncertain terms that they were there to work hard and to play hard, that being, he claimed, a rough translation of the new school motto he had chosen: "Abeunt Studia in Mores". "Your holidays ended last night", he continued. "If you do not wish to work hard, I suggest, gentlemen, that you take a walk on the King's highway."

This beguiling alternative was, needless to say, declined and the very new boys trooped off to their respective classrooms. The youngest group, ranging from eight to ten, were designated Form I and the remainder, the eleven to fourteen year-olds, were split into forms IIA, IIB and IIC.

Soon lessons were underway. English and French were in the hands of Mr Cook and Maths was the province of Mr Banfield. Mr Palmer taught Geography and History while Mr Parsons dealt with all the sciences, banished, as he was, to a hutted and oddly-shaped laboratory some distance from the main building. The Doctor taught about half the 36 timetabled periods, mostly French but with a little English and Latin as well.

At the dedication service held eight days later, on Friday September 25th and attended by the boys, parents, local dignitaries and officials from the Education Department in Maidstone, proceedings opened with the hymn: "The Church's One Foundation" and a reading by the Headmaster from Philippians IV. Canon Basil Spurgin, the Vicar of Sidcup, then gave the address. He welcomed Dr McGregor Williams and his staff, saying that a great deal of time and trouble had been spent by the authorities in their eagerness to choose the best men. He expressed his confidence that subsequent events would vindicate their decisions and urged the boys to develop what he called: "a really strong brotherhood" so that the School would be a credit to the Sidcup district. Canon Spurgin concluded with prayers that the School might know the glory of God's service and that they might labour without asking for reward save that of knowing that they did His will. No doubt the five members of staff on the platform nodded their approval but a week later the irony of the Canon's behest became apparent. Ramsey McDonald's "National" government announced that, in view of the financial crisis, the "Geddes Axe" would be wielded and all teachers throughout the country would take an immediate pay cut of 10%.

Into these turbulent waters thus was the School launched.

C.R.McGregor Williams by Jeff Hoare, R.A.

CHAPTER TWO

Doctor Mac

CHARLES REGINALD McGREGOR WILLIAMS was born in Newport, Monmouthshire, in September 1889, the son of a Glamorgan tailor. He attended Newport High School where he won a scholarship to Cardiff College, University of Wales, graduating in 1910 with an honours degree in modern languages. His love of France and all things French derived from a series of boyhood holidays on the Brittany coast. Having travelled there from South Wales by coal barge he used to stay with a French family, thus becoming fluent in the language at an early age.

There are relatively few Welsh surnames and confusion is inevitable, as when another C.R.Williams walked off with a school prize that should rightfully have gone to Charles. With the aim of avoiding a lifetime of such annoyances, he adopted his grandmother's maiden name, McGregor, as a distinguishing mark, though he never hyphenated it to form a "double barrel" as many do.

McGregor Williams was the cousin of J.H.Thomas the Labour politician who, having served the Party with great commitment for many years, becoming Colonial Secretary, resigned in disgrace from Baldwin's "National" cabinet in 1936 after being found guilty of disclosing budget proposals to a wealthy businessman at the Savoy Hotel.

He began his teaching career at Cleobury Mortimer College in Shropshire. Despite being a tailor's son he was rebuked by his first headmaster for dressing scruffily. "Only dukes and dustmen are allowed to dress like that." Even in his later years, as a headmaster himself, he was described as a "walking ragbag". Although he bought a new suit every year, he had a mysterious knack of transforming it, within days, to the rumpled condition of its predecessor.

After two years in Shropshire, McGregor Williams spent a short period teaching in Liverpool before taking the post of Senior Modern Languages Master at Lincoln School in 1914. Within a few months he was commissioned into the Royal Horse Artillery and served in France as a liaison officer with the French Army, his linguistic skills being put to good use and further honed. So fluent was he by now in the language that he even deputised as Mayor of St Gratien when the shell battered town found itself temporarily without a suitable civic leader. His role soon expanded into the field of military intelligence.

Twice wounded on the Somme, Williams was severely gassed in 1916 and invalided back to England where he spent time convalescing in a military hospital at Queen Victoria's Osborne House on the Isle of Wight. In 1917, back in his native Newport, he married Susan James.The Welsh town had lost far more than its proportionate share of young men on the Western front and, distressed by this appalling carnage, Miss James felt it inappropriate to wear white for her wedding, opting instead for a sombre shade of violet-purple, traditionally associated with war wounds (as in the American "Purple Heart" medal) and with liturgical mourning. This unusual decision is said to lie behind her husband's choice of purple as the School colour some fourteen years later. Fortunately such solemn thoughts seem not to have spoilt the day itself, since the new Mrs McGregor Williams, we are told, embarking on her honeymoon, lost her knickers out of the lavatory window aboard the train as she attempted to shake them free of the accumulated confetti.

At the end of the War, McGregor Williams worked as chief assistant to Dr James Garnett on the London District University Committee, which gave him valuable experience in educational administration.

As a teacher at heart, he soon found himself missing the classroom contact with pupils which was his first love and so, in 1921, he obtained a post at what later became Varndean School in Brighton. While there he obtained his M.A. from the University of Wales with a thesis on Molière's religious philosophy and began work on his doctorate during the holidays. His research was on the poet and editor John Payne (1842–1916), a Francophile like himself and perhaps best known for his translations of Villon. In 1926 Williams became "Docteur de l'Université de Paris", a distinction rarely granted to a "foreigner". Thus armed, he was in a position to compete on level terms with "Oxbridge" men and, in 1927, he was appointed headmaster of Uckfield Grammar School in Sussex.

Unfortunately this post proved short-lived since, despite outstanding academic success, the school was closed three years later for purely administrative reasons, being amalgamated with a newly-built school in Lewes. The Doctor now found himself unemployed. Anxious to return to Wales, he applied for the headship of a school in Haverfordwest. He was offered the post but at a slightly lower salary than the official Burnham rate which, at that time, was not mandatory in Welsh as it was in English schools. On a point of principle, for which he was greatly admired in the profession, McGregor Williams turned down the appointment and Pembrokeshire's loss eventually became Kent's gain. Impressed by such a courageous moral stance, the Headmaster's Conference raised, by voluntary subscription, sufficient money to keep him going for some eighteen months until, against intense competition, he obtained the post of founding headmaster of the new school at Sidcup.

Few people become legends in their own lifetime but C.R.McGregor Williams, over the twenty-three years of his headship, can surely lay claim to that distinction. In the half century or so since his death his reputation may be said to have expanded into the realms of the epic, perhaps even the mythical, at least as far as Sidcup is concerned.

McGregor Williams was a larger than life character in every sense other than the purely physical one. He was of short, stocky build but powerful, even bull-like in his younger days. As a boy his flaming red hair had earned him the nickname "Copper-knob" but, by his early forties, when he began in Station Road, photographs show him bald, with a small "toothbrush" moustache. Despite his lack of vertical inches the new headmaster undoubtedly possessed a commanding presence, a fact attested to by all who crossed his path.Though essentially a kindly man, McGregor Williams was not to be trifled with. His belligerence, on occasion, could be alarming. If he witnessed queue-jumping in a public place, for instance, the Doctor was quite likely to seize the culprit by the lapels and thump him before forcibly depositing him back at the end of the line. At school he had been a formidable boxer and he retained his enthusiasm for the sport throughout his life, in later years as a recognised referee. His son, Roger, recalls one famous occasion when his father took him to see building work in progress at the Crittall's Corner site. His entry was unwisely barred by a large Irish foreman who refused to let him pass, headmaster or not. McGregor Williams' uncomplicated response was to fell him with a blow to the jaw while his horrified son looked on. Kneeling on the prostrate figure the Head threatened to "punch him into the ground". Fortunately the Irishman, upon brief reflection, had a change of heart and this alarming follow-up proved unnecessary.

Boxing was by no means the only sport at which Charles excelled. He was a powerful swimmer and especially interested in life-saving techniques, perfecting a particular grip which was officially adopted by the Royal Navy in its Admiralty Fleet Orders of 1941. A film demonstrating this method, featuring P.E. teacher Milton Williams "saving" young Roger, is lodged in the National Maritime Museum at Greenwich. Lacrosse was another of the Doctor's passions. He introduced the game to the School and, in due course, became vice-president of the S.E.England Lacrosse Association. A keen soccer and rugby player at school and college, "Mac", as he was generally known, also enjoyed water-polo and tennis, besides turning out regularly for the Staff against the Boys during the annual Cricket Week which he instituted. Such was the Doctor's sporting versatility that, according to one entertaining but probably apocryphal story, he competed in a sack-race between a team from the University of Wales and the Japanese Universities Olympic Team. Williams knocked himself out hurling himself headfirst over the finishing line, thereby bringing about, in their final contest, the visitors' only defeat of their U.K. tour (improbable though all this may sound). This technique – the term "kamikaze" seems appropriate in the context – tells us, some might say, a great deal about the man.

The creating of "instant tradition", of course, is an essential task in the founding of any institution. Never short of energy and enthusiasm, as has already been amply demonstrated, Dr Williams himself wrote the words of the School Song (not, perhaps, the very pinnacle of his many achievements) and introduced a house system, though the original four names: "A", "B", "C", and "D", may have left something to be desired, later being changed to honour early benefactors such as Colonel Edlmann.

Drama was probably the Doctor's greatest love. The current *Sedcopian* editor, William Bray, refers to him as "an actor manqué" both on and off the stage. He was famous for his flamboyant entrances into morning assembly, sweeping magisterially through the silent ranks of boys, gown flapping out behind him. On special occasions, such as the last day of term, it would be his Sorbonne doctorate robes rather than the plainer stuff of Cardiff College. Often the tense wait for proceedings to begin was prolonged by his late appearance. Despite the fact that he lived a mere ten

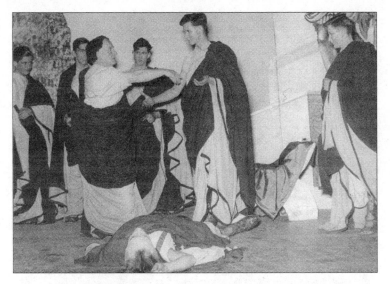

Julius Caesar, 1949, with C.R.McGregor Williams (L.foreground)
as Mark Antony.

minutes' walk away, boys and masters with a view through particular Hall
windows were used to seeing him enter by a side gate and hurry across the
playing fields towards the (Crittall's Corner) school building. Punctuality,
it seems, was not among the Doctor's leading virtues. Mac made up for his
late arrivals, however, by ensuring that assemblies frequently lasted over
half an hour as he indulged himself in one of his famous perorations. First
lesson, in consequence, often existed in little more than name, no doubt
much to the relief of both teacher and taught, upon occasion.

Quentin Blake, the celebrated artist and illustrator, looks back at
McGregor Williams as, in his own words, "a slightly grotesque figure" who
liked to take a leading role in the annual Shakespeare play which he usually
directed into the bargain. As Sir Toby Belch in *Twelfth Night* he was to
the manner born but, middle-aged, stout and bald, he made a less than
wholly convincing Mark Antony, especially in an implausible ginger wig.
Blake could not resist surreptitiously sketching some of his now famous
caricatures. Ever well informed, the Doctor learnt of their existence and,
sending for the perpetrator, demanded to see them. Quentin nervously
selected three of the least incriminating. The Headmaster surveyed them
in silence while the artist sweated. After what seemed a very long time he

remarked: "Yes, you've caught something of the energy of the man."

Williams' acting was in the grand manner in direct line, as William Bray puts it, from Garrick, Irving and Beerbohm-Tree. He was, nevertheless, by all accounts, a remarkable Shylock and many recall to this day his exit at the end of the Trial Scene. The knife dropped from his nerveless fingers and stuck, quivering, in the wooden floorboards of the stage as the humiliated Jew slunk out.

Though not devoid of pomposity at times, an undoubted showman always and with occasional touches of the poseur, Mac won the heartfelt affection and respect of virtually all who knew him, staff and boys alike. Many and warm were the tributes paid on his retirement and in the obituaries that, sadly, followed just a few months later.

He was a shrewd judge of men as well as of boys, much of the School's early success undoubtedly stemming from his wise choice of staff out of the huge numbers that applied in that time of horrendous unemployment. One appointment is of particular note. A.E. ("Joe") Parsons had been the headmaster of his previous school in Tetbury, Gloucestershire, and obliged to leave it in unfortunate circumstances involving a fifteen year old girl, or so the story goes. Urged on by his ambitious (and no doubt furious) wife, Constance, Parsons was understandably desperate to take the Senior Master post on offer. His career was under a cloud and such a move would, after all, take him just one rung back down the ladder, a better outcome than might have been expected, given what had happened. Such was the pressure upon him at his interview that he broke down in tears and threw himself, in effect, upon the Doctor's mercy. McGregor Williams is reported to have been touched and to have felt for him in his plight. Wisely or not – opinions differ – he gave him the chance to rebuild his career. In so doing he showed great humanity, letting his heart rule his head as he often seems to have done. Several suspected, however, that an additional motive may have lurked somewhere in the recesses of his mind. It can be useful, in dealing with one's second in command, to know where the body is buried, so to speak. Certainly one of Mac's colleagues maintains, to this day, that the Head "had a pull" (as he rather quaintly expresses it) over his faithful deputy and that this factor was well known in the Common-room.

Some of Dr Williams' prodigious energy was spent in the organisation and leading of holiday trips abroad to such countries as Switzerland, France and Germany. One visit to the Rhineland, in 1937, gave rise to what is, arguably, the most bizarre occurrence in the entire history of the

School. The hostels into which the party had booked were, it turned out, run, to all intents and purposes, by the Hitler Youth Movement. In order that they might take full advantage of all the facilities on offer, including free admissions, cheap travel, subsidised meals and the like, the Sidcup pupils were given "official" swastika armbands which they cheerfully wore throughout the duration of their stay in Germany. The true nature of Nazism was not, of course, widely appreciated at that time and it should be quickly pointed out that the Doctor was soon to look back upon this episode with horror, especially after he had spoken, secretly, to some German Jews and been told what was really going on in the Third Reich. He later took several Jewish refugee boys into the School and, during the War, gave a job to a Viennese-Jewish medical student called Erich Geiringer who taught Biology from 1941 to 1943.

In the immediate aftermath of war the Summer visits were not abroad, understandably, but to harvest camps in Somerset and elsewhere, boys and masters alike engaging in the back-breaking activities of pulling flax and lifting potatoes to aid Britain's economic recovery.

In the early days of World War Two McGregor Williams joined the Home Guard and was soon in charge of the Chislehurst platoon. His son Roger, now in his seventies and living in Sussex, describes his father as a "Captain Mainwaring look-alike" and there certainly are touches of *Dad's Army* about some of their escapades.

The platoon was in the habit of repairing, after evening drill sessions, to the Tiger's Head, where refreshment was provided by the buxom Mrs King. Timing their departure carefully, the men would then stagger out into the night and make their way home across Chislehurst Common, stopping off in Camden Close where, at that precise hour, two well known local characters, the Tiarks sisters, could be relied upon to be undressing for bed. Apparently, oblivious of both blackout regulations and the possibility of an admiring audience, they never drew the curtains and hence provided an enthralling and completely free Windmill Theatre-style spectacular for the appreciative group of military gentlemen assembled in the darkness below. In due course the ladies concerned were to become great friends of the McGregor Williams family (besides, incidentally, becoming aunts to the current Duchess of Bedford) though whether Mac ever informed them of his covert nocturnal visits history does not record.

The Doctor was, undoubtedly, far from immune to the charms of the fairer sex. On one occasion, some years later, a young science master (whom we will call Mr Smith) had cause to slip out of his laboratory during a lesson in order to fetch something from the Staff Common-room. Next to the Headmaster's study, at that time, was a cubby-hole in which tea was made. As he hurried past "Mr Smith" happened to glance in and could not fail but notice Mac in there with his arms around the young woman from the kitchen whose official duty was limited to the provision of more traditional forms of refreshment. The young teacher in question, deeply shocked, made his way quickly back to his class and, at the end of the lesson, received an urgent summons to the Headmaster's room. Would he, he wondered, as he made his way along the corridor, be sworn to secrecy? Not a bit of it. "Mr Smith," said the Doctor, curtly. "Don't ever let me catch you out of your lesson again!"

Quitting the Home Guard after a row with the district commander, McGregor Williams threw his energies, instead, into the founding and running of an Air Training Corps at the School. In due course he rose to the rank of Squadron Leader and oversaw the building of a working glider, a remarkable achievement of which fuller details will appear in a later chapter. Desperate for further involvement in the war effort, the story goes that he prevailed upon an old friend, who had become Commanding Officer of R.A.F. Tangmere, to let him help out on occasion, when they were short of manpower, as a stand-in rear gunner on operations over occupied France. His wife knew nothing of these activities, according to daughter Norah, and would doubtless have been appalled had she heard of them. As it so happened, and surely much to his regret, the pugnacious emergency gunner never had the opportunity to fire his weapon in anger.

Another war-time anecdote is worth inclusion here, shedding, as it does, a little more (dimmish) light on the rum character of our subject. Bill Freeman, the young biology master, then a sergeant, encountered Mac, muffled in a long, military-style greatcoat, on Waterloo Station one evening. "Why no salute, Mr Freeman?" The young teacher confessed to being unaware that a salute was required. "Intelligence," muttered the Headmaster, enigmatically, and pointed to a small, indecipherable mark on his left shoulder. "Full colonel!" No explanation for this intriguing encounter has, to date, been forthcoming.

According to son Roger and daughter Norah, Mac was rather in awe of his wife Susan, or "Floss" as he affectionately called her. On one famous occasion he was waiting on Sidcup Station with a group of boys at the start of a holiday visit. Just before the arrival of their train, Mrs McGregor

Williams, like her husband small but forceful, came hurrying along the platform and, in front of numerous fascinated witnesses, handed an envelope to an accompanying master, physics teacher Cedric Morley. "His pocket money's in there", she told him in her pronounced Welsh accent. "He can't be trusted with it all at once. Don't let him have more than a pound a day."

Though occasionally turbulent, the marriage was a strong one and Mrs Williams very much the anchor to her husband's successful career. She regarded the boys as her extended family and came to be, in effect, the "mother" of the School community.

In his later years the Headmaster took up golf. A cherished anecdote has him playing a round with Cedric Morley and George Goddard, by then both senior members of the Common-room. Mac, of course, teed off first but sliced his drive badly into a thick clump of trees. Morley and Goddard, however, both drove down the centre of the fairway. As they moved on they were aware of crashing noises and expletives coming from the undergrowth to their right. Eventually Mac caught up with them on the green where, mysteriously, there were now three balls close to the hole. "How many are you, Morley?"

"Four, so far, Doctor."

"What about you, Goddard?"

"I'm four as well, Headmaster."

There was a slight pause and then Mac announced: "I'm three."

McGregor Williams was a complex man. He was famous for his kindness and consideration to his pupils, habitually stuffing his untidy pockets with sweets, biscuits and even school meal vouchers which he would cheerfully distribute to the deserving and undeserving alike. Yet he was very strict, a martinet even, as Dr Richardson, one of his original Station Road pupils, still recalls. Beatings were often administered with a sawn-off cricket bat which, over the years, acquired almost legendary status. It is still in the Williams family to this day, currently residing in the possession of his grandson (and namesake) Charles.

"Tough but fair" is a recurrent phrase one hears when former pupils look back across half a century or more. Those guilty of serious offences such as stealing were offered a choice between expulsion and a public thrashing. The latter, which was invariably chosen, would be administered on the stage in front of the assembled School in a manner reminiscent, almost, of Nelson's Navy. Bare-bottomed, the culprits might receive as many as nine strokes at a time. Roger Dracup recalls one such "nine of the best" administered as he lay stretched across a table with his trousers around his knees. He went on to become a teacher himself in Australia and, though more than half a century has passed, still stoutly maintains his innocence.

Unthinkable now, such punishment was, of course, regarded as pretty normal in the thirties and forties, though the Doctor's zeal in such matters led to his twice being prosecuted in court. One of these cases received considerable prominence in the *Daily Mirror*. On both occasions, it should be stressed, the magistrates acquitted and he returned, character un besmirched, to continue meting out condign punishment without fear or favour as, for that matter, did the rest of the staff.

Charles McGregor Williams merits a full biography all to himself and, perhaps, one will eventually be written. A few further points must suffice here, however, in this all too brief attempt to do justice to the memory of the man who founded the School and guided it through its formative years.

Mention should be made of the School's first "golden period" aca demically. Examination results in the late forties reached new heights and, for a short time, surpassed (pro rata) even those of Manchester Grammar School. Naturally the Doctor took great pride and satisfaction in his boys' successes, particularly in the "Oxbridge" awards that began to roll in.

He was a staunch Conservative most of his life and greatly valued his connections to the famous and influential, many of which he turned to the advantage of the School. Local M.P.s Patricia Hornsby-Smith and Sir Waldron Smithers were close friends and his archive is full of letters to and from the pair of them as well as such celebrated personages as Compton McKenzie, Field Marshall Wavell and John Masefield. One note, from Winston Churchill's Downing Street office, thanks the Doctor for "the sonnets which you enclosed." Unfortunately these seem to be no longer extant. The young Margaret Roberts (later Thatcher) visited his Leas Green home during her unsuccessful campaign for the Dartford constituency in 1951. McGregor Williams himself would have stood as a Conservative candidate for a seat on the Kent County Council in the Spring of 1955 had death not intervened. At a political meeting in Chislehurst five years earlier, reported in the *Kentish Times*, he spoke on the theme of juvenile delinquency, attributing it to "Godlessness" and recommending more police patrols in the local parks. A fellow speaker at the same meeting, incidentally, placed the blame for such behaviour on the malign influence of "tawdry girls", but on this particular topic the good doctor appears, for once, to have remained silent. He was a founder member of the Sidcup Rotary Club and went on to become its president in due course.

Among the indefatigable Mac's numerous achievements should be mentioned the writing of several books, notably a primer, *La Formule*, which he made sure was on the French Department syllabus.

A heart attack suffered in 1949 caused the Doctor's lengthy absence from his beloved boys and the resultant health problems cast a shadow over his final years. The proposed move to Hurst Road distressed him greatly, so fond had he grown of the "glass house" at Crittall's Corner which he had helped to design. His opposition to the new building was increased by a conviction that it formed part of a "comprehensive" scheme (as we would now call it) which involved the grouping together, on one extended site, of three secondary schools, each catering for a supposedly different category of pupils in accordance with the new "tripartite" doctrine of Butler's 1944 Education Act. So adamant was the Doctor in his views that he refused even to visit the new building as it took shape on the golf course at Lamorbey in 1953. He once dutifully enquired of Bertha James how it was progressing, only to receive the sarcastic answer: "Oh, you know, brick upon brick!"

The combination of deteriorating health and the change of site precip-itated the Headmaster's retirement. "Doctor Bill", as he was known by the Station Road boys at least, handed over the torch to Richard Pedley in the Summer of 1954.

To the surprise of many, he announced his intention of taking holy orders. His two children, certainly, had never regarded their father as a par-ticularly religious man, although he had, admittedly, always given up smoking for Lent.

Sadly, the Doctor's retirement was to be a brief one, barely four months, in fact. On New Year's Eve, 1954, as he sat reading (according to his son) the meditations of Dean Inge upon life after death, he suffered a further heart attack and died. St John's Church was packed for his funeral on the morning of Wednesday, January 5th, the feast-day of St Simeon Stylites, perhaps appropriately, since both men, from their lofty perches, dispensed kindliness, sympathy and practical common sense advice to all their many adherents assembled below. Tributes poured in to all the local newspapers and numerous former pupils wrote of the great debt they owed to the School and to the Doctor in particular.

Few headmasters, it is safe to say, can have cared about their charges more than Mac did, have followed their subsequent careers with greater interest or have rejoiced more sincerely in their achievements in life. Rarely was he at a loss for the correct name when students returned to visit the School, as many did, often long after they had left. A passage from a letter sent to the Doctor on his retirement by a pupil from way back in his Brighton days sums up, in a few simple words, the feelings of so many: "I think that looking back on the happy times of one's youth is always very pleasant. With kindest regards (in spite of the numerous stripes!), Yours sincerely, Cyril Goldstein." Here perhaps we have, in chiaroscuro and in essence, the measure of a truly remarkable man.

CHAPTER THREE

27 Station Road

THE FIRST EDITION OF *The Chronicle* appeared on December 19th 1931, three months after the School opened its doors to the boys of Sidcup. Unsurprisingly it exudes eagerness and optimism despite the national economic crisis that loomed over the microcosm of 27 Station Road. "Already our school has assumed a distinctive and vigorous personality. It has, in a short time, developed into a sturdy, self-reliant child, throbbing with energy and pulsating with life, its numerous and varied activities pursued with a joyful zest", enthused Geoffrey Cook, the School's first English master. It is, of course, the sort of comment that an editor was required to make in such a context but there seems good reason to find it, for the most part, justified. As he warmed to his theme, Cook's prose becomes (appropriately) purple. "The future lies before us. With our Headmaster to lead us and our own strong hearts to give us courage, we shall tackle, with a song on our lips, all the tasks that await us, striving ceaselessly to make the world a better place to live in than it was before we entered it." What, after all, could be more exciting than "the launching forth" of a new school? asked McGregor Williams, rhetorically, addressing the boys in an open letter. "To fit yourselves adequately for your place in the world should be your object, and, by pursuit of that aim, to set up for those who will follow you a tradition worthy of your best."

This reference to the setting up of tradition reminds us that a new school necessarily lacks one. Since a school without traditions comes close to being a contradiction in terms it can be easily appreciated that the creation of 'instant tradition' must be amongst a founding headmaster's earliest priorities. Into the first couple of terms, therefore, were crammed a host of innovations, many of which were destined to survive for the rest of the century and beyond: a school badge and motto, school colours, a uniform, a school song, a house system, form captains, a tuck shop, sporting trophies, concerts, an assembly pattern and much else besides.

Among these instant traditions was the parroting of the Latin "adsum" ("Here I am") by each boy in turn as the four assistant masters read out their form-lists at the end of that memorable first assembly on the morning of Thursday, September 17th. The teaching of Latin was, at the outset, entrusted to Mr Cook along with his English, French, editorial and other responsibilities. No doubt he discussed with his charges the motto chosen by the Head: *Abeunt Studia in Mores*. The quotation is taken from Ovid's *Heroides* (No.15 line 83). The Lesbian poet Sappho, in a love letter to Phaon, declares that her upbringing and education have formed her character. The Doctor had translated this, in assembly, as "Work hard, play hard " but, even as a loose rendering, it leaves much to be desired. Cook's own attempt: "The pursuits and interests of school develop into the habits of later life" is much closer to the Latin original if somewhat cumbersome in its phraseology. Not that such concerns would have been uppermost in the boys' minds as they trooped after their black gowned teachers along the corridors and up the staircases towards their new classrooms, knobblykneed in their light grey flannel, short-trousered suits. The privilege of wearing long trousers, according to the School Uniform Regulations booklet, was reserved for boys of fifteen years or over. The only purple to be seen at this early stage was in the three hoops atop the long, grey socks and in the diagonal stripes alternating with silver-grey on their school ties. Caps were, as yet, plain grey and lacked the purple piping along the segment seams that followed later, together with the School badge. This, designed, of course, by Mac himself, consisted of a quartered shield. Two identical, opposite, sections included the white horse of Kent. The third (bottom left) featured a mitre representing, apparently, the Diocese of Rochester and the fourth a plumed helmet which, it is said, was in honour of Edward the "Black Prince" (1330–1376) who, according to local tradition, courted his future wife, Joan the "Fair Maid of Kent", on the banks of the Cray near Hall Place.

The smallest boys, several as young as eight, had been designated Form I and the sixteen of them, their shoes, in these tough times, protected with metal blakeys, clattered up the narrow staircase to their room at the top of the building. The others, for the most part aged eleven to thirteen, were allocated to three "Year II" classes – A,B and C- with form captains Cyril

Tomlin (at 14 the oldest boy in the School), Richard Dale and Alan Murray respectively.

One of their teachers' first tasks was to collect the weekly contribution of a half-penny from each boy for the School Gift Fund. Before long IIC trooped out of the main building to the hutted laboratory to be greeted by the tall, balding figure of A.E.("Joe") Parsons, the Senior Assistant Master and first teacher of science. Parsons had been Senior Chemistry Master at Cheltenham Grammar School before spending six years as Headmaster of Tetbury Grammar School, Gloucestershire, as previously mentioned. He had served in the final months of the First World War and this experience left him asthmatic, with a persistent cough. At thirty-seven considerably older than the other three masters, Parsons was to suffer recurrent bouts of ill health throughout his career, a particular problem, of course, when he had to take over the running of the School during McGregor Williams' own lengthy absence in the early 1950s. A London University Chemistry graduate, Parsons single-handedly launched all three science subjects in the new school and was largely responsible for building the thriving departments that would, in due course, be handed over to the illustrious triumvirate of Freeman, Morley and Goddard, men who would carry them to great academic heights in the post-war years. Somewhat lugubrious but with a puckish sense of humour and the occasional wide-mouthed grin, Parsons made "Stinks", as the boys invariably called it, one of the most popular subjects on the early curriculum. Soon eager heads were buried in their first textbook, *General Elementary Science*, a work written by a man with the not inappropriate name of Willings.

Meanwhile, in the main building, J.R.Banfield was introducing his young charges to the mysteries of Mathematics. The chalk clattered over the small blackboard which balanced rather precariously on its easel, angled slightly to one side at the front of the classroom. An accomplished pianist and the School's first games master, in addition to his principal role of mathematician, James Banfield was an instant success with small boys. He roared up Station Road. every morning on a Sunbeam motorcycle with sidecar which he might, on occasion, be persuaded to let specially favoured pupils drive across a field. From his breast pocket hung a chain that attached to a massive watch which he hauled out, periodically, like a bucket from a well, to ascertain how much of the lesson remained. As Music Master and Director of the School Choir as well as football and cricket coach, Banfield's energies were as prodigious as his versatility.

Immediately *below* Year I, much to their juvenile delight, were their elders in II B. We can picture them in an English lesson with Mr Cook. Fair-haired and boyish, "Cookie" quickly enthused his charges with his own love of words. Before long nibs were dipping into porcelain ink wells and scratching across the flimsy paper of the exercise books as the boys recorded what they had done during the Summer and their first impressions of the new school.

Along the corridor II A were meeting the youngest member of staff, 23 year-old Cambridge graduate Tom Palmer. Dapper, bespectacled, a Lincolnshire man and in his first appointment, he was destined to take over, 27 years later, from A.E.Parsons as Deputy Head. As the boys began their study of Geography, seated attentively in rows beneath the Mercator-projection wall-map, with the British Empire daubed in deep pink across huge swathes of it, who among them could have foreseen that their youthful teacher, in his dark, pin-striped suit and brilliantly polished shoes, would go on to achieve the staggering, and record-breaking, total of 42 years service to the School?

At 10.45 the bell rang for break and small boys hurried along towards the trestle table in the passage, where a tuck-shop had been set up by Mr Phillips, the School Caretaker, and his wife. Unwrapped bars of muddy textured chocolate were on sale at a halfpenny each, while the wealthier could buy coconut squares for 1d. Crisps and wine-gums were also available, as was milk in third-of-a-pint bottles with cardboard tops from which a small, central disk could be detached with a firm press of the thumb. When lessons resumed at eleven, Mr and Mrs Phillips cleared up and then hastened off to prepare two-course dinners in the assembly-hall cum dining-room at 10d per pupil. Somewhat bizarrely to modern thinking, the School Prospectus for 1931 stated: "Boys bringing their own luncheon are asked to pay a small charge for the use of table linen, cutlery etc." Quite how small this "small charge" was is, unfortunately, unrecorded.

Morning periods lasted 45 minutes. Lunchtime was a generous hour and a half, from 12.30 to 2.00. Afternoon school consisted of three forty-minute lessons and ended at 4.00. Each class had a weekly General Knowledge period and Fridays finished with what was termed an 'elective class', the boys choosing from Dramatics, Photography, First Aid and Musical Appreciation. The whole of Wednesday afternoon was given over to sport. Saturday morning school was from 9.00 until 12.00, the last lesson being the shortest of the week at just thirty minutes. Three years later, however, Saturday lessons were replaced by organised games. From September 1933 the lunch break was cut by fifteen minutes and the start of the school day brought forward from 9.00 to 8.55, thus creating an extra hundred minutes per week of contact time. By this stage numbers had risen to around the 200 mark and so the administration of school business was becoming a more complicated matter.

The 1931–2 timetable, happily still preserved in the Bexley Borough Archive, makes interesting reading. Jim Banfield appears to have drawn the shortest straw, teaching no fewer than ten subjects, though this number drops to a mere eight if the separately-timetabled Arithmetic, Algebra and Geometry are all grouped together under the heading of Mathematics as would be the case today. Tom Palmer appears to have worn the smallest number of hats, being required to teach just six different subjects every week!

That first day ended with II C back again in the laboratory-hut with "Joe" Parsons, this time for Biology; Year I having a General Knowledge session with Mr Banfield; II B with Cook again, though now studying French, and II A with Mr Palmer, the Geographer helping out by teaching English for five periods per week. At 4.00 sixty-two tired but animated boys flocked out into Station Road., chattering excitedly. Most of them would have made their way home on foot, even where their journey was one of several miles. The blakeys beneath their feet were a sound investment in terms of the shoe leather that they saved.

The next day, being a Friday, began with Mr Palmer taking his weekly Handwriting session with Year I, after which the youngsters turned their minds again to General Knowledge, this time delivered from the lofty height of Mr Parsons. James Banfield gathered II A and II B together for a combined singing lesson while II C had English with the hugely popular Geoffrey Cook. At 3.20 all pupils went off to the 'elective ' classes referred to earlier. At noon on Saturday lessons ended for the week. The staff, having spent the first three days preparing hard for the new school year, were, no doubt, particularly glad of the weekend, or what was left of it. The boys, one imagines, were equally pleased to rest, even though, in their case, they had worked only two and a half days.

On Monday the 21st – the Autumn equinox – school began in full earnest. There would be no more time off – apart from Sundays – until late October when there would be a two day break for Half Term. Remorselessly now the timetable rolled on. All classes studied English and

Mathematics, together with French, History and Geography. Each group had one weekly session of 'Physical Exercise', Religious Knowledge and Singing. The youngest had General Knowledge four time per week, the other three classes once. Additionally, Year One had five periods of Nature Study and two of Art (delivered by who else but J.R.Banfield?). The weekly Handwriting class and their elective session last period on Fridays made up the curriculum for the youngest boys. Year Two pupils took Chemistry, Physics and Biology. II A, the ablest group and the largest with twenty students, carried the additional burden of Latin, with all those conjugations and declensions to be filed away in the memory alongside their French irregular verbs and rules of agreement.

The Autumn of 1931 was wet and windy, so noses were more willingly probed into textbooks than might have been the case had an Indian Summer ensued. Distractions were far fewer at that time. Television still lay in the future and radio programming was not designed with early teenage boys in mind. It is worth recalling that 'teenager' is a post-war concept, the word itself not attaining currency until the 'Teddy Boy' era of the 1950s. With little or no economic autonomy at the best of times, never mind during a major recession, children did not constitute a 'market' in anything even remotely resembling the modern sense and, in consequence, few commercial concerns were at all interested in aiming products or activities in their direction. Sidcup was no Las Vegas and most of Dr Williams' boys had little choice but to study hard. In the unlikely event that the combined weight of pedagogic and parental pressures had proved insufficient, the lack of seductive alternatives to academic slog provided any additional incentive that might have been needed. These, after all, were serious times. Unemployment was rampant and those at school needed little reminder that exam success was crucial to their prospects of a living wage, let alone anything that could be termed a career. A profession, of course, was the highest aspiration and the Headmaster allowed few days to pass without reminding his charges of the way things stood. "England has her back to the wall and is fighting for her life", wrote Waldron Smithers, M.P. for Chislehurst, that September, in the *Kentish Times*. It was almost as true in 1931 as it would be ten years later.

Week two of the School's existence began with II A, the elite group, having their first session of French under the rigorous regime of Mac himself. Wednesday afternoon saw the first games session, the boys marching off to the sloping, hummocky football pitches at the back of the Sidcup

Recreation Club, later part of the grounds of Sidcup Place. For those of less sporting inclination, entertainment was derived from the frequent forays into the adjacent frog pond to retrieve the ball.

With the shortening days the smell of hot tar that had drifted in through the open windows during the heat of mid-September was replaced by the stench of scorching paint as radiators were turned on in classrooms newly decorated a fetching combination of green and brown. This assault upon the nostrils was compounded by offence to the ear-drums as boys discovered the pleasing cacophony that could be made by the flapping of many brass ink-well covers in concert. In English Horatius stoutly kept the bridge while History took pride in Magna Carta and Britannia's ruling of the waves. Geography, too, was British Empire focused, with much time devoted to the white man's burden in Africa and the Raj. Pythagoras' theorem ruled in Mathematics and Religious Knowledge, uncontroversially, saw maps drawn of St Paul's travels around the Levant.

There was, in most subjects, much time spent in the laborious copying down of notes and diagrams from blackboards. Chalk dust hung everywhere, dancing in shafts of sunlight, whitening varnished desk-tops and the dangling sleeves of masters' gowns. From up the staircases and along the corridors came the low hum of teachers' voices and the occasional higher sing-song chant of boys: "...the square on the hypotenuse...freezes at 32 degrees Fahrenheit...je vais, tu vas, il va...at Oxford, in 1258, Simon de Montfort...every sentence needs a finite verb...the prairie provinces, Alberta, Saskatchewan and Manitoba...amo, amas, amat..."

School societies flourished. First Aid, overseen by Tom Palmer, attracted 22 members with ages ranging from 8 to 14. Early sessions concentrated on the treatment of fractures, many younger boys cheerfully volunteering to act as accident victims. The Wireless & Meccano Club was enthusiastically attended at lunchtimes. One of its first tasks was to dissect a valve. "We were rather disappointed to find that it only contained a bit of wire and a piece of tin", Jim Banfield later recalled. "What we expected to find we were not quite sure." The Photographic Society established a darkroom at the end of the annexe and work began on the construction of an enlarger. Members had to purchase their own films. One small boy was bitterly disappointed when his film emerged from the developing dish completely blank. No one had explained to him, apparently, that there was a necessary process between the obtaining of the film and the appearance of the finished picture which involved the use of a camera!

Geoff Cook's Dramatic Society acted out a number of one-act plays, the first being *Shivering Shocks* by Clemence Dane, but as yet their performances were for internal consumption only. The Debating Society, again under Cook's aegis, held fortnightly meetings on Friday afternoons. The very first motion, "that school games should be compulsory", was carried by 21 votes to 3.

Football was played on Wednesdays and Saturdays, despite the muddy conditions. There were, in this first term, no matches against other schools. In the inter-form competition IIB, captained by "Toddy" Barber, emerged as winners with two victories and a draw. "Boys, shoot hard and shoot often!" enjoined Jim Banfield in *The Chronicle*. Badminton proved a popular indoor sport when atrocious weather merged football pitch and pond.

The fortnightly 'lists' provided another competitive element. Regular 'speed-accuracy' tests in mental arithmetic and spelling were held with a £1 prize awarded at the end of the year to the boy with the highest marks, the first winners being Arthur Stanyon and Kenneth Stuart. The first departure was that of William Stanley Morton Duck who was expelled on October 9th, barely three weeks into the opening term, apparently for spitting at passers-by from an open-top bus amongst other misdemeanours. His record card reads simply: "Removed from School at the request of the Headmaster."

On the afternoon of Saturday December 12th the first school outing took place when thirty-five excited boys travelled by private bus to see *Henry V* at Sadler's Wells. The following Tuesday their visit was followed up in History by Tom Palmer's lesson on the Battle of Agincourt. In that time of austerity left-overs were frowned upon.

A week later, on Saturday December 19th,the Autumn Term came to an end, thirteen weeks and two days after the School opened its doors on that sunny day in mid-September – a crowded, tumultuous three months which laid the foundations upon which so much would be built in the years that followed. Christmas celebrations, however, were subdued. Launched during a worldwide economic depression with its collapsing currencies and soaring unemployment, the as yet tiny craft had ploughed on through seas that grew increasingly mountainous. Whether one looked at local eddies such as the collapse of the Labour Government a few months earlier, mutiny in the Royal Navy, the abandonment of the gold standard during the School's second week of existence or the savage cuts in unemployment benefit that followed, or whether one cast one's eyes towards the horizon and contemplated Hitler's imminent rise to power in Germany, panic and mass suicides in Wall Street or the Japanese occupation of Manchuria, with the fall of Shanghai awaited daily, the news was universally grim.

Spring Term 1932 saw many more innovations. The first of these was the creation of a house system, the School being divided into four groups with the uninspiring titles of 'A', 'B', 'C' and 'D', captained, respectively by Alan Murray, Peter Ost, John Whitbread and Norman ('Toddy') Barber. At the time declared 'temporary', these house names remained in force until 1953, though two additional houses, 'E' and 'F', were introduced in 1937. The first cross-country race was held over three miles on January 17th, the winner being Murray in a time of 20 minutes 19 seconds.

The School's first sporting contest against a rival establishment took place towards the end of term, the football XI taking on Dartford Technical School. It was a momentous occasion in every sense. Not only was it the first of thousands of matches against other schools in a whole variety of sports but it also turned out to be an extremely close and exciting game in its own right. Ahead 4–3 at halftime, Sidcup eventually lost 6–7 against bigger and stronger opponents. Waters, Murray and Ost were singled out for particular praise in the *Chronicle* report, though the six goals were apparently shared between Batchelor and Cade. A second match followed soon afterwards, the School side again going down to a narrow defeat in another high-scoring match, losing 3–4 to Bromley County.

In March the whole school, virtually, attended another Shakespearean production at Sadler's Wells – this time *Julius Caesar* – a double-decker bus being hired for the occasion. At the invitation of governor and local philanthropist Hugh Marsham-Townshend, another whole-school outing took place that Spring, this time by bicycle to view the bluebells in Scadbury Park.

With the cherry blossom in full glory along Station Road. the School's first public performance, a concert, took place. The choir sang well-loved songs such as *Loch Lomond* and *The Lass of Richmond Hill*, performing "tunefully and with good, clear articulation", according to the *Sidcup Times*. Boxwell gave a piano solo, Form One recited nursery rhymes in French and the Dramatic Society performed a one-act play, *The Hordle Poacher*, the actors being Whitbread, Stuart and Dale. Several items from the staff followed and the evening concluded with lusty community singing.

The smell of hot tar returned through the open windows and, with Summer, began School cricket. The house competition was won by 'B' house with victories over all three of their opponents, Stonham major scoring a fifty and Dale taking 7 wickets for 5 runs in one splendid stint of bowling. The School XI, captained by Toddy Barber, played Upton College, the first contest to be staged on the new field at the Crittall's Corner site. Despite Barber's brilliance with both bat and ball the School lost by 36 runs. In the return match, however, played at Bexleyheath, the School gained its revenge, scoring 114 and winning by the triumphant margin of 75 runs. This victory was doubly momentous in that it marked, at the fourth attempt, the first sporting success in inter-school competition.

The last major event of the academic year was the first annual athletic sports, held on Saturday July 23rd 1932 at a Crittall's Corner still, as yet, devoid of any building work. Mr Hugh Marsham-Townshend and Chairman of Governors Colonel Francis Edlmann, resplendent in his Cambridge cricket blazer, acted as judges. By now school numbers had risen to 96, an increase of over fifty percent during the academic year. On an overcast day 44 competitors entered for 18 events ranging from the familiar sprints, middle-distance and jumping to more bizarre contests such as a sack race, a tug-of-war and a pick-a-back race for fathers and their sons. An additional event, the 'house hundreds', obliged the rest to join in with their more athletic colleagues. 'B' house, in green, finished in fourth place, rather strangely in view of their footballing and cricketing triumphs earlier on. Winners were the reds, 'A' house, whose star athlete, Cyril Owen, took the silver 'victor ludorum' individual trophy from Mrs Marsham-Townshend, the guest of honour. And so the Summer term and the School's first year drew jointly to their close.

September saw the arrival of Charles Mitchell, a young Bristol graduate, to add a new subject, German, to the curriculum and to help Geoffrey Cook with the teaching of English. Mitchell was a rugby enthusiast and a dead shot with the wooden-backed board-rubber if a boy's attention lapsed. Although he remained at the School for only five years before moving to Hackney Downs, he is revered by those he taught and has a strong claim to be considered one of the most brilliant teachers to have served at Chis and Sid. There were now 140 pupils on the roll and five masters, in addition to the Head.

The second Autumn term witnessed the formation of the School Scout Troop by Tom Palmer with two patrols, the 'Bulldogs' and the 'Peewits'.

Palmer also arranged for a fives court to be built in the south-west corner of the playground, the game, which he had enjoyed at Cambridge, being ideal for such a restricted area. Some might have rested on their laurels for a time but Palmer, indefatigable, started the Chess Club and organised an inter-house tournament for those sportsmen of more sedentary inclination.

The School's first Speech Day was held on December 8th 1932 in the assembly hall of the County School for Girls, Chislehurst, the Station Road equivalent being adjudged too small for such an occasion. Indeed, the already cramped conditions were commented upon by several speakers that evening who pointed to the rapidly rising level of intake, while noting that there was still no indication of when building work would commence at Crittall's Corner. Guest of honour Lord Hayter, the walrus-moustached steel magnate, urged the boys to use their common sense, though he confessed his inability to define the phrase. The principal prizes were won by Kenneth Stuart, John Whitbread, Arthur Stanyon and Frank Norris.

As Year Two progressed, the kicking-in of adolescent male hormones, the lengthening of gangling limbs and the over-crowding of stairs and corridors built with sedate young ladies in mind ganged up with those well known conspirators familiarity and contempt to produce the first stirrings of recalcitrance. Douglas Flindall remembers such pranks as electrifying the brass doorknob to administer a (mild) shock to teachers entering the classroom and joining the four hanging lights with near-invisible piano wire so that they swayed in unison, balletically, in the draught from an open window, their rhythm increasing until they reached a spectacular crescendo as they collided overhead. Another favourite trick was to loosen the pegs in the easel so that the blackboard would come crashing down when the master attempted to write on it. Such became his reputation that, by his own admission, lessons would often begin with the words "Outside, Flindall!" To be sent out meant an automatic beating from the Head who commanded a view of the corridors from his study. Flindall's technique was to hide for a few minutes in the cloakroom, then slip back into the room, rubbing his posterior and mumbling the apology he declared that Mac had instructed him to deliver on his return.

Mac ran a tight ship, there is ample testimony to that. An unfortunate boy called Gunner, who lodged with the McGregor Williams family in Chislehurst, was hoisted on the back of caretaker Phillips and soundly thrashed by the Head in front of the whole school during assembly, according

31

to an eye-witness account. What he had done to merit such a drastic reprisal is not recorded. Attitudes of course were different then and one should not, perhaps, judge such practices by the standards of today. It is interesting to note, in this context, that the Debating Society, that very term, rejected overwhelmingly, by 40 votes to 7, the motion that corporal punishment be abolished in schools.

Relations between staff and boys were, for the most part, cordial, however and in the Summer of 1933 a cricket match was held, the first sporting contest between the two great 'opposites'. The *Chronicle* does not name the Staff XI but the laws of arithmetic suggest that at least five players must have 'guested' for them. At all events the game was won by the boys who scored 160 runs to their opponents' creditable 113. It was somewhat unkindly suggested that the Staff were a little slow in the field. This result established a norm for such contests that would, with rare deviations, persist into the next millennium.

July saw the first tour abroad take place, the Head, with Messrs Mitchell and Palmer, taking nineteen boys to the Rhineland, the whole trip, astonishingly, costing less than £5 per pupil, all included! With Hitler now Chancellor and possessed of full powers to rule by decree, the Third Reich was underway and Germany was becoming an alarming place to be.

Next term the School roll reached 190, the staff being augmented by the arrival of Maurice Gridley, a U.C.L. graduate, to teach Maths and Physics, together with Edwyn Birchenough, a Balliol man, whose subjects were Religious Knowledge and History. A controversial figure, Birchenough lived up to his name by establishing a fearsome reputation as a disciplinarian. 'Birchie', as he was universally known, has been called a holy terror, being particularly notorious for his vigorous use of rubber tubing according to several pupils who survived to tell the tale. The story goes that in his early days at the School Birchenough so upset Pead minor that an enraged Pead major, (his elder brother by some five minutes or so) pursued the master around the building with a knife. Incidents of this kind do not find their way into the *Chronicle* and it has not proved possible to ascertain the outcome of this alarming episode but it is reasonable to suppose that Mac's wrath was awesome to behold.

That same Autumn saw three pioneers – Cyril Tomlin, Gerald Boxwell and the new School Captain, Kenneth Stuart – begin work for their London General Schools examination, reconnoitring a path that would be trodden, under different signposts, by many thousands destined to follow

1st XI football team, 1933–34. (Back row, L to R: J.Banfield, Waters, Barber, Smith, McCulloch, Cade, Boxwell, Dale, Headmaster. Front row: Crittenden, Stonham, Murray, Ost, Stubbs).

them. Again the footballers, under Murray's captaincy, found themselves considerably shorter and lighter than most of their opponents and predictably lost six of their eight matches against other schools. More worryingly, Christmas arrived with Maidstone's sanction still not given for building work to begin on the Crittall's site.

Spring brought with it the third, and to date most ambitious, School Concert which included the operetta *Hearts are Trumps*, in addition to various solo items and some pieces by the percussion band. The Dramatic Society performed a one-act play, *The Captain of the Gate*, and a surprise was sprung by the unexpected appearance of the Comedie Francaise, whom discerning members of the audience identified as various members of the staff.

In June 1934 the first public exams were sat at the Sidcup County School, the three aforementioned candidates all getting through satisfactorily. The School Cricket Team, still led by Barber, enjoyed a spectacular change of fortune, winning eight of its ten games, one of them being the first ever sporting fixture against a parents' side. At the annual sports championship in July Colonel Edlmann was at last able to announce, to great applause, that an immediate start was to be made on building the new school. The 'victor ludorum' cup went this time to Richard Dale. The academic year finished on an unhappy note with the death of Thomas Beeton, Secretary to the Bromley Rural and Chislehurst District Education Committee throughout the twelve years of its existence and a prominent figure in the establishment and early fostering of the School. Shortly afterwards the Sidcup Urban District Council ceased to exist, its role being taken on by the new Chislehurst and Sidcup U.D.C., a move which would lead, four years later,to the renaming of the School.

The Autumn term, 1934, already the tenth in the School's existence, ushered in some more major innovations. The pupil roll passed the two hundred mark and three new masters joined the staff, bringing it into double figures for the first time. E.S.Jenkins, soon to become 'Teddy' or 'Jenks', was a native of Aberdare, less than thirty miles from McGregor Williams' Newport and, like the Head, a graduate in French from Cardiff College, University of Wales. Scarcely had he arrived before, with the help of Charles Mitchell, he introduced rugby to the School, acknowledging that the move was 'greatly daring' in his article entitled 'Rugger' in the seventh issue of the *Chronicle*. As Head of Modern Languages he organised and led trips to Paris for twenty-five Easters in succession, eventually becoming Head of Junior School in 1958 and then in 1973, after 39 years of service, Deputy Head.

Another 'giant' who began his Chis and Sid career on this same auspicious September day was John Walsh, like Gridley a U.C.L. man, who had been a pupil of Mac's at Varndean. Tall, gently spoken, an acknowledged expert in his field, Walsh went on to spend 37 years at the School, most of them as Head of English following Geoff Cook's departure at the end of the war. During his long and distinguished career Walsh directed plays, edited the *Chronicle* and found time to write a number of books including volumes of poetry and editions of Wordsworth, Keats and Clare.

The third new member of staff was Edward Raynham, another Varndean old boy and conspicuous for wearing size twenty shoes. Raynham taught Maths for just three years before moving to Raynes Park and thereby sharing with Charles Mitchell the dubious distinction of being the first masters to leave the School. Another first this September was a full class of 26 boys studying for their General School Certificate in what had become the Fifth Form. Furthermore the School had now acquired a bona fide Sixth Form, with two students, Boxwell and Stuart, studying for

The Staff, 1934: (Back row, L to R: E.Birchenough, M.Gridley, C.Mitchell. Front row: E.Palmer, A.Parsons, Headmaster, J.Banfield, G.Cook).

their Higher Schools.

This Autumn saw the discontinuation of the unpopular Saturday lessons, the time being given over to official sporting activities instead. Those not actively participating were expected to turn up to give support. So overcrowded were the Station Road premises by this stage, despite the acquisition of a second hutted laboratory during the Summer, that accommodation was leased in Sidcup High Street with an annexe opening above the Midland Bank. This consisted of two classrooms and a tiny staffroom and was occupied by the youngest boys who entered the main building only for morning assembly and for the assembly that concluded the week on Friday afternoons, an arrangement that was known as 'central control'. The boys travelled between the two buildings in 'crocodiles' under close staff supervision.

The School's first Open Day, on November 16th 1934, consisted of a two hour session, from 6.00 until 8.00, during which parents could watch their sons in the process of being taught. There were displays of arts and crafts, gymnastics and drama and the experiment was judged a great

The Charcoal Burner's Son, 1935. (Staff – 2nd, 4th & 6th from L: E.T.Palmer, C.N.Mitchell, E.C.Birchenough. Pupils – 1st, 3rd, 5th & 7th from L: G.Martin, D.McJames, A.Murray, J.Keard).

success. Badminton and philately now competed for the pupils' interest. Some ninety boys went swimming each week at the Orpington Lagoon, this activity being, of course, very dear to the Doctor's heart as we have seen. Whether he, or the parents, come to that, would have been so happy watching the young cyclists clinging to the backs of lorries en route to the baths is another matter.

Those passing Crittall's Corner could now see an army of workmen preparing the site. The first stumbling block was the clump of elm trees beneath which the boys changed for games. Shifting the stubborn roots proved quite a challenge but deracination was eventually accomplished. As the Spring and Summer months rolled by, a new grove slowly replaced the old one but this time consisting of concrete trunks and steel branches. 1935 was the King's Silver Jubilee year and the School celebrated in style, travelling by special train from Sidcup Station direct to Southampton Docks where they saw many ships, including the *Mauritania*, and toured the *Majestic*, until recently the largest ship afloat. Schools were granted a three day holiday for the Jubilee and, on May 5th, a chosen few pupils were picked up by coach from each local school and taken up to the Mall where spaces had been reserved for them, though it meant camping out on the pavement overnight. The magnificent procession clattered past the following morning. Many more went up to London that evening and stood in the enormous crowd outside Buckingham Palace as King George V and Queen Mary appeared on the balcony.

Problems with the dye having at long last been resolved to meet the Head's exacting specifications, the now famous purple blazers began to make their appearance at about this time. Given their high cost and the straitened circumstances of many parents, they were deemed to be optional and the majority of boys remained in their grey flannel suits. The few boys who were able to take advantage of this splendid new sartorial flourish were visited in school by the local tailors who came in to measure up their customers. School photographs show that it was not until well into the 1950s that purple began to predominate over grey.

Finance for the swimming bath scheduled for Crittall's Corner was proving problematical and so proceeds from the School Concert at the end of the Spring Term went to form the nucleus of a fund that would be devoted to bringing this much desired amenity into being. The hall was filled on four successive evenings. The string orchestra made its debut and, for the first time, full stage lighting was employed. A successful cricket season followed, the School now fielding two elevens and playing, in all, 21 matches of which no fewer than 16 were won. Two dozen sat, in June, for their General Schools, all but five successfully.

At the fourth Annual Sports Day on July 27th Lady Kemnal presented the 'victor ludorum' cup to H.G.Stubbs and the Colonel looked forward, in his speech, to occupying part of the new school building the following term. During the Summer holiday one group of boys went on a Scandinavian cruise and the second German tour took place. R.Greenaway of IV A, in his *Chronicle* report, described with evident distaste what he called "this Heil Hitler business" and "much evidence of Jewish persecution". Conscription had just been reintroduced and the formation of the Luftwaffe officially announced. The sinister implications of this latter event as far as Sidcup was concerned would not, of course, be revealed for another five years or so. In Station Road eyes were focused on issues much closer to home, the School reassembling in September with its numbers now above three hundred and with much excited speculation about *the move*.

CHAPTER FOUR

Into the Glasshouse

AT THE START OF the Autumn Term, 1935, the School entered its fifth year and the teaching staff reached a dozen with the recruitment of Sidney Martin, a first class graduate from U.C.L., who served for eight years as Head of Classics before being killed in an air-raid, and K.Mortimore, from St Edmund Hall, Oxford. There were now some three hundred pupils on roll, about two dozen of whom were in a sixth form divided into three sections: an Upper Sixth and two Lower Sixth groups, "S" and "M", for Science and Arts respectively. The letter "M" denoted "modern", as opposed to "classical", studies.

Even with the extra facility at the Midland Bank, overcrowding in Station Road was becoming critical. A mixture of enthusiasm and relief, therefore, greeted the announcement that, on Armistice Day, November 11th, one wing of the new building would open for business. It was a date, of course, that held particular poignancy for three of the key figures involved: Colonel Edlmann, Dr McGregor Williams and Arthur Parsons. The four youngest groups – IIa, IIb, IIc and Year I – were chosen as the pioneers and, when the great day dawned, duly sent into exile at Crittall's Corner. They occupied a newly completed section that would later be known as the "Kitchen Wing". This future Dining Room was temporarily divided into several classrooms. Ironically, hot food had to be ferried up to the boys in churns from the Station Road canteen. The caretaker's laden car became a familiar sight as it made its daily trip up the cinder track from the by-pass.

Further temporary accommodation was secured at the Sidcup Art School in Grassington Road, which meant that four sites were now in use and co-ordinating them caused a major headache to the timetabler, James Banfield, to say nothing of the principal administrators of the system,

Arthur Parsons and the Headmaster. Day to day organisation was greatly assisted by the appointment of Mary Burnell, who would prove a tower of strength as School Secretary over the next nineteen years. To avoid utter chaos the system decreed that, for the most part, the boys stayed put while the masters hurried from one building to another. The scope for disruption was, of course, immense and the fact that little materialised is a tribute both to the discipline instilled by Mac and his staff and to the self-restraint and innate common sense that, by and large, characterised well brought up, middle class boys of that era. In these litigious days such a set-up, involving, as it necessarily did, leaving large numbers of boys unsupervised for considerable periods of time, would be quite out of the question.

Further evidence of the School's steady growth can be found in the addition of a second Scout Troop and the division of the School Library into two sections, Reference and Lending. In the *Chronicle* of December, 1935, Geoffrey Cook declared: "The 'vigorous infant' of four years ago has developed into a not inconsiderable youth standing on the threshold of manhood."

The Spring of 1936 brought two new masters, both Cambridge graduates, G.R.Gibbs from Emmanuel College and E.C.Pettett from St John's.

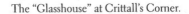

The "Glasshouse" at Crittall's Corner.

A visit to Portsmouth Dockyard on July 7th involved not only a tour of the *Victory* but also sightings of the aircraft-carrier *H.M.S. Courageous* and what was then the world's largest battleship, *H.M.S. Hood*. As they gazed at her in awe, none of the boys could have imagined that this formidable vessel would, less than five years later, be sunk by the *Bismarck* in the North Atlantic with the loss of over 1400 lives.

This year saw further developments at the Crittall's site with the erection of two temporary huts to house four more classes. The School now boasted a three form entry, with "a", "b" and "c" classes in Years II and III as well as a Year I which still catered for younger boys, for the most part aged nine or ten.

In the Autumn arrived R.D.Clarke to run the History Department and W.H.Freeman as Head of Biology. Both men would go on to make a major impact upon the School over many years. Dennis ("Nobby") Clarke was, like John Walsh, a former pupil of Mac's at Varndean School. After graduating from London University he taught, briefly, at Uckfield Grammar School under the Doctor's headship before joining him, yet again, in Sidcup. Better the devil you know! Clarke served the School for thirty years – if one includes his wartime service in the R.A.F. An expert chess player, his party piece was "kriegspiel", a variant of the game in which the participants sat back-to-back and made their moves without being able to see the board. During his last decade the History Department was widely acknowledged to be one of the finest in the entire state sector.William Harvey Freeman, known universally as "Bill", was educated at Haberdasher's Askes and King's College London. Father of six children and husband of Beryl, another to figure prominently in the history of the School, Bill was an outstanding teacher and largely responsible for launching numerous young men on their medical careers, many of them going on to achieve eminence in their particular fields. A prolific writer of scientific textbooks, he was also an accomplished draughtsman and artist as well as an outstanding cricketer. After forty years of service to the School, including four years overseas in the Royal Artillery during the War, Bill devoted his retirement to reviving the flagging fortunes of the Old Boys' Association, a torch which was picked up by Beryl upon his death in 1980.

Under the acronym "SCOBA", the Sidcup County Old Boys' Association came into being in the Autumn of 1937 when some ex-members of the School First Eleven and a few of their friends got together to run a football team. Leading spirits in this venture were P.C. Mitchell, A.J.Stanyon, C.P.D.Tomlin, A.Spicer, B.J.Grassby, A.Martin and J.Ernsting, who went on to become an Air Vice-Marshall. A near unbeaten record in the first two seasons attracted many keen new recruits but the outbreak of war caused the club to fall into abeyance until its revival in 1946. The organisation's subsequent name, Old Sedcopians, has its origin in this football side since, when they joined the Old Boys' League, a name of that kind was de rigueur. Apparently it was Mac himself who persuaded the organisers that "Sidcupians" lacked euphony and suggested changing the first two vowels.

Founding caretaker L.H.Phillips gave way to L.R.Barrow and, two years later, he in turn was succeeded by E.R.Green who was charged with the onerous duty of safeguarding the pristine new premises.

The Autumn Term, 1936, ended on a sombre note with the death of a young pupil, Derek Carter, in an unspecified accident, this unhappy event marking the first fatality to befall the School community. It had been a year of three monarchs, the old King, George Vth, dying in January and Edward VIIIth abdicating, uncrowned, on Speech Day, Friday December 11th, to marry Wallis Simpson and be replaced by his brother, Albert, thereafter George VIth. The year also saw the outbreak of the Spanish Civil War and, this time too close for comfort, Mosley's black-uniformed Fascists marching through the East End. These momentous events, however, appear to have made little impression upon the County School, Sidcup, which pursued the unruffled tenor of its way if one is to judge from the written record and from the recollections of those who have survived to reminisce.

A generous three day holiday was granted the following May for the purpose of celebrating the new reign. When combined with the Whit Monday and Tuesday traditional at half term this meant a full week's freedom for Dr Williams' boys, several of whom had official places reserved for them on Constitution Hill. Fifth-former K. Thomson recalls seeing a man (presumably a republican) spend hours perched precariously up a lamppost merely so that he could ostentatiously read a newspaper as the coronation procession passed by.

At the end of term the first staff resignation took place, Charles Mitchell crossing the Thames to teach at Hackney Downs. Another – and more welcome – precedent that Summer was the birth of the first "School" baby, a daughter, Margaret, to Tom and Enid Palmer, the news being announced in assembly to spontaneous applause.

The School's third Summer visit to Germany took in Cologne and Berlin. R.Greenway of the Lower Sixth stayed with a family near Dortmund and, in his *Chronicle* article, describes the father going off, in full uniform, to his S.S. meetings while the sons attended Hitler Youth rallies. At 9.30 each evening Greenway joined the hushed family around the radio "to hear their Fuhrer broadcast to his people" and observed, with some misgiving, their enthusiastic response. "If you wish for peace, prepare for war" was, ominously, the first proposition put before the Debating Society the following month. The result was a tie with the chairman's casting vote ensuring that the motion was carried. It is doubtful whether any of the participants could have appreciated, at that time, the true significance of their deliberations though, barely two years later, it is likely that some of those there present would have looked back and recalled which way their particular vote had been bestowed.

Three new teachers joined the staff in September 1937: P.H.Taylor, a mathematician from an English school in Istanbul; H.J.Martin, a German teacher with a Manchester degree and physicist C.R.Morley, the latter destined to become, over the next 39 years, a semi-legendary figure around whom would accumulate a stock of anecdotes to rival those of Mac himself. More of him later. That Autumn the pupil roll crossed the four hundred mark and just over half that number could now be catered for on the new site. Space was available for the first full season of lacrosse, a game dear to the Headmaster's heart and one that was embraced with enthusiasm. So rapid was the progress made that a squad of players, together with teams from St Dunstan's and Henry Thornton, had the honour of representing the English Lacrosse Union in the march past the King and Queen at Wembley in the Festival of Youth. The *Chronicle* report of this occasion is written by R.W.("Bob") Ims the Head Boy who, years later, was to embark upon a distinguished career as Head of Geography and Head of the Arts Sixth. The swimmers, however, were less fortunate. A letter from the Kent Education Committee, dated June 16th, casts serious doubt upon the construction of the long-promised pool. Despite Mac's plaintive protests and the School's own considerable fund-raising efforts the project fell into abeyance and was never to be revived.

The obstinate row of elm trees having finally capitulated and the underground stream having been located and suppressed, work at Crittall's Corner moved on apace, often in front of an admiring audience. The smaller boys derived great amusement from racing each other along the half-completed corridors until seen off by a fierce watchman with a big, ashwood stick – very possibly the same gentleman whose ill-advised confrontation with McGregor Williams was described in Chapter 2.

Issue Number 13 of the magazine, dated December 1937, expresses the hope, in its editorial column, that a few, at least, of the original 1931 intake would still be on-roll to share in the School's rebirth in its new buildings, now confidently expected for the following year. In the event, five very senior boys did indeed achieve this feat. Arthur Spicer, Geoffrey Ford, Derek Croxson, Hedley Madgett and Stuart Pead all left the School in the Summer of 1939, having completed eight years in grey and purple.

This time the optimism proved well-founded and the next issue, July 1938, proclaimed itself the last *Chronicle* to be issued from the original building. Many waxed sentimental and declared that they would greatly miss the dear old place for all its inadequacies. Fond memories abounded and staff and boys vied with each other in pointing out that such and such would be the last ever whatever it was in Station Road. Much space was devoted to anticipating the great move South though, in truth, the two sites were only a mile apart. The Headmaster, in a letter to his "dear boys", observed that "the passing of time brings many a change". He warmed to his theme. "The long-hoped for School building, the vision splendid, is to actualise." He continued, rhapsodically: "Its ferro-concrete structure stands for strength and strength of purpose, its design for simplicity, its vast window spaces for open-mindedness, its unusual lines for a modern outlook and independence of thought, its proportions for harmony of development and discipline." Space was somehow found to welcome three newcomers. F.H. Bramwell from the Royal College of Art, E.J.Dellar from Goldsmiths' to teach P.E. and F.W.Dutton, a short, peppery Geographer from the Naval school H.M.S. Worcester were the first appointments to the staff of the School in its new, post-Sidcup incarnation. Nor was the imminent move the only good news at this point. Colonel Edlmann was made High Sheriff of Kent, a well-deserved honour which gave great pleasure to his many friends and it was announced that Kenneth Sander had won the School's first State Scholarship, to the Royal College of Science, starting him off on a distinguished career that would see him Senior Wrangler at Cambridge University.

At the start of the Autumn Term, on Thursday the 15th of September 1938, the School mustered for the last time in Station Road. After a short religious service the boys fell into line and were marched by the prefects, supervised by the new Head Boy, J.R.Bechervaise, crocodile-fashion up the hill towards Mac's "vision splendid" at Crittall's Corner. As they crossed the border that separated Sidcup from Chislehurst a new chapter was opened in the annals of the School which had, at that moment, acquired, of necessity, a new and more cumbersome name.

A fortnight later another symbolic, cross-border march took place. Hitler's Wehrmacht crossed the Czech frontier and occupied the Sudetenland. Many in the grey and purple column were but a year or two younger than their counterparts in field grey. It may not be entirely fanciful to suppose that several young men from either group would meet, eventually, on the battlefield, for the Second World War lay less than a year ahead. On that September morning, though, as the boys wound their way from Sidcup to Chislehurst, all thoughts would have been on the edifice that loomed up before them, its acres of glass reflecting back a dazzling sun. In his poem inspired by the approach to a still more famous educational establishment, Ode on a Distant Prospect of Eton College, Thomas Gray wrote:

> *Alas,regardless of their doom,*
> *The little victims play!*
> *No sense have they of ills to come,*
> *Nor care beyond to-day:*
> *Yet see how all around them wait*
> *The ministers of human fate.*

The words seem curiously apt, as does the poem's celebrated conclusion: *Where ignorance is bliss,'tis folly to be wise.*

Happily unaware of the misery so soon, in a very literal sense, to descend upon them, the boys of the Chislehurst and Sidcup County School – to use its official new name – filed inside the building, having first removed their outdoor footwear and put on the elastic-sided, soft-soled "house shoes" which they carried with them in cloth bags. The gleaming new parquet floors were to be preserved at all costs.

Four years under construction – the firm in question being H.Friday and Sons of Erith – the completed building was a sensation and widely enthused about in architectural journals and the popular press alike. Local and national newspapers carried photographs of a structure praised for its daring modernity and its imaginative employment of innovative tech-

44

1st XI cricket team, 1938, with James Banfield and Dr McGregor Williams.

niques such as the handling of reinforced concrete. The use of frames and columns meant that the outer walls had no structural importance and were, effectively, mere panels, making use of red facing bricks with horizontal raked joints. What most took the eye were vast expanses of glass with a consequent abundance of natural lighting and ventilation. The famous glass tower, surrounding the main staircase, was soon to become a familiar landmark in North West Kent. The metal-framed windows came from the Crittall's factory opposite, whence the location drew its popular name. The design was by John Poltock, a man still in his twenties, later to be best known, perhaps, for Victoria College, Cairo, working under the overall supervision of W.H.Robinson, the County Architect. Mention of architecture prompts the reflection that one of the new boys who entered the School that Autumn, John Leaning, was destined to become famous in this field. In the 1970s he was principally responsible for the redesigning of Central Ottawa. He was a contemporary at the School of another famous architect, Frederick Lloyd Roche, who went on to be Vice-President of the R.I.B.A. and heavily involved in the expansion of Milton Keynes.

Mac, as may readily be imagined, had kept closely in touch with the work as it slowly unfolded and many of his suggestions were incorporated into the scheme. The gallery at the back of the hall is an instance of this and proved so successful that it was perpetuated at Hurst Road some twenty years later. The new School was built to accommodate 660 boys although, at this point, it had rather less than two thirds of this number. *The Kentish Times* compared its airy lightness to what it recalled as the dim, unhealthy surroundings of the schools attended by the previous generation and made extravagant play with metaphor arising therefrom. "Too many of them were dark, not only with the darkness of unhealthy architecture but with the darkness of unbridled pedagogy which stifled free criticism and independent thought." Now well into his stride, the anonymous journalist continued: "It is a matter for solemn thanks that in these days, when it is more than ever necessary for people to do their own thinking … modern teaching aims to produce a free man or woman rather than a regimented adding machine."

Modernist in influence, owing much to the purist manifesto of Le Corbusier, the building was splendidly functional as well as strikingly original in its appearance. To Kenneth Sander, the School's first State Scholar, writing later in *The Housewife*, it was "like something from an H.G. Wells film fantasy". As an icon of thirties school architecture it has become, in its latest incarnation as Kemnal Technology College, a grade two listed building. The Chairman of Kent Education Committee, W.R. Nottidge, however, apparently took far greater pride in the fact that, in terms of cost per place, the new school was the cheapest ever to be erected in the county.

The building was set in 23 acres of land and, as a noise reduction measure, positioned as far back as possible from the adjacent Sidcup and Orpington by-passes along which traffic tore at speeds of up to 60 m.p.h. "More glass than grass", observed one local wag and, when Summer came the following year, the boys nearest the windows were, in the words of sixth-former James Murray, "reduced to perspiring desperation". In the depths of Winter, equally, it was the opposite side of the classroom, nearest the radiators, that was competed for. Grass too there was aplenty, however, and in the middle of the turfed quadrangle, surrounded by cloisters, sat, rather smugly, Mr Palmer's famous white meteorological cabinet.

As the excitement of the move began to subside, school settled back into its accustomed routine. The workmen wandering about the premises putting the finishing touches to fixtures and fittings were soon ignored, though many lessons were interrupted by the hammering in of nails and the whirring of drills. A striking feature of the Autumn Term, 1938, were two debates which caught the prevailing anxieties of the time. The motion

"There it stands, a building of glass, brimming with light and air, immense,
unorthodox, yet nevertheless infinitely majestic."

that "this house welcomes the future with hope and optimism" was, unsurprisingly, though rather sadly, defeated by 17 votes to 12. A few weeks later the motion that "this house favours the introduction of conscription with immediate effect" was defeated by the wider margin of 21 votes to 5. A little over twelve months later, on New Year's Day, 1940, two million men aged between 19 and 27 were called up to the armed forces.

The last peace-time Christmas for seven years came and with it issue number 15 of the *Chronicle*, the first, of course, to emanate from Chislehurst and, appropriately, with an updated cover design, featuring the new building, courtesy of Mr Bramwell. Much space, as might be expected, is devoted to the splendours of the new edifice. A sixth-former, J.H.Hall, must be allowed to speak for all. "There it stands, a building of glass, brimming with light and air, immense, unorthodox, yet nevertheless infinitely majestic." Praise indeed.

Early the next term, on February 9th 1939, the new school buildings were officially opened by Charles Robertson, Chairman of the London Education Committee. The boys, all but a chosen few "helpers", were given the morning off but, on a cold, blustery afternoon, they paraded in front of the main entrance where the ceremonial unlocking was performed. School Captain "Sammy" Spicer (who went on to become Professor of Linguistics and Pro-Vice-Chancellor at the University of Essex) stepped forward and handed the guest of honour a silk-lined case from which he took a golden key that had been made in the School's metalwork room. With this the door was opened. Gowns flapping in the stiff wind, the staff led the way into the main hall where parents and dignitaries were assembled. Among the platform guests were Mr P.R. Norris and Mr Rolfe Nottidge, respectively the Director and Chairman of Education for Kent. A dedication service conducted by Canon Webb and the Rev. T.W.Bond was followed by the sort of speeches usual on such occasions. The School Choir sang *To Youth* by Alexander Smith and the School Song and the National Anthem followed. Staff and senior pupils then began to show visitors around the building but proceedings were cut short by a power-failure and the great day ended earlier than planned. The superstitiously inclined no doubt saw, in the sudden going out of the lights, an omen foretelling dark days ahead. If so they were, on this occasion, right.

In the months that followed, two visits, in particular, gave strong hints as to what was to come. On Empire Air Day, in May, Hawker Hurricanes performed aerobatics over Biggin Hill and Blenheims carried out a mock bombing raid, much to the excitement of the watching boys, many of whom would, before long, be in the R.A.F. themselves. On July 18th a large group again visited Portsmouth. In pouring rain they steamed round the harbour where, amongst battleships and destroyers, the aircraft-carrier *Ark Royal* lay at anchor. Like the Hood she too would shortly be sunk with horrendous loss of life. No cameras were allowed this time but the boys, as they sat, dripping, on the electric train laid on for them by the Southern Railway and headed back to Sidcup, had some powerful images imprinted on their minds and had ingested plenty of food for thought.

The School's first full year at Crittall's Corner thus came to an end. The boys dispersed for their Summer holidays, aware, obviously, of the grave news arriving almost daily from overseas but little imagining how different life would be upon their return to the "glasshouse" in the Autumn.

CHAPTER FIVE

War

ON AUGUST 23RD 1939 German foreign minister Von Ribbentrop flew to Moscow and signed, with Molotov, the Nazi-Soviet Pact. The new alliance stunned Britain and France. Reservists were hurriedly called up to the forces, F.W.Dutton, the new Geography master, being the first from Chis and Sid to go. As a Territorial Army officer he was recalled to the Royal Tank Corps in July. The digging of trench-shelters in the School grounds was begun and, on August 29th, the staff were summoned back from their holidays and told to stand by for emergency duties. Geoff Cook and Edwyn Birchenough received orders to report to Control H.Q., Bromley, for A.R.P. (Air-Raid Precaution) activities. The evacuation of children began in parts of Kent. At dawn on September 1st German soldiers crossed the border into Poland and a new word entered the language: *blitzkrieg*.

Like the rest of the population throughout the country the people of Sidcup and Chislehurst gathered around their radio sets just before 11.15 on the clear, bright morning of Sunday, September 3rd. Prime Minister Neville Chamberlain's voice reached them across the air-waves, flat, weary, infinitely sad: "This morning the British Ambassador in Berlin handed the German Government a final note stating that, unless we heard from them by 11 o'clock that they were prepared, at once, to withdraw their troops from Poland, a state of war would exist between us. I have to tell you that no such undertaking has been received and that, consequently, this country is at war with Germany." When "God Save the King" was played many families stood to attention in their living rooms. Shortly afterwards the air-raid sirens wailed and everyone took cover. It was a false alarm.

The Autumn Term was not scheduled to begin until September 14th and so the boys joined in the great digging of trenches and filling of sandbags which took place over the next few days. Nobody went out without a gas-mask slung over one shoulder in its cardboard box. The air filled with barrage balloons and hospitals were cleared to take the million casualties confidently expected in the first two months of war. A good few patients duly appeared, though the vast majority were the victims of the blackout. Regarded as something of a joke to start with, the absence of street lighting and normal car headlights led to many collisions on the roads.

At the behest of their parents, one and a half million children were evacuated from towns and cities, particularly in the South East. Surprisingly, considering that Kent was very much in the front line, only fifteen boys from Chis and Sid were among them. The expected air-raids, however, failed to materialise. Two hundred thousand British soldiers embarked for France.

September 14th duly came and went. Term could not begin because the shelters were unfinished, the delay in their completion being exacerbated by their tendency to flood. Boys were brought back over the following weeks, a few forms at a time. Not until October 26th was the entire School (minus those few evacuees) reassembled. School was now a very different place. Hall assemblies, for example, were discontinued. Given the numbers involved it would have been impossible to carry out a hurried evacuation safely. Air-raid drill was practised frequently. Perhaps the most famous photograph in the School's history shows lines of boys in gas-masks descending the glass-enclosed main staircase. The Head and his Deputy needed no reminders about the effects of poison gas.

And then ...nothing happened. It seemed there had been a reprieve. People settled down to enjoy the warm Autumn weather. There was even, briefly, a sense of euphoria, this period being referred to, in retrospect, as the "phoney war". Once fully back in residence the School carried on with its normal routine of teaching and learning although many activities were unavoidably hampered or curtailed. As the days shortened, blackout regulations necessitated that the afternoon session finished early and after-school events had to be cancelled.

Mac's letter to his "dear boys", dated December 1st 1939, declared: "Everyone of us is called upon to play his or her part and to accept with fortitude the role allotted by fate and circumstance." He called for "vigour and efficiency" from the boys in war-time which he contrasted with "the piping times of peace", borrowing Richard III's contemptuous phrase.

Gas mask drill, 1941. (Photo courtesy of Imperial War Museum).

Among the first Old Boys to join the forces were Norman Barber and Arthur Stanyon (Queen's Westminster Rifles), Raymond Greenway (Royal Army Medical Corps), Douglas Flindall (Royal West Kents), Geoffrey

"This way round!" More gas mask practice. (Staff, L to R: L.Stringer, Headmaster, R.Clarke).

Hunt and Peter Marchant (Royal Corps of Signals) and Francis Whitehorne (New Zealand Artillery). The first fatality seems to have been that of Godfrey Wood, one of the original Station Road pupils, who died of an illness in February 1940, just two months after volunteering for the R.A.F. at the age of eighteen.

The first Winter of the War was Kent's coldest for half a century. The sea froze at Folkestone. Fuel shortages made it difficult for the boys to keep warm in a building consisting largely of glass. On the Maginot Line all was quiet. France had a hundred divisions dug in on the Western Front, augmented by the ten of the British Expeditionary Force. The defences were deemed impregnable. The cold gave way to a remarkably sunny Spring and confidence grew. Nine months of war had passed yet, on the home front at least, all remained calm.

Suddenly, on May 10th 1940, everything changed. At 5.30 a.m. Hitler's troops invaded Holland and Belgium. Later that day a single German plane dropped bombs near Chilham in Kent, the first attack of the war upon the British mainland. That evening Churchill succeeded

Chamberlain as Prime Minister. Two days later German armour crossed the Meuse into France. All was now frantic activity. E.J.Dellar left to join an R.A.F. that was taking heavy losses over France and the low countries. Holland surrendered, Brussels fell and twelve million refugees crowded the roads of Northern France. The Wehrmacht advanced 200 miles in a week and, on May 27th, reached the Channel. June 4th saw the evacuation of British forces from Dunkirk and on the 14th the German army entered Paris.

Invasion was now a very real possibility and discussions began about procedures for evacuating the School should this become necessary. "So long as we are able to keep our present humour and courage we should be able to pull through anything," declared Geoffrey Cook, defiantly, in his *Chronicle* editorial the following month. Poles were erected on the playing fields and a heavy roller and a farm-waggon placed as obstructions to enemy gliders seeking to land. Grass was left to grow with the intention of gathering it later as hay. Twenty or so boys answered the Government's appeal and worked on the land, mostly in the Chelsfield and Swanley districts, during the Summer holidays. They toiled away in the heat from early morning until eight o'clock in the evening, weeding potatoes, harvesting, rick-making, plum-picking and the like, unsung heroes all.

At the start of the War teaching had been a reserved occupation but this ruling was now rescinded for those under 35. Everybody on the Chis and Sid staff was therefore liable for call-up other than the Headmaster and Arthur Parsons, both of whom, of course, had served in the previous war. In the event, fourteen teaching staff joined the forces, about two thirds of those employed on a full-time basis. Hugh Oddie, a young Cambridge graduate who had joined to teach Chemistry at the start of the War, was one of the first to go and, sadly, one of the first to lose his life, shot down over the Ruhr in June 1943. Oddie remained at the controls of his crippled Halifax bomber while several of his crew baled out and parachuted to safety, by which time it was too late to save himself. Dennis Clarke was another to join the R.A.F., spending most of the War in the Middle East where, quite by chance, he met colleague Bill Freeman who had joined the Royal Artillery. Bill's letter, dated August 20th 1940, apologising to the Head for his abrupt departure, survives in the School Archive. Maurice Gridley was called up to the Royal Navy with similar abruptness, being required "to report at Portsmouth tomorrow, 10th September, 1940." G.R.Gibbs, F.H. Bramwell and P.H. Taylor were called up to the R.A.F.

K.Mortimore and Victor Cullingworth joined the Medical Corps and Edwyn Birchenough the Royal Artillery. Cedric Morley, the physicist, was called up to work in the R.A.F. research establishment at Farnborough.

Replacing staff at such short notice, of course, proved a nightmare for McGregor Williams and the Education Department. So many staff vacancies occurred that they could be filled only by employing, for the most part, older, often retired, schoolmasters and – to the horror of certain traditionalists – women. Many of the replacement staff were not used to handling lively boys and some had serious disciplinary problems. Malcolm Bowden remembers leading 'Bud' Simons a dog's life and describes Joe Fox being pelted with flour bombs. One unfortunate Biology teacher named Froud refused to return after just one day in the classroom, thereby earning for himself the unenviable record for the shortest ever teaching career at Chis and Sid.

Many of these war-time appointments were temporary ones and it has been calculated that about forty teachers "filled in" during this six year period. Shortage of space precludes mention of more than a few. The cachet of being the School's first female teacher fell to Enid Palmer, wife of Geography teacher Tom. Mrs Palmer, a graduate of Newnham College, began teaching Mathematics in January 1941 and stayed until the end of the Summer Term. Jean Anderson, a physicist on the brink of her sixtieth birthday, joined the School just two days later than Mrs Palmer but found the boys too much for her and left within a month. Nevertheless she holds the dubious distinction of being the eldest-born teacher ever to work at Chis and Sid, having entered this world in 1882, seven years before Mac himself. A very different kettle of fish was Lily Cunningham. Described by one of her numerous adolescent admirers, Roger Dracup, as "gorgeous and curvaceous" she was known, universally, as 'Diamond Lil' in consequence of the flamboyant jewellery with which she encrusted her fingers. Hundreds of boys discovered a new interest in Biology during her occupation of Bill Freeman's lab.

Eva Jackson was another to arrive as a "stop-gap" teacher but she remained for twenty-six years, for most of them as Head of Classics. A brilliant scholar, with a first class degree and an M.A. from Sheffield, Mrs Jackson is remembered with great affection by her former pupils. One of her eccentricities was to keep a tennis ball tucked into the sleeve of her gown which she brought down on the table with a wallop, the terrific noise it made frightening inattentive boys out of their skins. Another of her favourite methods of dealing with miscreants was to make them sit under her desk. From time to time she would administer a kick. During these wartime years a stray bullet from an aerial 'dog-fight' ricocheted around her bath but she escaped with a small cut to her cheek from a splinter of enamel. Eva Jackson died in the Spring of 2002, just a few months short of her one hundredth birthday.

Two other wartime appointees deserve particular mention, both of whom clearly qualify as members of the sizeable 'Chis and Sid Eccentrics Club.' Naim Basri, born and educated in Baghdad, joined the staff in November 1940, at the height of the Blitz, to teach Physical Education, replacing E.J.Dellar. Alan Hanson recalls being sent out by him, in the depths of January, to play at snowballing dressed in nothing but a pair of shorts. Basri joined the boys on an icy playground slide and succeeded in colliding with some metal railings and knocking himself out. On another occasion Basri threw the aforementioned Hanson, fully clothed this time, into the swimming pool at Dunton Green. At the end of the War he left to join the Arabic section of the B.B.C. World Service.

Erich Geiringer, a Jewish refugee from Austria, arrived to teach Biology in November 1941, leaving behind him a half-completed medical degree course at the University of Vienna. Geiringer, though only 24, had already acquired a colourful past. Having escaped via Switzerland in 1938 he was interned for six months with the celebrated Austrian philosopher Ludwig Wittgenstein. Geiringer endured considerable teasing on account of his strong accent and was once reproved by Mac for failing to leap to his feet at the start of the National Anthem. He was fond of playing the mouth-organ and is said to have done so even while invigilating exams. One of his more alarming habits was to wave a revolver (presumably a toy one but nobody was sure) at pupils who were not attending to their studies. Sometimes he carried in his pocket a live rabbit which he would produce at unexpected moments, hugely to the enjoyment of small boys, though his propensity to slap pupils around the face for no very observable reason was felt by some to be a less endearing feature of his personality. Erich Geiringer left in the Summer of 1943 to continue his clinical studies, this time at the University of Dublin, and went on to enjoy an illustrious career in medical research after the War. It would be fascinating to know whether his face-slapping proclivities continued into professorhood in New Zealand but such extended investigation is beyond the scope of this history.

The Blitz began in earnest on Saturday, September 7th 1940. Three hundred bombers – Heinkels, Dorniers and Junkers – accompanied by six hundred Messerschmidt 109 fighters, swooped low across Kent around five o'clock on a hot, sunny afternoon in a surprise attack on London. Hurricanes and Spitfires of Fighter Command climbed to meet them. Third-former Derek Guyatt still vividly recalls the bombers passing overhead in groups of sixty, each formation chevron-shaped like the stripes on an N.C.O.'s sleeve.

In the weeks that followed, as the raids intensified, barrage balloons filled the sky and, at night, hundreds of searchlights probed the darkness, coalescing into a single cone so bright that those in the blacked out street below could read of the destruction in their newspapers. The School was firmly in "Bomb Alley", as it came to be called, and the drone of enemy planes, the sharper whine of R.A.F. fighters and the deafening thump of (largely ineffectual) anti-aircraft fire became familiar sounds to every pupil. With Biggin Hill, most famous of the Battle of Britain fighter bases, only about seven miles away, the boys soon became accustomed to the sight of dog-fights taking place overhead. P.Gross of IVA recalls the air "filled with the sound of screaming planes, bursting bombs and the staccato rattle of machine-guns" and Kenneth Greenway of VB described planes, lit up from the brilliant sunshine, appearing "as silver dots, dashing here and there, turning, twisting and tumbling in and out of one another, leaving a pattern of streaks in the sky". He watched one go into a steep dive, nose first, with white smoke pouring from its tail until it "burst into flames, turning and twisting", before crashing to earth behind a clump of trees.

"After a particularly busy night there was always a competition in School to produce the largest piece of shrapnel from the roads," wrote Guyatt in his account of this memorable period. Of particular danger were the unexploded incendiary bombs that the boys gathered up despite strict instructions not to do so. On the night of September 17th a landmine fell on houses in Valley Road, at the far end of the 1st XI cricket field, many of which were destroyed. The School, three hundred yards away, was severely damaged. Unsurprisingly, countless windows were shattered and one side of the assembly Hall was blown out, leaving it open to wind and rain. At first only a small part of the building remained usable so boys went in for one day per week and returned with work for the next six days to be completed at home. Gradually the number of schooldays was increased as repairs progressed.

The full opening of the new academic year was postponed until September 30th while staff set about sweeping up jagged mountains of broken glass and fastening anti-splinter netting to the remaining window panes, their work constantly interrupted by enemy planes and the firing of the ack-ack batteries nearby. Machine-gun emplacements were dug outside the front gates of the school. The Blitz was popularly supposed to be the prelude to invasion and Crittall's Corner lay astride one of the most obvious routes to London from the Channel ports.

The corridors outside the Hall and Gym were blocked in to form anti-blast shelters for use when the Luftwaffe came in so fast and low that there was no time to reach the deep shelters that had been dug on the field parallel to the avenue and near the cycle sheds. When the sirens wailed, as they did with ever-increasing frequency during that most traumatic of terms, the boys hurried in pairs to the shelters, carrying with them the textbook appropriate to the lesson that had been interrupted, together with exercise book and pencil.

Sport was severely restricted. Not only inter-school matches but even form games had to go. Boys came to school with emergency "iron rations" (biscuits, chocolate etc.) for when stays in the shelters were particularly lengthy. All too often they were consumed early in the day, however, and did not fulfil their purpose. The installation of electric lighting in the trenches made conditions more bearable although frequent power-cuts had to be endured. The *Chronicle* for December 1940, now in the hands of E.C.Pettet, begins as follows: "This editorial is being written by candlelight in a small dug-out. For a while the night is comparatively quiet – nothing to be heard except an occasional buzzing of German bombers in the distance … and the remote, gruff-throated woofing of the guns towards London. The usual sounds, but any moment they may sweep up into a crescendo of fury and danger." In the circumstances it is remarkable that the magazine appeared at all.

Each of the six houses was allotted a plot of land in the School grounds as part of the "Dig for Victory" campaign. Inter-house rivalry was encouraged and some volunteers even gave up their Saturdays, becoming enthusiastic gardeners in the process. The land, just under an acre in total, was put to the growing of potatoes, cabbages, turnips and carrots which went, in due course, to the School kitchens and made a welcome addition to the daily diet. Indeed such was the Government's emphasis upon nutrition during the war years that, it has been plausibly argued, children, at least, were better nourished than in the period immediately preceding the conflict or in the years of recovery that followed.

News arrived, belatedly, that Stanley Flaxman, a lieutenant in the King's Own Yorkshire Light Infantry, had become the first ex-Chis and Sid pupil to fall into enemy hands as a prisoner of war. One is sharply reminded how young these soldiers were by the recollection that Flaxman was the quickest 1st XI bowler during the Summer of 1939.

Christmas 1940 was darkened by grim news crowding in from every side. Cyril Owen, the brilliant young athlete, one of the original sixty-two and first holder of the 'victor ludorum' trophy, was killed in a raid on a research establishment in Wales where he was working as a chemist. He was twenty-one. Gerald Dale died in a German concentration camp and David Powell became the first of the many Old Sedcopians to be killed in action with the R.A.F.

With the coming of Spring the number of daylight bombing raids diminished and school work proceeded with fewer interruptions. By mid-February the school day was extended to its original four o'clock finish. Time was still spent in the trench-shelters, though, and this was made less uncomfortable by the introduction of an electric heating system. The night of March 19th 1941 is memorable for numerous incendiary bombs falling on the flat roof of the School and on the surrounding field. Fortunately many failed to ignite and the fires that did break out were capably extinguished by a team of firewatchers led by Mr Fox. Staff, in pairs, subsequently took turns to fire-watch overnight.

That same month the School's Air Training Corps, known as 1227 Squadron A.T.C., was established under the command of Flight Lieutenant McGregor Williams. By the end of the Summer term its ranks had swollen to over 180 cadets one of whom, J.Syms of VB, brimming with pride and excitement, was taken for a "flip" in a Miles Magister trainer by Squadron Leader John Mungo-Park, the celebrated night-fighter ace who was killed in his Spitfire shortly afterwards over Belgium. At least thirty of these cadets went on to join the R.A.F. (or the Fleet Air Arm) before the end of the War, some half dozen being killed in action.

By the Summer the threat of invasion from the air had sufficiently receded to permit the removal of the obstructions from the field and the recommencement of cricket against other schools. Boys in the Fifth Form and above volunteered as fire-watchers or as messengers attached to A.R.P. or first-aid posts. Now that clothes rationing had been introduced and coupons were in short supply school uniform regulations were relaxed. This, together with hot, sticky weather, lent a somewhat casual air to the final weeks of term. At the end of the academic year the mood was far more optimistic than it had been at its outset the previous September. Hitler had hurled a hundred divisions against the Soviet Union and, in mid-July, Britain concluded a mutual assistance pact with Stalin.

The new school year began with some rare good news. It was announced that Cyril Cooling had won an Open Scholarship to University College, London and November's half term holiday was extended by a day in celebration. Another notable success that Summer was the first class degree achieved by Kenneth Sander, the School's previous State Scholarship winner, who had entered Imperial College in 1939. Inter-school football resumed with a full programme of matches and morning Hall assemblies were restored, daylight bombing raids now being few and far between. Night-time attacks continued, however, and Colin Suddards of 5A describes being awakened by the siren in the early hours of the morning and stumbling out of the house on incendiary patrol: "Suddenly a whistle, rising in intensity to a shriek, rent the air. We instinctively fell flat on the pavement and felt the vibration of the bomb as it exploded." At two a.m. his shift ended and, after a cup of hot cocoa, he tumbled back into bed to arise five hours later and begin a full school day. This experience typifies the routine to which the more senior boys, at least, had become accustomed.

In October the A.T.C. Squadron, now officially affiliated to R.A.F. Biggin Hill, began building its own glider, an ambitious project not attempted in any other state school. Gas-mask drill and air-raid warning rehearsals continued on a regular basis. There were complaints about the quality of wartime ink, now a dirty grey-blue colour and sometimes hardly any colour at all.

On December 7th the Japanese bombed Pearl Harbour and the United States entered the War. The German advance ground to a halt in appalling weather outside Moscow. Christmas 1941 was therefore celebrated more wholeheartedly than its predecessor had been. The mood darkened early in 1942, however, with the news that Singapore had fallen to the Japanese. In March the R.A.F. began its round-the-clock offensive against munitions factories in the Ruhr. At least a dozen Old Sedcopians were now serving in Bomber Command. Pilot-Officer David Powell was the first of them to be killed in action, shot down over Germany in June, 1941, at the age of twenty.

Lieutenant Douglas Stonham (R.A.S.C.)
Killed in action, 1942.

As our pilots headed East the Luftwaffe was still sweeping up "Bomb Alley" from the opposite direction and the decision was taken to camouflage the large expanse of conspicuously white concrete that constituted the flat roof of the School building. Huge quantities of 'clinker' from the School's furnace were spread across it by Mr Stacey the caretaker and an enthusiastic young team of volunteers for whom the task of raking cinders, dirty though it was, seemed more enticing than the alternative of grappling with French irregular verbs. Besides, it gave them further opportunity, from their lofty vantage point, to ogle Joan Partridge, the chimney sweep's pretty daughter, who worked in the School canteen and was much admired by hundreds of pubescent boys. Wartime austerity provided few such welcome distractions. Even the Tuck Shop had been forced to close since most of the boys used up their sweet coupons elsewhere.

The Summer Term saw the School's first General Inspection. From May 19th to May 22nd inspectors "prowled around the building with silent, rubber-soled shoes on. If they saw anyone misbehaving they would pull out a green note-book and write something down", observed fourth-former Robert Craven, while his classmate Peter Veness lamented that, for a few days at least, they were unable to put the traditional wastepaper basket on top of Mr Fox's door. "In fact there was no fun during that week at all." Apparently the elderly gentlemen were satisfied with what they saw, though, after the passage of some sixty years,a copy of their eventual report has proved difficult to track down.

That same term, Miss Mennie took a party of pupils to Kingsway Hall, in central London, for the "Greetings to Soviet Schools" rally and money was collected for the "Aid to Russia" fund. The British people were very grateful for the fact that the Eastern Front was tying down the vast majority of Hitler's forces and affording them, in consequence, a temporary respite in the West.

The new academic year began on September 17th with things "more normal than at any time since the outbreak of war", according to *Chronicle* editor 'Spike' Pettet. Work pursued a steady course, uninterrupted by air-raid alerts. Societies and games flourished again and the number of visits greatly increased. Several trips up to London were made to watch Shakespeare productions, one of them the John Gielgud *Macbeth*. This more relaxed regime was symbolised by the fact that, for the first time since September 1939, boys were no longer compelled to trail their gas-masks with them wherever they went.

In October 1227 Squadron A.T.C. spent the day at Biggin Hill, six cadets going for a twenty minute flight in a Lancaster. Such initiations, of course, helped to secure for the R.A.F. a steady supply of replacements to feed into the great mincing-machine that was Bomber Command. Of the School's 45 war dead 27 flew with the R.A.F. or (in two cases) the Royal Navy's Fleet Air Arm. Bomber Command lost about 47,000 aircrew, the highest pro-rata loss of any Allied military unit. Nevertheless this figure represents only about 15% of total British military fatalities during World War Two and renders startlingly disproportionate the 60% of the School's roll of honour who perished in aerial combat. At least 113 Sedcopians served in the wartime R.A.F. and a further 13 in the Fleet Air Arm. Pilots and navigators were largely drawn from the universities and the grammar schools. It should also be remembered that, although conscription meant all healthy males between 18 and 40 had to be either in uniform or a reserved occupation, all aircrew were (uniquely) volunteers.

Gym Club, 1944. (Naim Basri, far right).

That same October Montgomery's Eighth Army defeated Rommel's Afrika Korps at El Alamein and, within weeks, the Red Army had forced Von Paulus' surrender at Stalingrad. The war had turned decisively in favour of the Allies. At Chis and Sid the mood brightened perceptibly. The Model Railway Club was formed under Mr Mann. A track was laid in 4B's form-room and some small children from a neighbouring kindergarten were invited in to admire it. For all Mr Basri's efforts, however, the 1st and 2nd XI soccer teams contrived only one victory between them from the fourteen matches played, though this was one better than the Rugby XV managed from their five. The iron railings round one side of the field were removed and sent as salvage to aid the war effort. In the Spring of 1943 the cadets spent an entire week at Biggin Hill and learnt how to fire a machine gun as well as enjoying flights in various types of planes. Sports Day was reinstated after three years in abeyance and much excitement was occasioned by a small boy called Davies who, in rashly attempting to slide down the banister-rail, fell thirty feet down a staircase. Miraculously he landed on a pile of sandbags and survived the experience, none the worse for wear apart from some minor cuts and bruises.

The main event of the Summer Term was undoubtedly the Dramatic Society's production of *Henry Vth*, an appropriate choice for the School's first ever Shakespearean play given its military theme and patriotic tone.

The Headmaster himself directed as well as playing the Chorus. Geoff Cook took the title role. Given the problems of the previous few years this was the first time that the School had felt able to use its well-equipped hall and stage for an event on this scale. The production ran for five performances and drew lavish praise from the *Kentish Times*. H.J. Anderson, one of the many temporary appointees on the staff, mustered a capable sixteen piece orchestra – another important 'first' in the history of music and drama at the School. Norah Williams, the Headmaster's daughter and an experienced actress, made a "delicious" Katherine, by all accounts and the reporter expressed the hope that this would be the first of a long line of Shakespeare productions by the School – an aspiration that time would amply fulfil.

All connected with Chis and Sid were deeply saddened by news from Tunisia that Norman Barber, a lieutenant in the Royal West Kents, had been killed in an attempt to rescue a wounded comrade from a minefield. 'Toddy', as he was universally known, was one of the original Station Road pioneers, a notable athlete, first captain of cricket and hugely popular with boys and staff alike.

The end of the academic year, 28th July 1943, saw the departure of Edward Pettet who left to become Senior English Master at Kilburn Grammar School, bequeathing the *Chronicle* to John Walsh. Caretaker Stacey, who – usefully at times – gave warning of his approach by the obnoxious stink of his pipe, made way for his successor R.G.Baynham. Just days before the start of the new school year word came that Italy had surrendered. German troops were now in full retreat on the Eastern Front. This good news, however, was overshadowed the following month when one of the now sporadic enemy air-raids struck Sidcup, killing six people and injuring many others. Among the dead was Sidney Martin, the Senior Classics Master, whose house in Old Farm Avenue was destroyed by a direct hit though, amazingly, his wife and small son survived. A large contingent from the School, staff and boys, attended his funeral at Holy Trinity Church, Lamorbey. McGregor Williams' tribute refers to his sporting prowess, particularly in tennis, and his brilliant scholarship, together with a charming modesty and natural dignity.

It was new editor John Walsh's sad task, in his first issue of the *Chronicle*, dated December 1943, to record five more deaths on active service: those of Hedley Madgett,who was posthumously awarded the Distinguished Flying Medal, Alan Gardner, Bernard Wright, Peter

Collins and Hugh Oddie, all of them flying with the R.A.F. In his editorial Walsh refers to a large wooden structure, located just outside the Staff Room, known as the 'Queen Mary', which consisted of two stacks of shelves, placed back to back, for the depositing and receiving back of exercise books. One side was labelled with the names of the teaching staff. As the War progressed these labels changed with ever greater frequency and the English master lamented the unsettling effect upon the School. "The series of rapid departures brought about a temporary restlessness which not even air-raids and shelter-life had previously been able to produce."

There were, of course, arrivals too and an important addition to the Staff during this period was Harold Brooke, a veteran of the previous War, who came to teach French. A famously severe disciplinarian and an accomplished pianist, Brooke served the School for nearly thirteen years up to his death in 1956.

Innovations that Autumn Term included the playing of classical music "on our powerful electrical reproducer" during Friday assemblies and the dreaded Fortnightly List, which ranked boys in mark order as "an admirable antidote to listlessness" and " a useful spur to those who cannot work for love." The Debating Society decided, by 95 votes to 15, that war did not bring out the best in man.

The following Spring Southern England became one enormous armed camp as preparations for the Normandy invasion intensified. Huge columns of military vehicles rumbled past the School on the Sidcup Bypass. Then came the brief radio announcement: "Allied forces have landed on the coast of France." Jack Watkins (at the School from 1932 to '37) was one of a number of Old Sedcopians who took part in this greatest of all invasions, landing on Sword Beach in the first wave alongside Lord Lovat and his famous bagpiper. Later he was one of the first Allied soldiers to enter Belsen.

Few at school on that memorable day, Tuesday June 6th 1944, will forget hearing the news as it circulated like wild-fire. Middle-aged masters, as excited as their charges, put their heads round classroom doors to report the long-awaited event.

As so often in this war, however, good news all too quickly gave way to bad. Within a week Hitler's new secret weapon, the V1,rained down on London and the suburbs. The flying-bomb, quickly nicknamed the 'doodlebug', was, in effect, an unmanned plane with a primitive jet-engine at the rear. It carried nearly a ton of high explosive and was launched from the Calais area with just enough petrol to reach Greater London. When the fuel supply cut out the engine stopped and the bomb nose-dived silently to earth, taking about fifteen seconds before impact. Its targets within the conurbation were, of course, entirely random and this factor alone made the missile even more alarming than the bombs that had blitzed the capital four years earlier when there had been at least some element of precision in their deployment. Once again Crittall's Corner lay in the centre of 'Bomb Alley'.

On the morning of Friday June 16th a flying-bomb fell in the Avenue and again the School's windows were shattered, iron frames being wrenched out of the concrete on one side of the Assembly Hall leaving it gaping open as before. T.Oesterreicher of the Upper Sixth describes riding to school that morning, his steel helmet slung over his shoulder. "Just as I came to the cycle-shed the guns opened up. I took a flying leap for the shelters where I found the Headmaster, the staff and most of the boys. Mr Parsons was conspicuous in a brilliant yellow helmet."

It had been assumed that bombing was over, apart, perhaps, from the occasional token foray, and the 'second blitz' came as a terrible shock to the population of Northern Kent who found themselves, without warning, back in the front line again. The timing was particularly unfortunate as far as the School was concerned since public examinations were in full swing. With new surface-shelters adjoining the Hall the candidates were able to continue. A spotting system was quickly established. When the look-outs on the roof saw a doodlebug approaching the School a whistle was blown and a bell rung, whereupon the examinees left their desks and hurried into the shelters. Strict silence was, naturally, enforced until the word was given to return. The rest of the school 'camped out' on the field for the remainder of the Summer Term. At 9 a.m. each form arranged wooden benches near the mouth of its allotted trench-shelter and here the day's lessons were held, except when interrupted by the spotter's whistle whereupon the boys disappeared, mole-like, underground. Fortunately the weather was kind and boys acquired healthy tans in the June and July sun.

Rex Watson, whose work on hydrogen fuel cells at Cambridge led to their use in the Apollo moon flights and who went on to become Director of the Chemical Defence Establishment at Porton Down, recalls one lunchtime when a flying-bomb's engine cut out, it seemed, directly overhead. With no time to reach even the surface shelters the boys all dived under the tables. The bomb landed with a stupendous crash a few hundred yards away. Over the summer months eight thousand flying-bombs were launched on England, the vast majority landing in the South East suburbs, the Chislehurst, Sidcup and Orpington districts being amongst the most badly hit. Hundreds were killed and thousands of homes destroyed or badly damaged. But worse still was to follow. On September 9th, a fortnight after the liberation of Paris, the first V2 hit London. This ballistic missile travelled much faster than its predecessor, was virtually impossible to shoot down and packed even more high explosive into its warhead. Chis and Sid, however, carried on while most other schools in the area were partially or completely closed. Although the building itself sustained no more serious damage the carnage round about continued. One V2 rocket-bomb exploded in North Cray during morning assembly and another landed near the Girls' School in Beaverwood Road. The sound of ambulances and fire-engines on the by-pass became a familiar background to academic study. Perhaps worst of all was when word reached a boy that a bomb had fallen in his road. In such cases he was allowed to go home at once and many returned to find houses damaged or destroyed. Several boys were injured, some even hospitalised, though no such incidents occurred on the School premises themselves.

There were, nevertheless, happier moments intermingled with the panic and the grief. Volunteers at work in the neighbouring fields and orchards took advantage of the chance to fraternise with the Land Girls who frequently toiled alongside them. Pulling flax, potato-lighting and wheat-stooking thus became more bearable despite the stifling heat.Caretaker Talbot's attractive daughter Anne was much seen about the School and raised temperatures still further if the numerous appreciative references to her charms that slid their way, thinly disguised, into the pages of the *Chronicle* are to be believed. The much-postponed production of *The Merchant of Venice* at length went ahead in March 1945, Mc Gregor Williams (who else?) giving a memorable performance as Shylock. The boys beat the staff 3.1 at soccer, undeterred by a V2 exploding in the neighbourhood during half-time. News came that Walter Smith had been admitted to Pembroke College, Cambridge, the first in an illustrious line of 'Oxbridge' successes for which the School achieved national celebrity over the next few decades. Smith's achievement was rapidly followed by that of Irving Browning, the School's poet, who won an Open Scholarship to read English at Magdalen College, Oxford. Browning, who possessed a very light voice, had achieved great success playing female leads such as

Portia and Lady Macbeth. Some years later he attained further academic distinction through his election to a fellowship at Merton College, Oxford.

On a more depressing note, the members of the Debating Society decided, by a majority of 70 votes to 35, that another world war was inevitable in their time. This war, however, in Europe at least, was drawing to its close and, on May 8th, Field-Marshal Wilhelm Keitel surrendered unconditionally on behalf of the German people as a whole. After a brief period of wild celebration the mood quickly turned to one of sombre reflection into which the pent-up exhaustion of six long years could finally be released. A few weeks later McGregor Williams addressed the School in the following terms: "The feeling of grievous loss of over forty Old Boys who, barely come to manhood, have made the supreme sacrifice…is sustained by a pride of consolation that their sacrifice for humanity was made ungrudgingly and not in vain. To the boys who have served our country in the armed forces of the Crown, I want to express the School's greatest admiration of your selfless devotion to the call of duty and congratulations on your achievements. To have hundreds serving with distinction in the forces is no mean achievement for a school which did not come into being until 1931." He went on to praise the boys who had endured war-time conditions at Crittall's Corner, expressing his admiration for them too, particularly their "spirit of calm endurance during the trials of 'blitz' and V1 and V2 attacks … when screaming engines of death were passing over and falling around for most of the day." It was, he said, an achievement of which they might feel proud. They had more than justified the confidence he had expressed at the beginning of the War and proved themselves "in England's finest hour, the equals, in achievement and promise, of those whose doughty deeds have forged her glorious name."

It is difficult to arrive at precise figures but at least 280 former pupils are known to have served in the armed forces during the Second World War. Of these 113 were in the R.A.F., 94 in the Army and 73 in the Royal Navy, of whom 13 flew with the Fleet Air Arm. These numbers are augmented by a further thirteen members, and one former member, of the teaching staff. Many of their names have been mentioned already in this chapter. To these should be added those of Alistair Wilson, John Goldby, John Cooksey and Michael Carreck, all of whom were awarded the Distinguished Flying Cross. The purple and silver colours of the D.F.C. ribbon seem, in their cases, peculiarly apt. Michael Carreck, the very first to enrol as a pupil in 1931, flew fifty missions over enemy territory as a

Michael Carreck, D.F.C. (Bomber Command).

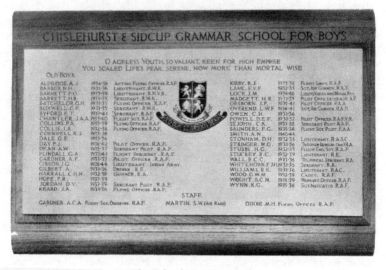

The School War Memorial.

navigator and cheated all the odds to survive. His experiences in what he calls "the flaming coffins of Bomber Command" are conveyed in his powerful, semi-autobiographical novel *Blaze of Glory*, published by Robert Hale. There were, of course, numerous other examples of heroism, many known only to the men concerned and perhaps their close friends and families. It was, unfortunately, far beyond the powers of this chapter to do more than refer, all too briefly, to just a few.

The School's roll of honour, now engraved on a new memorial plaque and placed above the entrance to the Hall in the foyer of the current building, displays the names of the 45 who died in World War Two. Some were still in their teens. The others, almost all of them, were in their early twenties. One may pick out their faces, some serious but most smiling confidently, from the ranks assembled for the School photographer in the years leading up to the conflict. Their identity is captured and held in the celluloid of the picture and in the brass of the plaque. Both these selves – the grinning boy and the charred body in the plane – are frozen in time, contradictory, permanent. The two images refuse to come together and yet cannot be prised apart, the chilling irony of which is enough, in the words of the poet Ted Hughes, to "shoulder out one's own body from its instant and heat."

CHAPTER SIX

Moving On

IN DECEMBER 1945 THE A.T.C.'s splendid glider, four years in the building, was finally handed over to the Air Ministry. Christened "Homewood" after the cadet whose brainchild it had been, the aircraft was made almost entirely of materials from the School's metal workshop. Because of torrential rain the presentation took place in the Hall where there was just room for the glider to spread its enormous wings. Group Captain C.F.Gordon received it on behalf of the R.A.F. and the achievement was deemed remarkable enough to warrant coverage on B.B.C. Radio's evening news programme.

Shortly before Christmas a start was made on removing the clinker from the roof, a tedious business that involved shovelling the filthy stuff down canvas chutes and into lorries. Though rather less pristine than of yore, the pale concrete, when it again saw the sky, might have symbolised an optimism about the future that had been strikingly absent both before and during its interment as, on Tuesday January 8th 1946, the School embarked upon its first peacetime year since 1938, during the Autumn of which it had completed the movement to Foot's Cray. Any likelihood of euphoria taking hold, however, was soon dampened by a number of factors, some of them more immediately apparent than others.

Severe rationing – in many ways harsher than that in force during the war years themselves – weighed heavily upon a population anxious to return to what they fondly remembered as "normality". A national paper shortage, for example, meant that even such basics as exercise books were hard to come by and every last gap had to be filled on every page before a new one could be sought. Boys resorted to microscopic handwriting, though this may have had less to do with patriotic duty than with a desire to irritate their teachers, particularly the more myopic amongst them.

The fact that school ink was little better than "bluish water" did not help in this respect.

Far more seriously, incipient heart trouble, not helped by heavy smoking, led to Mac's protracted absence and Arthur Parsons was obliged to step into the breach, a situation that occurred with increasing frequency over the next few years.

Thirdly, a hidden time-bomb had begun to tick. Two years earlier, in 1944, R.A.Butler had steered his Education Act through the wartime Parliament. In schools, as everywhere else, attention was focused on great world events such as the Normandy Invasion and it was not until much later that the Act's full implications began to be understood. A radical reshaping of the education system was now embarked upon and embraced with enthusiasm by Attlee's new Labour Government, elected the previous July with a mandate to create a modern, less class-ridden nation with opportunities for all. Churchill's unexpected defeat at the polls made it clear that the British had not made enormous sacrifices over so many years in order to return to the social divisions of the nineteen-thirties. Butler, a Conservative minister in the Coalition Government, introduced what was dubbed the "tripartite system". There would now be three categories of secondary school: the grammar, the technical and the "modern". Each would cater for a perceived different level of ability and aptitude but, crucially, parity of esteem was held to be essential if the new set-up was to be fair to all and it was this principle of fairness that now, for the first time, held centre stage. Intelligence testing was in its heyday and few, at the time, questioned its validity even if there was disagreement about the details. What could be easier, therefore, than to stratify the nation's eleven year-olds (excluding, of course, the small proportion in private education) into three uneven layers and to provide the buildings accordingly?

Thus it was that as early as March, 1946, a new scheme for schooling in the Chislehurst-Sidcup and Orpington area was presented to the Divisional Executive by the Development Planning Sub-Committee. The meeting was chaired by E.V.Mills and amongst those present were Colonel Edlmann and the District Education Officer Enid Appleby. The re-organisation of schools into Butler's tripartite structure in itself necessitated a radical rethink of building availability in the Division. Coupled with the raising of the school leaving age to fifteen (in 1947) and – with demobilisation – a rapidly rising birth-rate, it soon became clear that further changes were essential. It was felt that two new grammar schools were required within easy reach of Orpington and its expanding population. The inexorable logic of this led to the conclusion that the current divisional boys' grammar school, though admirably sited in relation to the district as a whole, would better serve the needs of the hitherto neglected northern sector if it were to move to a site nearer the population centre in Sidcup which was itself expanding apace, particularly in the neighbourhood of Lamorbey.

It was suggested that a boys' grammar school be sited on the golf-course at Lamorbey Park, together with a boys' technical school and two modern schools, one for boys and one for girls. A girls' technical school would occupy the old building at 27 Station Road. The extensive acreage at Lamorbey would allow for ample development whereas the Crittall's Corner site was now deemed too small, besides being too far to the south to fit in with the new scheme of things. An additional advantage of this plan, as far as the Butlerites were concerned, was the fact that the three different categories of pupil would be close together on one site, the tripartite system in miniature, so to speak. There would, it was held, be scope for much social integration which could only be to the benefit of all concerned.

Rather than establish a new, more northerly grammar school from scratch it was suggested that Chis and Sid be uprooted and relocated back in the Sidcup of its birth – indeed within a few hundred yards of its original home. This would leave the "glasshouse" at Foot's Cray free to provide accommodation for a much-needed secondary school in that area.

Mr Mills apologised for the haste with which his plans had been drawn up. He pointed out that his committee had been given so little time in which to arrive at conclusions that it had been obliged to hold meetings on Sundays. They had, nevertheless, he insisted, managed to inspect every site in the entire division.

The effect of this news, when it reached the ears of Doctor Williams on his sick bed, is dreadful to contemplate. His beloved building, which he had watched take shape over the early years of his headmastership and into which so many of his own ideas had been incorporated, was to be cruelly snatched away. John Poltock's famous concrete edifice with its much admired glass staircase tower, the talk of Europe's architectural journals, would become home to others. It was not even as though its academic standards would be maintained since it was destined for the least able category of pupils, those given the depressing designation "modern". Mac, despite

Milton Williams, 1946–1981.

ill health, was not one to take such a decision lying down and he fought manfully against it over the next few years. His struggle is a topic to which we will return more than once during the course of this chapter but other events must command our attention too.

On the night of Thursday February 14th, St Valentine's Day, little love was shown by two burglars who, in the early hours, stove in the stationery room door and made off with the petty cash. The alarm was raised by Micky, the School cat, whose mewing awoke art master F.A.Williams, sleeping overnight in his room. The police were called and the thieves apprehended, each receiving two months'imprisonment and, one trusts, learning their lesson, even though the School was officially closed during their brief visit.

Another Williams, Milton, fresh from service in the Royal Navy, arrived to replace Naim Basri in the P.E.Department, embarking upon an illustrious thirty-five year career at the School. A Welshman, like his name-sake, Milton was a gymnast of international repute and also a great exponent of boxing and rugby, coaching boys to the highest standards in all three sports in addition to fencing, swimming, athletics and much else besides. He and the Head had met years before during a life-saving demonstration. It is said that his interview for the P.E. post was somewhat unconventional, consisting largely of a competition to see which of the two could hold his breath the longer. Mac later claimed four minutes. Milton's time is not recorded but it was apparently impressive enough to get him the job.

All staff on war service returned to Crittall's Corner during the year with the exception of Messrs Dellar, Gridley and Mortimore who went to teach elsewhere. The most notable departure was that of Geoffrey Cook who left to become headmaster of a school on the Romney Marsh. After fifteen years Cook was, remarkably, the first of the original five staff members to depart. John Walsh took over the reins as Head of English, a post he would hold with distinction until 1971. The gap was filled by Roland Rahtz, a graduate of Keble College, Oxford, who contributed greatly to the development of drama in a long career that ended a year after Walsh's, in 1972. Walsh, like McGregor Williams, would enjoy a mere sixth months of rest before his death but Rahtz enjoyed many peaceful years in Italy before dying in 1995.

Although the War was over there was a constant reminder of it just beyond the school gates in the early months of 1946. Each lunchtime boys would wander down to watch a group of German prisoners, in their green uniforms, constructing a roundabout and subway on the A20. They made friends, through the railings, with a man called Heinz and practised their classroom German in the process. Some of the prisoners were scarcely older than sixth-formers at the School. The results of their labours stood for forty years before the new flyover replaced them, slicing off a large portion of the old soccer pitch in the process.

On March 7th the School's first post-war speech day was held with Colonel Edlmann yet again in the chair. The most popular item on the agenda was the announcement of a day's holiday to celebrate Irvine Browning's achievement in winning scholarships in English at both Magdalen College, Oxford and Jesus College, Cambridge, the former being the one that he took up.

The July issue of the *Chronicle* for this year contains articles and illustrations by a fourth-former called Quentin Blake. Of him, far more would be heard! The same magazine carries a fascinating survey into what the boys were carrying about their person while at school. Although only 13%

wore a watch almost as many (11%) carried cigarettes. When one translates this into actual numbers it emerges that as many as sixty pupils came thus equipped, a startling difference (one assumes) between then and now. Mysteriously, over 30% had either a box of matches or a lighter in their pocket, the mere thought of which would inspire nightmares in the head teachers of today. One sixth-former, apparently, never left home without tobacco pouch and pipe.

The academic year ended with a production of *Macbeth*, the first tragedy to be attempted by the Dramatic Society (the Head contenting himself with upstaging everybody in the cameo role of Porter) and with news that Cyril Cooling had, by graduating from U.C. Medical School, become the first in a long and distinguished line of doctors whose science education had begun in the laboratories of Chis and Sid.

The provision of free milk that Autumn – one third of a pint per pupil – reflects concern about malnutrition during this period of post-war economic stringency. The new Education Minister, Ellen Wilkinson, was no stranger to deprivation having, as the Jarrow M.P., led the hunger march to London in 1936. After her premature death in 1947 she was succeeded in office by George Tomlinson who had left school at the age of twelve to work in a Lancashire cotton mill. Unsurprisingly, the outlook of these two ministers was somewhat different from that of their Conservative predecessors, a significant factor, of course, in the fortunes of Chis and Sid during this decade.

In the eight years that followed the War, academic achievement at the School went from strength to strength. State (or Royal) Scholarships were won by Rex Watson, Donald Kidney, Alec Hester, John Ernsting, Roy Rand, George Vignaux, Anthony Edwards and Barrington Stead, the latter pair joining Irving Browning at Oxford University. Additionally, ten places were won at Cambridge and a further two at Oxford making fifteen in all. The successful students were: Peter Cornish, John Swift, Edward Wright, Quentin Blake, A.S.Gordon, P.G.White, J.B.Yeoman, John Bradley, William Bennett, Donald O'Connell, Clifford Barnard and Barrington White. The secret, it seems, was to be called either "White" or "Barrington". One successful student managed both. The English Department led the way with five of their students going on to read the subject. Maths, History and Chemistry claimed two each. The "Jubilee" *Chronicle* for July 1952 announced that, since the foundation of the School in 1931, some eighty university degrees had been gained by former students, nine of whom had gone on to earn Ph.Ds. Other academic distinctions at this high level included Cyril Cooling's election to a fellowship at the Royal College of Surgeons and, in due course, I.R. Browning's research fellowship at Merton College, Oxford. In considering these achievements it should be borne in mind that very few, at that period, gained university admission in any given year.A figure of 3% of the relevant age-group would not be far from the mark. Today, of course, the number is at least twelve times greater and may well be higher still. To quote the names of all those who have graduated over *recent* years would require another book that would rival this one in length, a fact that is, in no sense, intended to denigrate their achievement but serves merely to put into perspective the performance of their predecessors as set out above.

These outstanding successes were echoed in the impressive pass-rates achieved in the G.C.E. examinations at both Ordinary and Advanced Levels and by a steady rise in university admissions generally, particularly to the London colleges. Shortage of space precludes fuller details here but further testimony to the School's rapidly growing reputation can be found in the fact that, as early as 1947, the number staying on into the Third Year Sixth – for the most part "Oxbridge" candidates – had reached double figures. Few state schools could boast such a figure at that time.

Chis and Sid then, it is safe to say, was gaining widespread recognition for its high academic achievement before the forties were out. However Dr.Williams' pleasure in seeing his efforts, over twenty years, bearing such abundant fruit was, sadly, much diminished by the growing realisation that its days at Crittall's Corner were drawing to a close unless the politicians could be persuaded to backtrack. More power to the Doctor's elbow was provided by the Old Boys' Association which was reborn at a meeting held in the School on October 11th 1946. As "SCOBA" such an organisation had enjoyed a brief existence between 1936 and 1939, only to fall into abeyance on the outbreak of war. Former Head Boy P.C. Mitchell was elected Chairman. The Secretary was C.P.D. Tomlin (oldest of the original 1931 entrants) and the Treasurer A.J. Stanyon, another who had been in at the beginning in Station Road. They quickly adopted the role of pressure group and put their resources behind the campaign to stay at Crittall's Corner.

The Winter of 1946/7 was particularly harsh – made all the more miserable by power cuts and the severe rationing of fuel. On the night of February 26th the temperature recorded on the School roof by Tom

Palmer's instruments dropped to a record low of minus 24 degrees centigrade. Finally the cold relented and, in April, new trees, the gift of Colonel Nash, were planted around the perimeter of the field in what was seen by some to be an ostentatious declaration of confidence that Chis and Sid would be there to see them in their prime. If so it was a sadly misplaced gesture since seven and a half years would prove all too short a time in which to watch them grow.

Along with the new poplars, hawthorns and horse-chestnuts arrived Edgar Martin, a graduate of King's College, London, to join the Physics Department and to involve himself in the musical life of the School over the next three decades. He came just in time to see McGregor Williams back centre stage, this time as Sir Toby Belch in *Twelfth Night*.

The Headmaster modestly confessed, afterwards, that he had found the role a particularly easy one to play, a remark which drew an interesting variety of response. Edwyn Birchenough left at the end of term to become Head of History at Archbishop Tennison's School in Kennington.

The new academic year witnessed the arrival as laboratory assistant, technician and projectionist of Shirley Quinnell who, perhaps unsurprisingly, preferred to be known as "Bill". During his thirty year stay at Chis and Sid, Quinnell was to acquire an aura few others have achieved, certainly as far as the non-teaching staff is concerned. Brave indeed the pupil, or even teacher, who ventured to seek him out by penetrating the mysterious sanctum on Staircase One into which he locked himself for long periods in the latter stages of his career.

On September 27th 1947 the Old Boys' Association held its first annual dinner, at Chiesman's in Lewisham. Two months later the current pupils enjoyed a day's holiday in celebration of Princess Elizabeth's marriage to Philip Mountbatten. A scrapbook arrived from Brooklyn High School, New York, in return for one the School had sent to them during the War. The following Spring Mac's dramatic career continued, again in an appropriate role, this time as the exiled Duke in *As You Like It*. Unhappily his banishment to the Forest of Arden reflected rather aptly the situation in which he would shortly find himself as the enforced move to wooded Lamorbey loomed up on the horizon. Unlike Shakespeare's Duke, however, Mac could not find it in his nature to bear such misfortune with equanimity. While there were heads that might be knocked together he remained convinced that officialdom could be made to see sense and that the death sentence hanging over the Glasshouse would be repealed.

That Summer Bill Freeman, the Staff's lanky fast bowler, took all ten wickets for just nine runs in the annual cricket match against the School 1st XI. Even more remarkably, perhaps, the Staff team still contrived to lose, scoring 41 in reply to the School's meagre 43. Freeman's feelings at the end are not on record but are not difficult to imagine. The pugnacious F.W.Dutton chose this Summer to leave, after twelve years' service, to become Head of Geography at Whitby Grammar School.

The following term, Autumn 1948, brought great sadness with the sudden death of Frank Bramwell, the hugely popular Head of Art. The large sum of money, in excess of three hundred pounds, that was raised by donations from his pupils to help his widow and two young children is, in

itself, testimony to the affection in which he had been held during his ten years at the School. Stanley Simmonds, a graduate of the R.C.A., who replaced him, proved to be an able successor, running his Department with great skill and commitment for the next thirty years. During the War he had served on aircraft carriers from the decks of one of which, H.M.S. Arbiter, he witnessed the dropping of the atomic bomb on Hiroshima. Jack Burnip and Frank Tomlinson, who joined the staff in January 1949, were two more who went on to enjoy careers of considerable length, both contributing, before their retirement, a quarter of a century's service to the School. Burnip, a historian in his mid-thirties, had already gained experience in two well known grammar schools, Parmiter's and Harrow, since graduating from Merton College. He was rumoured to have

Staff Room, 1948.
(L to R: A.Parsons, R.Clarke, E.Palmer, P.Taylor, L.Stringer, H.Morris, G.Goddard, Mrs E.Jackson (almost obscured), H.Brooke, C.Morley).

Lacrosse practice, 1949.

had an "interesting" war in military intelligence and spoke fluent Bulgarian in addition to the Russian which he taught to small Sixth-form groups. He was also, improbably, a skilled electrician and plumber. Tomlinson, a contemporary of Roland Rahtz at Keble, completed a notable trio of English teachers who, between them, clocked up eighty-nine years at the School before their retirement in the early 1970s.

In this context it is interesting to examine John Walsh's research into the reading habits of the boys in 1949. Most popular fiction in the Lower School included the "Biggles" stories of W.E.Johns, Arthur Ransome's *Swallows and Amazons* series and the "William" books of Richmal Crompton. The older boys opted for "Sapper" of Bulldog Drummond fame, P.G.Wodehouse and his Jeeves stories, the futuristic H.G.Wells novels and the detective fiction of Dorothy Sayers and Agatha Christie.

A production of *Julius Caesar* at the end of March saw Roland Rahtz in the title role and the inimitable McGregor Williams orating as Mark Antony in the aforementioned ginger wig. One of his sharpest critics, the sixteen year-old Quentin Blake (whose response to this performance is recorded in Chapter Two) launched his own career with a drawing in the *Punch* magazine of June 22nd. He was at the time – and very probably still is – the youngest contributor to that illustrious magazine.

That Summer sweets came off ration for the first time in a decade, much to the delight of small boys such as L.Brown of IIIA who joined a queue twenty-five yards long at his local shop. The appropriately named B.Sweet of IVC was clearly anxious to make up for lost time: " I went in and bought two quarter boxes of chocolates, two quarter bars of Cadbury's whole-nut, two Mars, two Crunch, a quarter of liquorice allsorts, a quarter of Everybody's Mixture and a quarter of toffee." One hopes that he was violently sick.

Thoughts turned at frequent intervals to the School's future at Crittall's Corner. Responding to a suggestion that the long-promised swimming pool should finally be constructed, Quentin Blake, as letters editor for the July 1949 *Chronicle*, remarked: "There seems a likelihood that in the future the school will be removing from this building. We don't want to leave our swimming pool behind." It was the first mention of this contentious issue to emanate from the School itself.

The following term Blake, still only sixteen, was entrusted with the full editorship of the magazine, with Messrs Walsh and Rahtz in an advisory capacity. He was the first pupil to undertake this responsibility. Blake's drawings were now appearing regularly in Punch and he was praised by John Walsh for his "serious and enquiring mind" and the "range and sympathy of his interests". Blake edited three issue of the *Chronicle* before handing over to another pupil, J.B.Yeoman, in 1951. One of his earliest tasks was coverage of the School's first boxing tournament, organised by Milton Williams and Sydney Grindrod. Eighty-three boys participated and "D" House emerged the winners. Not long afterwards P.J.Smith

The highly successful Colts Rugby Squad, 1950, with Bill Freeman
(centre of back row).

became Kent Schoolboy Champion at 11 stone 6 pounds. In the Summer
of 1950 1st XI Cricket Captain, Roger Dracup, scored 155 not out, still the
highest score by a School batsman. Rugby, it should be said, was now flourishing in competition with soccer. During the 1949–50 season three rugby
XVs turned out, playing in all 24 games against other schools compared to
the 60 or so matches played, in total, by the three soccer XIs. The soccer
players, incidentally, won two thirds of their matches and the rugby players
half of theirs. The following season, 1950–51, it was decided that all boys
would play rugby in the Autumn Term and then soccer after Christmas.

After nineteen years in charge of Mathematics, James Banfield left, in
July, 1950, for a post on the Isle of Man. His contribution to the School had
been invaluable, not only in launching and developing a key department
but also in such areas as sport, music, timetabling and the scouts. The
amount of his own out-of-school time he devoted to such activities was
remarkable and his rather sudden and unforeseen departure left a great
gap to be filled. Into his shoes stepped Lionel Pascoe, a graduate of
Hertford College, Oxford. Pascoe had served as a Lieutenant Commander

in the Royal Navy during the War and had fought at the Battle of Narvik aboard H.M.S.Warspite. He was an expert on early English silver and had taught for some years at the Skinners' Company School in Tunbridge Wells. Walter ("Wally") Moat arrived to take charge of the Craft Department, a position he held with no little distinction until 1971 when he became Deputy Headmaster of Marlborough Special School. Moat was famous for the difficulties he experienced behind the wheel of a car and managed, on two separate occasions, to crash into the same tree in Old Farm Avenue. Other new appointees in September 1950 were Eric Side, to teach Maths and Physics and Bob Cole to become the fourth member of the English Department. Both remained for fifteen years.

The Merchant of Venice, postponed earlier because of the Head's absence on sick leave, was finally performed at the end of the Summer Term, the first time a Shakespeare play had been revisited. Unable to reprise his celebrated Shylock of five years before, Mac reluctantly handed the role over, at short notice, to Roland Rahtz. Portia was played by W.J.C.Pinnell and Launcelot Gobbo by William Bray, a name that would be heard with increasing frequency over the next half century by those connected with Chis and Sid.

The new academic year was scarcely into its stride before the sad news came that Lieutenant-Colonel Francis Edlmann D.S.O. was dead. Chairman of Governors for all of its nineteen years, Edlmann, courteous, conscientious and dignified had been a great friend to the School. The chairmanship passed to Harry Lester, J.P.

In the *Chronicle* for December 1950 came the official announcement that "on a date not yet settled the School will be moved to a new and larger building on a new site." The choice of "moved" rather than "moving" was surely significant. The next issue, for July 1951, records a visit to Lamorbey to inspect the chosen location. The scene was described as "idyllic", the background of woodland giving way to "sylvan glades, through which purl-ing rills ran down to a reed-fringed mere." One is reminded of the New Ideal Homesteads prospectus quoted at the start of Chapter One. Very dif ferent this picture, certainly, from the cacophonous Sidcup By-pass. Roland Rahtz's article soon drops its tongue-in-cheek tone and goes on to describe a golf course on which "rising above a morass of builder's rubble was the Modern School, already completed in what Osbert Lancaster calls the "Public Convenience" style of architecture." This unflattering descrip-tion of Hurstmere might have been paraded with less relish had it been realised, at the time, that its sister-school-to-be, the new Chis and Sid, would be, if not its mirror image, then certainly a lot closer to Lancaster's dismissive epithet than to the brave new architectural world of Poltock's pre-war vision. "The new Grammar School is, we gather, to be built somewhere on the golf course," continued Rahtz, adding optimistically that "what we have seen of the K.E.C. architect's work, together with the elaborate and far-reaching suggestions made by the masters and boys, encourages us to look forward to the new building with composure."

McGregor Williams had been indisposed throughout the term but, rising from his sick bed, he appeared on the platform at Speech Day, December 8th. In a powerful address he lamented the problems experienced by grammar schools in appointing staff of sufficient calibre and expressed his fears that such establishments were losing their former prestige and their ability to foster an academic culture. In the New Year, despite continuing health problems, he divided his formidable energies between directing a production of Much Ado and drafting a series of increasingly irate letters to local and national politicians and to the press on the subject of the School's return to Sidcup, a move that he was still determined to prevent despite all the preparations going on apace.

The return of a Conservative government in October increased his confidence of success. Mac's files still bulge with copies of the letters he sent to the new Minister of Education, Florence Horsbrugh, and to local M.P.s Sir Waldron Smithers and Patricia Hornsby-Smith and, of course, with their replies to him as well as their correspondence on the subject amongst themselves. Some flavour of their content may be conveyed by a few representative quotations.

McGregor Williams to Rt. Hon.Florence Horsbrugh C.B.E., M.P. 20th February 1952

"I thank you for your letter and the trouble you are taking in what to us is a matter of great importance. I expressed the hope that the [work] should be deferred 'sine die', thereby saving the cost of the proposed new building (£285,000) on the Lamorbey site and the additional saving of £300,000 for a new grammar school at Orpington which, it is declared, would be necessary if our grammar school is removed from its present site. I have never budged from my opposition [to the plan] which I explained to the County

Education Officer in person two years ago, when I was first informed of the new building scheme, after it had already been decided upon, without consultation.

The School [should remain] where it is and an additional storey for 200 be built on the present flat roof site, where it was originally intended to expand, if necessary, at a later period. The cost should not exceed £70,000 and the whole saving could mean £500,000. There is not the slightest doubt that, were a gallup poll ...taken on the matter, the vast majority in the district would plump for it remaining where it is."

McGregor Williams to Sir Waldron Smithers M.P. 23rd September 1952

Your points defining the situation emphasise all the more the great need to keep this school on its present site. The present building, enlarged at a relatively small cost ... can satisfy all requirements, even over the bulge period of 1956. The enlargement of this school should be a matter of priority once the major question of staying put has been settled.

Sir Waldron Smithers to Florence Horsbrugh 2nd October 1952

You will remember that you met Dr McGregor Williams with me ... some months ago. He has been an outstanding success at Chislehurst and Sidcup County School for Boys and has got a real public school spirit into that school. He has now written me a letter, which I send you in confidence, because it will help you in being better aware of the details in Kent and perhaps help you to reply to the letter which I sent you from the deputation. We on the spot know the value of Dr.Williams' work and it seems a thousand pities that anything should be done to break up such a fine tradition.

Florence Horsbrugh to Sir Waldron Smithers 15th October 1952

I don't think I can re-open at this stage the question of resiting the Chislehurst Grammar School, which we went into earlier. It will make no difference to the total provision whether it is enlarged on the present site or rebuilt at Lamorbey Park as a larger school.

85

PAST PURPLE

Sir Waldron Smithers to Florence Horsbrugh 14th November 1952

> At a time like this when moral standards are crashing everywhere
> and our prisons have never been so full, it is unthinkable that any
> such change should be made, not only from the moral and spiritual
> standpoint, but also, in these difficult days, from the point of view
> of keeping public expenditure to a minimum.

Dr. McGregor Williams to Sir Waldron Smithers 12th December 1952

> I must again raise the question of Chislehurst and Sidcup
> Grammar School being forcibly moved, for no apparent good
> reason, from its present excellent site and modern buildings. The
> School, on its present site, is geographically a centre for pupils
> from Mottingham, Chislehurst, St Paul's Cray, Sidcup (up to
> Blackfen), the Kent side of New Eltham, parts of Bexley and
> Bexleyheath, Swanley, Orpington and Petts Wood. It was wisely
> chosen almost twenty years ago and has proved completely ade-
> quate for all the demands made upon it.

Florence Horsbrugh to Patricia Hornsby-Smith M.P. 16th March 1953

> I have had a good deal of correspondence about this matter with Dr
> Williams through Sir Waldron Smithers. I do not think there is
> really any uncanny secrecy about this proposal. It was included in
> the Authority's development plan which was approved in February
> 1949. My predecessor then decided that notice of approval should
> be published in the local press, indicating where copies of the plan
> could be examined. The fact that nobody apparently troubled to
> examine them need not cause surprise, but it is hardly the Local
> Education Authority's fault. There is, of course, no question of
> wasting the present building. It will be used either as a secondary
> modern school ... or as a technical school for boys. It does seem to
> me that Dr Williams is perturbing himself groundlessly. *How many
> headmasters would consider it a hardship to move into a new and
> larger building?*

Mac's rage on reading this last sentence (which seemed to deserve
editorial italics), with its tone of lofty dismissal, must have bordered on the

apoplectic. It now became clear to him that the battle was lost and he resigned himself, as best he could, to the sacrifice of his beloved "Glasshouse". The fact that the final decision had been made by a minister of the Conservative Government which he supported so strongly made matters, if anything, even worse. His only consolation was the thought that he himself, at least, could avoid treading the unhallowed ground of Lamorbey by timing his retirement to coincide with the move that now lay just eighteen months ahead. He would be sixty-five and, with his health deteriorating, it was clearly the right moment to leave the stage.

From this point onwards the Doctor averted his gaze from that stretch of parkland a mile and three-quarters to the north. Apparently he refused even to visit the site of the new building as it took shape and, as far as possible, avoided all discussion of the subject. Whenever his duties left him with no choice but to address issues arising therefrom he responded professionally (of course) but with scant pretence of interest, far less enthusiasm. Chronic heart problems obliged him, in any case, to delegate much of his work-load to his senior lieutenants, Arthur Parsons and Tom Palmer, onto whose capable shoulders fell the main burden of the transition.

Mac's production of *Much Ado*, when it belatedly opened in mid-March, 1951, did so without the master himself who had intended to play Dogberry, the dim-witted constable. Sadly he was too ill even to see a single one of the five performances given.

The Summer brought with it the retirement of E.Selvey, the School groundsman since its birth twenty years before. It also witnessed the departure of Quentin Blake to read English under the famous F.R.Leavis at Downing College, Cambridge. Already a School legend, Blake would go on to enjoy an illustrious career as an artist and academic, being perhaps best known for his collaboration with Roald Dahl. In 1978 he became Head of the Illustration Department at the Royal College of Art and later Senior Fellow and Professor, being awarded the O.B.E. in 1988 and made the first Children's Laureate in 1999. The following year he was awarded an honorary doctorate at the London Institute and became a Fellow of Downing College. In 2001 he mounted an exhibition at the National Gallery and a school in Germany was named in his honour.

The warm weather enabled the windows on the Quadrangle side of the Assembly Hall finally to be repaired after the flying-bomb damage of seven years before, during which time a makeshift arrangement of plasterboards had patched the holes. The annual School v Staff cricket match was distinguished by what the match report describes as "aggressive wicket-keeping" by Cedric Morley. The present chronicler, for one, regrets that he was not there to witness the event. The School broke up in July with no summer harvest camp to look forward to, the scheme having been abolished with the return to peace-time normality in the countryside.

In October a mock election was held, three days before the real thing. The result in Chislehurst foretold the outcome nationally with Stead, the Conservative candidate, gaining 241 votes to Loakes' 141 for Labour. "Mr Attlee is making the country miserable", opined an anonymous pupil in IIIC. His misery was shared by others, apparently. The Debating Society motion "that our school days are the happiest days of our lives", proposed by P.Marvell and opposed by D.L.W.Gill, was defeated by 68 votes to 47.

The School's jubilee year of 1952 began with one of the worst of the notorious Winter "smogs" that made life miserable in that era, particularly in the great industrial cities. Traffic ground to a halt on the by-pass and, when the filthy air reduced visibility almost to zero, the boys would be sent home, sometimes as early as two o'clock.. The elderly and those prone to lung complaints suffered dreadfully. Many died, most notably King George on February 6th. McGregor Williams penned some unconvincing sonnets to mourn his passing and to welcome the new Queen and the School moved serenely on into the fourth reign of its still relatively brief existence. Despite the lengthening shadow of Lamorbey, life went on much as before. Boys continued to swing round the pole opposite the Geography Room to expedite their turning of the corner and to accelerate their dash to the Dining Hall and the clamour for buns and doughnuts that signalled Break. The voices of Frankie Lane and Doris Day were "all the go" – as the phrase had it – on household wireless sets tuned to the B.B.C.'s Light Programme. At Sunday lunchtimes boys would listen, mystified, as their parents enjoyed "Round Britain Quiz" on the Home Service, precursor of Radio Four. The Debating Society rejected by 37 votes to 15 the contention that television had become a menace, despite the morning fatigue attributed, by masters, to the new phenomenon known as "television hangover" which became, increasingly, a bone of contention as the fifties unrolled.

A Shakespeare play, *Richard II*, appeared with no input whatsoever from the Head, being directed by John Walsh with Frank Tomlinson taking the title role. No less a personage than Air Chief Marshal Sir John Baker arrived to inspect, and to congratulate, 1227 A.T.C. Squadron, now the largest in Kent.

1st XI soccer team, 1952–53, with Bill Freeman (far left) and
Cedric Morley (far right).

On September 17th the School "came of age", marking its twenty-first
birthday with a Service of Remembrance conducted by the Rural Dean,
Canon Webb. On November 8th a still more eminent prelate, Bishop of
Rochester Christopher Chavasse, processed through the Hall, crosier in
hand, to unveil and dedicate the School's war memorial plaque. The dead
having been thus honoured the living received their tribute with the erection, in the vestibule, of the first boards recording high academic success.
The year finished with a new craze sweeping the Lower School – cheese
label collecting – and the long-awaited switch from wickerwork wastepaper baskets to metal wastepaper bins in every classroom. These were less
fun for naughty boys, of course, since they could not be unravelled, talk of
which may remind us that it is this interweaving of the momentous and the
trivial, perhaps, that makes up the stuff of which all history is made.

John Walsh's editorial to the July '53 *Chronicle* refers to the construction work taking place in Lamorbey. He regrets the necessity "to move into
a new building not many years after our entry into this one" and adds that
"it is hoped our next move will be our last one." Some half-century on that
wish, at least, remains undashed.

Three days' holiday had been granted to schools for Queen Elizabeth's coronation celebrations at the start of the previous month. Again places were reserved for a party on the procession route – the Embankment, this time – and the boyish descriptions of the pageantry they witnessed are remarkably similar to those written by their predecessors some sixteen years before. This time, however, those unwilling to elbow their way through the crowds in Central London instead clustered in front of small, flickering black and white (or, more accurately, grey and grey) television pictures in neighbours' houses. Fifth-former W.J.Mitchell recalls that twenty-one people were crammed into the room in addition to the family dog. On Woolwich Common an ox was roasted but proved virtually inedible despite being carved by comedian Frankie Howerd. A few days later the Queen progressed through Eltham (as one does) with the School's A.T.C. Squadron lining a stretch of the route.

The summer break of 1953 was remarkable in that, for the only time in the School's entire history, there was not a single change in the Staff Room. Nobody left in July and no newcomer arrived in September. The following year, of course, was very different, featuring, as it did, perhaps the most significant change of all. It began, for some at least, with a Winter holiday in Klosters organised by Messrs Burnip and Sandercock. This was the School's first ever ski-ing trip and the first visit abroad since before the War. The ice having thus been broken, another foreign adventure followed hard on its heels, Edward Jenkins ("Jenks") leading the first of his many Easter trips to Paris. *Henry Vth*, first performed in 1944, was staged again in the Spring. Anthony Arlidge (who went on to become a Q.C. and, famously, defended the "Birmingham Six") took the title role and Mac, though still far from well, again played the Chorus in his own inimitable fashion. It was his final appearance upon a stage. How appropriate, then, the choice of April 23rd, Shakespeare's birthday, for the Headmaster's retirement dinner at the Black Horse Hotel in Sidcup High Street. It was a formal, black tie occasion. Mac made a witty speech and chairman Ben Grassby presented him with a silver cigarette case on behalf of the Old Sedcopians.

The unimaginative usage of the first six letters of the alphabet to designate the houses would, it was announced, be discontinued upon reassembling in Hurst Road. From September 1954 they would become (in this order) Davies, Edlmann, Williams, Staff, Townshend and Lester, honouring important figures in the history of the School.

As he entered 1954 and his last few months at the helm Dr Williams undoubtedly felt a sense of betrayal. Not only had the politicians proved obdurate but even some of his own governors had failed to support him. Most vociferous in her support for the move was Bertha James, a doughty opponent with a Roedean and Girton pedigree. Allegedly she undermined all Mac's efforts to remain at Crittall's Corner and he came to regard her as his sworn enemy. Despite his very understandable bitterness the central issue was starkly clear. The "Glasshouse" had been designed to accommodate five hundred boys and for some years, like its Station Road predecessor, it had become seriously overcrowded. The new building nearing completion in Hurst Road, however, was designed with eight hundred pupils in mind and had ample space for further expansion should that be needed, a factor clearly not applicable on the current site. Since 1931 the population of the Chislehurst-Sidcup area had trebled and the post-war birth-rate "bulge" generation would shortly reach secondary school age. The die was cast.

The Head's farewell message, dated July 11th 1954, appears in *Chronicle* number 46. "I have puzzled long to find something to say to you, my colleagues and my boys," he confesses. Appropriate words indeed failed him on this occasion, perhaps for the only time in his long stewardship of the School. Besides some brief words of thanks to his staff for their hard work and loyalty and, of course, of welcome to his successor, Richard Pedley, he falls back upon the remarks he had written in the Magazine of July 1938 when the school was poised to complete its previous move. This 500 word passage he caused to be reprinted in full and word for word. It is, obviously, all about the splendid new concrete and glass edifice into which he had poured so much of his energy and devotion all those years ago and which was about to become, in a sense, his mausoleum. Of the new building in Hurst Road he cannot, sadly, bring himself to speak a single word. On Friday, July 23rd Mac turned his back, for the last time, upon his beloved Crittall's Corner. Five months later he was dead.

Richard Pedley (1954–1967).

CHAPTER SEVEN

Hurst Road:
The Pedley Years

RICHARD RODMAN PEDLEY WAS born on September 23rd 1912 at Sherborne in Dorset and educated locally at Foster's School where he was captain of both cricket and football before becoming Head Boy and winning an Open Scholarship to Downing College, Cambridge, to read English. He began his teaching career in 1934 at the City Boys' School, Leicester and within three years was promoted to Senior English master. He served in the Royal Artillery during the War, leaving with the rank of major. From 1946 to 1950 "Dick" Pedley (as he was generally known) held the post of Senior English Master at St Olave's School in Southwark. He then returned to Leicester to take up the headship of his former school but remained only four years before being appointed, at the age of 41, Headmaster of Chislehurst and Sidcup Grammar School for Boys in its new location.

Those who served under him differ greatly in their opinions but all agree that he was a man of enormous energy and determination and it is undeniable that under Pedley the School's reputation, already high in North West Kent, grew to one of national proportions. He was a passionate believer in academic excellence and demanded the highest standards from staff and boys alike. Perhaps his greatest achievement was to increase the size of the Sixth Form from 80, when he took over in 1954, to 270 when he left in 1967, these figures representing, respectively, 13% and 31% of the total School roll.

Richard Pedley laid enormous stress upon sending boys to the more prestigious universities, particularly Oxford and Cambridge. An intensely competitive man himself, Pedley fostered a competitive spirit among his pupils and the ablest were encouraged to try for open awards which, together with state scholarships, were deemed, in the hothouse world of the grammar and public schools at least, to be the ultimate measure of success. An unofficial "league" ranked the nation's foremost schools according to such criteria, a precursor of the familiar tables which appear, nowadays, in the broadsheets every August. In the final year of Pedley's tenure 85 boys gained admission to university, 23 of them to Oxford or Cambridge (nine winning open awards). In terms of "Oxbridge" entrance this is a total which has never been surpassed at the School, before or since, and, in the eyes of many older Sedcopians, represents the high summer of what some have called the School's "Golden Age". In all, during his thirteen years as Head, 150 boys went on to Oxford or Cambridge, an average of almost twelve per year.

Pedley's critics argue that such undeniable – and highly visible – success at the highest academic level was achieved at the expense of the "less able", though this term is a relative one in that, despite the move, the School's catchment area still embraced such districts as Chislehurst, Petts Wood, the Crays and Orpington. A high proportion of the intake came from "professional" backgrounds and the brightest pupils were systematically creamed off from numerous primary schools with all of which Pedley kept closely in touch. It is impossible to be precise but the likelihood is that they represented the top 5% or so of the ability range. It could be argued that, in these circumstances, had the School not done exceedingly well academically then something would have been very seriously amiss.

Nevertheless, highly intelligent boys are not always easy to teach and a great deal of hard work had to be put in by all concerned, not least by the pupils themselves. In the maintained school sector (i.e. among those schools run entirely by the local authority) only Harrow County could rival Chis and Sid's achievements during this period and – major public schools excepted – only Manchester Grammar School could boast a consistently higher "Oxbridge" tally. Richard Pedley, one learns, was thrilled when, at one of the annual "Oxbridge" dinners attended by no fewer than forty of his ex-pupils, he learnt that, the week before, M.G.S. had mustered a mere thirty at a similar function.

Such achievement was gained, of course, at a price. Pedley could be highly autocratic. Brian Burgess recalls going into School one hot day during the Summer holidays to talk over a timetabling matter with the Head only to be sent home to put on a jacket since even such an informal, private discussion could not take place, apparently, while the young physics master was "improperly dressed". "Domineering", "imperious" and "intransigent" are adjectives frequently applied to Richard Pedley and he was certainly not a man to suffer fools gladly. He insisted upon his own standards being rigidly applied at all times and would himself be at the forefront of inspection and enforcement. Caps were worn to and from school and raised to any masters or masters' wives encountered in the street. Boys' hair was not allowed to touch the collar since, in the Head's oft-stated view, intelligence was inversely proportionate to hair length. With the advent of "Beatle-mania" in the early sixties the struggle to retain the traditional "short back and sides" became increasingly vexatious.

A heavily-built man, forbidding in manner with a deep, gravelly voice and quick on the repartee, Richard Pedley rapidly imprinted his own personality on the School. He was frequently to be seen around the building, checking up on pupils and staff alike. When the bell sounded for the end of morning break he would usually be standing by the Staff Room door. At Hurst Road lessons began on time – not always the case, it seems, at Crittall's Corner. Twice a term every form would receive a headmagisterial visitation when the sacrosanct marksheet, brought out from a drawer with a reverence normally accorded only to holy writ, was solemnly reviewed. Praise or criticism would be bestowed, individually, upon those who had ended up, when the marks were totalled, either side of some notional and narrow isthmus of respectable mediocrity.

Like his predecessor, Pedley was active in the community, becoming, for example, President of the Rotary Club and of the Sidcup Literary and Scientific Society. His articles appeared frequently in both the local and national press, many of them arguing the case for the grammar schools. It was a source of constant irritation to him that the author of a Penguin,published in 1963, extolling the virtues of the comprehensive system should have been written by a man with the temerity to call himself R.Pedley. Robin was, in fact, entirely unrelated to Richard but the coincidence led to much confusion among the general public. R. "Grammar School" Pedley responded by contributing to the controversial "Black Papers" which put the right-wing counter-argument to Labour's plans to abolish all selection at eleven.

Dick Pedley used the School's academic success as a platform from which to launch himself into educational politics at a national level. In 1963 he became President of the Incorporated Association of Headmasters and the following year was elected to the Headmasters' Conference, only the third person from the maintained sector to be accorded this distinction.

He was a staunch supporter of his staff and invariably gave them his public backing, even if he might criticise them privately later. This, together with his distinguished academic record, earned the loyal, whole-hearted commitment of the vast majority although Stanley Simmonds and Wally Moat felt strongly that the arts and crafts were poor relations and largely ignored in the Head's relentless drive for the academic laurels. More than once Simmonds (himself an artist of considerable repute) exploded in staff meetings, arguing that Pedley's obsession with "Oxbridge" was stifling creativity and everything worthwhile. Art, he held, was, in any case, the most academic subject of them all if properly understood.

It was, given his national profile, not surprising that it should be Richard Pedley who, by common consent, led the opposition in his own area to Labour's plans to reorganise education and, in particular, to abolish selection. This is a theme which was to dominate local politics throughout the sixties and seventies and it is, consequently, a topic which we will revisit before long. In the meantime, however, we must return to the beginning of the Pedley regime and to the inauguration of the new building on the edge of Lamorbey Park.

Staff and pupils gave up part of their Summer holiday to help with the move. By the designated first day of the new school year sufficient had been accomplished for term to begin on time despite a considerable amount of "finishing off" by workmen over the next few weeks. This was a major achievement given that the original contract had specified a completion date of December 31st. The firm concerned, Rush and Tompkins of Station Road, had agreed to finish the project four months early in view of the pressure for places in the area and, urged on by Clerk of Works J.B.Wood and the foreman, A.H.Wakeford, Mr Rush, for one, lived up to his name and the new deadline was met to the surprise of most. The Glasshouse, one recalls, had, by contrast, greatly over-run its own schedule, though more for financial reasons than any deficiencies on the part of the contractors concerned.

The new building was designed in 1950 by Howard C. Lobb and Partners of Gower Street, in conjunction with the Kent County Architects S.H.Loweth and E.T.Ashley Smith. The plan had been to accommodate

720 boys in sixteen general classrooms in addition to specialist rooms for Geography and History (one each), six laboratories, six so-called "division rooms", two art rooms, a woodwork and a metalwork shop. An assembly hall, dining hall and gymnasium completed the picture together, of course, with utility and service areas and rooms for the teaching and administrative staff. Construction, under the supervision of site engineers Scott and Wilson Ltd., was of reinforced concrete and portal frames with brickwork finish internally and externally. This latter detail, like the soon-to-become-notorious system of access to first and second floor classrooms by means of staircases rather than corridors was, of course, a money-saving measure, like the thermoplastic tiles used in preference to wooden floors. Such economies were typical of the period. It is remarkable to think that the initial building work cost less than £300,000 in total.

The early nineteen-fifties were still very much under the shadow of post-war austerity and the building was starkly utilitarian, making few gestures in the direction of elegance or architectural innovation, unlike its predecessor. A percipient comment by a fifth-former, K.G.Woollard, summed it up well: "The old school was modernistic whereas the new school is simply modern". A fellow fifth-former, W.Martin, was even more forthright: "The huge glass staircase gave the previous building character and earned it a name, the "Glasshouse". Now we are hidden away behind a row of houses in Hurst Road, little known to anyone, forgotten, abandoned in a building whose white paint is already turning grey and whose dominating feature is an ugly water tank!".

Gwen Chapman, the new School Secretary, replacing Mary Burnell who had retired after twenty years' service, dubbed the building "singularly unlovely" and the young biologist Wyn Lewis, with alliterative vigour, described it as "faceless, featureless and functional." John Walsh contented himself with what was, for him, a surprisingly mild comment: "It would be foolish to pretend that it has not some inadequacies and inconveniences." Ever the gentleman, John Weston, who arrived in 1955 to teach German and served the School for thirty years (fourteen of them as Head of Department) remarked: " Seeing that it had to be built at a modest price it was quite satisfactory." His comment seems to be the closest to a compliment that any adult at the time paid the building, although it did (and indeed still does) possess a number of redeeming features.

The vestibule or foyer, if hardly "majestic" (as Head Boy J.D.Kimber – who should perhaps have got out more – loyally put it) does at least give a sense of airy space to the arriving visitor and the main staircase, with the sand-blasted white horse of Kent on the glass balustrade, dividing to turn sharply back on itself in opposite directions, contributes an interesting series of geometric shapes and angles. The sliding and folding ashwood screens to the Hall, enable it to open out to incorporate the vestibule for grand occasions such as Speech Day, an idea which showed imagination on the architects' part and which has, on the whole, operated very success-fully over the years. Another pleasing touch was the placing of a gallery to overlook the Hall, along similar lines to the one at Crittall's Corner. The narrow room thus created at the front of the building, with a commanding view of all entering or leaving the site, was, initially, occupied by the pre-fects and much appreciated by them. It also proved invaluable for stage-lighting crews, directors, and, more recently, those operating video-cameras and the like.

It has, in its time, been much used for teaching purposes (generally, though by no means exclusively, with Sixth Form groups) and was even used as an emergency staff room for a few months during the mid-seven-ties. Many examinations and interviews have been held there and it has long been the favoured meeting place for such groups as the Departmental Heads and the Governing Body. All in all, by far the most versatile room in the School in proportion to its size.

The financial constraints under which the building was planned and constructed necessitated economies of space which, in turn, led to very little natural light in the main corridor since it had classrooms on one side and lavatories on the other, the latter being so positioned to afford access from outside while the building itself was closed. Consequently artificial lighting had to be employed at all times, as in other dingy areas such as stair-wells and the passageway from the Foyer to the Gym. This regret-table feature was not helped by an overabundance of maroon paint, though this was varied with areas of yellow, white and blue. Unusually, wallpaper was used in several locations. Many will remember the grey leaf pattern over the main staircase and the "ship in a bottle" design beside the locker-range.

There were corridors on the ground-floor only and everyone soon found that Howard Lobb's money-saving expedient of pairing classrooms (with a communicating door) on the two floors above led to much unnecessary congestion on the all-too-narrow staircases and to much wastage of time and consequent exasperation. To get from A to B anywhere in the

School other than on the ground floor necessitated a tiresome series of triple manoeuvres – vertical, horizontal and vertical again – whereby one progressed around the building by what amounted to a succession of awkward hops. The School had begun its new existence with about 600 boys (ten times the number that had first entered through the doors of 27 Station Road 23 years before) and had become four form entry, which meant 130 new boys in the Second Year instead of the previous 90. The School's rapid expansion would soon make the new premises even more cramped than the Glasshouse had become before the move.

Here, though, came into play the great difference between the two and the one feature which made Hurst Road undeniably superior to Crittall's Corner. The new school was built upon 29 acres of playing fields and therefore had about twice as much space as before – and this is without allowing for the scenic Glade which bordered the grounds to the North, extending on beyond into Lamorbey Park proper, and the broad expanse of Hurstmere's territory sweeping on to the east. Include the golf course as well, just beyond the lake, and the Crittall's Corner site could have fitted about seven times into the great swathe of green in which the new Chis and Sid found itself. The psychological benefits of all this open space – and the much admired trees – went a great way towards mitigating the frustrations induced by the School's cramped and uninspiring interior design, especially when the weather was fine. There was, furthermore, of course, plenty of room for extra classrooms to be added as necessary and it was not long before these were forthcoming. The first extension work – an extra laboratory, additional classrooms and an enlargement of the Dining Hall – was agreed by Kent Education Committee within a year or so of the buildings' opening and three further sections would be added during Pedley's time.

It is perhaps worth recording here that the new School grounds had once been part of the parkland surrounding Lamorbey House, originally a medieval manor belonging to Thomas Sparrow but rebuilt in the mid-eighteenth century by William Steele, a director of the East India Company. Today this building is in the hands of Rose Bruford College of Drama with which the School has enjoyed a mutually beneficial relationship over the years. In 1891 Sidcup Golf Club leased land from the Lamorbey Park Estate on which to construct their course. Kent Education Committee purchased the estate, under the Town and Country Planning Act, in 1947, intending to erect three schools on the golf course and turn the remainder into a public open space. In the event, however, only the land on the Hurst Road side of the lake was needed for educational purposes. The Club was thus allowed to continue, though with nine holes instead of eighteen. Derrick Aughterlony, at the time of writing Chairman of both the Old Sedcopians and the Sidcup Golf Club, points out that Chis and Sid now sits on the seventeenth and eighteenth fairways, much to the chagrin, understandably, of such luminaries as current president Maurice Court who was heavily involved in what the Council called "negotiations" but which, as far as the Club was concerned, was a pistol pointed at their head.

The Glasshouse, it should be said, was soon occupied by the Cray Valley Technical School for Boys. Today, much extended and refurbished, it has become Kemnal Technology College and is flourishing by all accounts.

On the afternoon of Thursday September 9th, following a morning spent on "exploration, discovery and adjustment", the School "settled very placidly to work" as Frank Tomlinson later put it. It was 1954, the year in which Roger Bannister became the first human being to run a mile in less than four minutes, in which Bill Haley and his Comets changed the course of popular music with "Rock Around the Clock" and in which Faber Books published William Golding's *Lord of the Flies*, soon to be the staple fare of secondary school pupils throughout the land. More portentously, 1954 was the year in which Kidbrooke School, the country's first purpose-built comprehensive, opened just a few miles up the road from Chis and Sid.

The Autumn Term saw the arrival of Bill Hamblen as caretaker and the retirement of the statuesque Miss E.Haye-Forbes who had been the much admired cook-housekeeper for the last ten years. It also brought sad news with the death of Dr Enid Appleby, Divisional Education Officer and a good friend of the School. She was succeeded by G.V.Welbourne.

Dr McGregor Williams paid his first official visit to the new building in October, appearing in morning assembly to greet the boys and to bid farewell to his erstwhile secretary, Mary Burnell, whom he escorted onto the platform for the purpose. On December 16th Pedley attended his first Speech Day and Mac made what proved to be his final public appearance, just a fortnight before his death on New Year's Eve. His old enemy, Florence Horsbrugh, yielded the Education Ministry to Sir David Eccles and, at the election the following Spring the Conservatives retained power under Anthony Eden. The School's mock election, held at the same time, resulted, alarmingly, in a victory for the Fascists whose candidate, Robert Evans, beat the Conservative Henry Kamen (later to become an eminent historian) by nearly a hundred votes. The official response was that the Fascists had run the most entertaining campaign and that the result was not to be taken too seriously. One wonders, nevertheless, what those named on the Roll of Honour might have thought. The year was also marked by the retirement of H.Mann who had taught Mathematics since 1940 and founded the highly popular Transport Club.

Another event that took place during the Spring of 1955 was the demise of soccer at the School, a 1–12 defeat by Roan being a fitting tombstone, one might say, to set above the buried remains of two dozen seasons with the spherical ball. The following Autumn rugby reigned supreme as the Winter sport. There was much discontented grumbling and, as an ex-soccer player himself, Richard Pedley had some sneaking sympathy with the protests. In his efforts to turn the place into a public school in all but name, however, he was happy enough to see the oval ball enthroned and new fixtures inaugurated against what he doubtless regarded as a better class of opposition. Cricket, of course, still reigned supreme as the Summer sport and, during the 1955 season, John Flower took 78 wickets for the 1st XI, a record which, by a considerable margin, survives to this day.

In January 1956 a General Inspection took place, the first by H.M.I. since 1942. The gentlemen it seems, like their predecessors, were happy enough with what they saw. Later that year Anthony Crosland (Highgate and Trinity College, Oxford) published his Future of Socialism which called for a social egalitarianism to be achieved through the comprehensive school system. He vowed that, when Labour next came to power, he would close every grammar school in the country. Among his friends, it is said, he habitually inserted the embellishment "f...g" between the words "every" and "grammar." With the Tories firmly in the saddle, and destined to remain so for a further eight years, the significance of his words was, if not totally ignored, certainly filed away in the further recesses of most minds at Hurst Road. With the School in its Silver Jubilee Year and, some now say, poised to enter its "golden age", the word "egalitarianism" was not found upon many lips.

The new building was officially (and somewhat belatedly) opened on May 11th by the Lord Lieutenant of Kent, Lord Cornwallis, and the Bishop of Rochester, the Rt. Rev. Christopher Chavasse. The Chairman of

School Boxing Squad, 1956 (Milton Williams, centre of back row).

Kent Education Committee, Alderman Redman, presided and votes of thanks were proposed by Chairman of the Governors, Harry Lester, and by the Chairman of the Old Boys' Association, Peter Mitchell. In his speech Lord Cornwallis declared that the function of a grammar school was " to provide literacy to counteract the onslaught of television." Nor was the one-eyed monster the only perceived menace of the day. Even the humble radio – or "wireless" as most still called it – was capable of driving wedges between the generations. Tuesday night was *Goon Show* night and for most schoolboys this programme was unmissable. Catch phrases like "He's fallen in the water!" and "Have a gorilla!", while not, perhaps, intrinsically hilarious, had devotees in hysterics as, the following morning, they relived, beside the bike sheds, the highlights of the previous evening's show. Anyone unfortunate enough to have missed it would soon find someone who could repeat it almost word for word and in accents not notably inferior to those of Messrs Milligan, Sellers and Secombe themselves. The Debating Society's motion: "The *Goon Show* is an insult to the public's intelligence", was, needless to say, overwhelmingly defeated.

Towards the end of the Summer Term a Silver Jubilee Ball was held and celebrations were all the merrier for the news that only four state schools had surpassed the total of eighteen high academic honours (six open awards at "Oxbridge" and twelve state scholarships) achieved that past academic year in Lamorbey. On July 14th the Jubilee Fete, opened by Patricia Hornsby-Smith M.P., raised over £500 towards the Sports Pavilion Fund, despite atrocious weather.

While the adult world wrung its hands over the Suez crisis and the Hungarian revolt, the youth of Sidcup argued the rival merits of American heart-throbs Johnny Ray and Elvis Presley, tuning their sets to Radio Luxemburg. Teddy boys preened and strutted at street corners, their covert admirers studying points and seeking ways to incorporate an oxymoronic touch of discreet flamboyance into their schoolday attire – an obligatory purple blazer with grey flannels (shorts, still, for the younger boys) since clothes rationing had come to an end. Devising some detail ostentatious enough to be noticed and admired by their peers while, at the same time, unobtrusive enough to escape detection by eagle-eyed form-masters was all but impossible. Hair offered the best opportunities and, with Brylcreem and busy comb, many cultivated a quiff though the more daring affected the crew-cut popularised by such screen idols as James Dean.

Hair-style was one issue that had not greatly exercised the mind of Doctor Mac, as was made apparent in the portrait by Jeff Hoare R.A. unveiled in the School Hall by Harry Lester on the 1st of February 1957. Mrs McGregor Williams said a few words and her late husband's School Song was sung. In the Summer Edgar Martin handed over his responsibility for music to Steve Dunball, the first full-time music master to be appointed by the School. For many years Martin had been responsible for the Musical Society and for the Choir. More recently, towards the end of the School's spell at Crittall's Corner, he had formed an orchestra and, over the next few years, built it up to a high standard at the expense of a great deal of his own free time. Dunball was to carry this work forward another decade or so into the mid-sixties, building upon the firm foundations that the physics master had laid.

In 1957 the Russians sent their *Sputnik* into orbit and Harold McMillan succeeded Anthony Eden as prime minister, telling us, soon afterwards, that we had "never had it so good." Two young schoolmasters, Alastair Wilson and Philip Geen, who joined the staff at this point, were given a similar message by the Head. The former, a Bristol University classicist from Mansfield mining stock, was taken to one side by Richard Pedley and told that he was to be given, as form-master, the thirty most able youngsters who were to be "accelerated" through to "O" Level a year early. "I expect all these boys to go to Oxford or Cambridge, Mr Wilson." In due course twenty-two of them did. At Wilson's urging Greek was introduced in 1959 and, five years later, he took over the Classics Department from Eva Jackson, going on to complete 36 full-time years at the School, the last 20 of them as Second Master. A further four years of part-time teaching brought him to the remarkable total of forty years at the School, a figure that only Edward Palmer has surpassed. Philip Geen, on the other hand, spent just three years at the School, teaching French, but went on to become Chief Education Officer for Bexley in 1975.

The following year, 1958, saw the arrival of J.K.Tabert to teach Maths and Science for the next ten years and Stanley Darke to teach Chemistry for eight. It also witnessed the retirement of Arthur Parsons who had held the position of Second Master since the foundation of the School. Fulsome indeed were the tributes paid to him by pupils, colleagues, governors and Old Boys alike. Dick Pedley spoke of the "pawky and puckish humour which, from time to time, lit up his conversation – and his face" despite the heavy burdens he had had to carry as Chemistry teacher, Head of Science and Deputy Head over 27 years, for many of them combining all three roles. It was in large measure down to the foundations he had laid that Science in the School had become so strong. "He has been our prop and pivot for so long that it is hardly possible to imagine the School without him," continued the Head in his tribute and Edward Palmer spoke of his earlier sporting prowess and his preservation "amid many difficulties, of a happy atmosphere among his colleagues in the Common Room where his efficiency and modesty have won him well-deserved affection." With Parsons' departure the baton passed to Palmer himself, youngest of the original five and now, of course, the last surviving member of staff from September 17th 1931.

At Speech Day in December Pedley launched into a vigorous diatribe against the comprehensive movement. Kent, admittedly, "had set its face resolutely against sabotaging its existing secondary schools" but other authorities were, as he put it, "bringing to an end the courageous experimentation" of the tripartite system and there were already, in England and Wales, some 160 schools that were broadly comprehensive in character if not necessarily in name. Around half of these were in London, two of them, Eltham Green and Crown Woods, on the doorstep, virtually. Shifting key, he welcomed Eileen Butler as School Secretary to replace

Gwen Chapman. Mrs Butler was to prove a tower of strength over the next twenty years and to make herself indispensable to three different heads.

Before moving on it is worth noting that the Film Society, founded by Bob Cole, was born in 1958, its first offering being *The Lavender Hill Mob*, with Bill Quinnell at the projector. This was also the year in which a new purple cap for Sixth-formers was introduced, differentiating them from the younger boys who continued to wear a grey cap with purple piping, the central button of which was ritually cut off as part of the initiation ceremony inflicted upon new pupils. Prefects were afforded the still greater distinction of a gold tassel appended to their cap, a public school touch which fitted well with Pedley's aspirations.

The hot September of 1959 brought with it Gerwyn Lewis from Carmarthen to teach Biology and a Californian, Bill McElroy, to join the English Department. Lionel Pascoe left for a headship in Manchester after ten years in charge of Mathematics and the Department passed to Raymond Payne from, appropriately, the Mathematical School, Rochester. "Wyn" Lewis would, in due course, inherit the Biology Department from Bill Freeman during a thirty-five year career at the School which encompassed, additionally, the headship of Years Three and Four, the commanding of the A.T.C. and a range of sporting involvement in such diverse areas as shooting, cricket and golf as well as his first love, rugby football.

As the fifties clicked over into the sixties the era of the teenager finally reached these shores. Cliff Richard and Tommy Steele vied with their transatlantic counterparts. Young men took to wearing jeans and young women flouncy petticoats which swayed and rustled intriguingly as they tottered on stiletto heels. A hundred thousand protestors marched the fifty miles from Aldermaston to Trafalgar Square in support of unilateral nuclear disarmament – a demand the Debating Society rejected by 35 votes to 18. John Kennedy became President of the United States, the Berlin Wall arose virtually overnight and Yuri Gagarin was the first man into space. The Cuban missile crisis soon had the older staff shaking their heads and recalling 1939. Conscription, it was said, so recently abandoned, would have to be reintroduced and Sixth-formers were seen anxiously scanning the headlines and asking the likes of Palmer, Jenkins, Morley and Freeman to tell them about gas-masks and air-raid shelters.

Another reminder of the thirties was provided by the arrival of hutted classrooms in Hurst Road. The "quadrangle" at the back of the building disappeared under what was at first the "Annexe" and then, imaginatively, huts "A" and "B". In Summer the occupants of these outposts baked and in the Winter they choked as "monstrous iron oil stoves belched out fumes".

The new sports pavilion was opened by Kent and England cricketer J.W.Martin in July 1961. The School Fund had contributed £2,300 to this project with the balance, £650, supplied by the L.E.A. In September the School became five form entry, the extra thirty bringing the total of new boys to 150. Clearly even the additional space provided by the new huts would soon prove inadequate as the roll edged up towards nine hundred.

Some idea of the School's socio-economic profile at this period may be gleaned from a survey published in the *Chronicle* for Summer 1961. By far the most popular newspaper was the *Telegraph* which was taken by a quarter of pupil homes and by over half the staff. Nearly every family now possessed a television set. The "square-eyed" (to use the popular expression of the time) would eat their meals off their laps – unheard of in a "respectable" home even a decade before – while watching Z Cars or *Emergency Ward 10*. The slow disappearance, over the last half century, of the traditional "knees under the table" family meal, and the conversation that went with it, has been one of the greatest (and least remarked upon) driving forces of social change.

In the Spring of 1961 arrived the young, red-haired and glamorous Ann Nex to teach Mathematics. In a virtually all-male establishment, where testosterone bubbled almost audibly on every staircase and corridor, her arrival caused something of a sensation. Fortunately her firm common sense and good humour (not to mention her mathematical prowess) kept the worst excesses in check, although the Head felt it necessary to put in a discreet word about length of skirt. This was, after all, the age of Mary Quant and the famous "mini", enduring symbol, along with the Beatles, mods-and-rockers and the "pill", of the phenomenon known, indelibly, as the " Swinging Sixties". One ingenious pupil cut up a cardboard Kleenex box so that the bold slogan "KLEENEX FOR MEN" lost its first four letters (and, in some versions, its final letter as well). The jest caught on and "Nex for Men" (or "Nex for Me") was proclaimed by Ann's admirers – who were legion – around the School. The fact that the first hutted classrooms were known as the "Annexe" provided another source for punning adolescent humour. Under her married name of Clifford her career at the School – with a child-rearing break – continued until her retirement in 1997. Ann Clifford's 36 years (some of them part-time) would put her very high up in the long service league table were one ever to be drawn up.

Staff changes in the early sixties included the arrivals of Messrs Willingham ('61), Maylam ('61), Jewson ('61), Berry ('62), Burgess ('62), Brand ('62), Bratcher ('62), Lilly ('62), King ('63) and Roberts ('63) as well as the departures of Messrs Davies ('62), Cullingworth ('63), Pickard ('64), Cole ('64), McElroy ('65) and Side ('65).

Keith Willingham's appointment is of particular interest in that it involved two firsts: he was the first teacher of Economics (introduced by Pedley as a supposedly easier option for the less academic sixth-former) and the first former pupil of the School to return as a teacher there. Terry Maylam, like the present author a pupil at Hastings Grammar School, went on to serve Chis and Sid for 35 years, 14 of them (between 1973 and 1987) as Head of French. He will be remembered, among much else, for his Gilbert and Sullivan productions and for his dry wit in the Common Room. Brian Burgess and Martyn Berry, graduates of Imperial College and Pembroke, Oxford respectively, started together in September 1962 and would, between them, amass some seventy years of service to the School. When they joined the departments of Cedric Morley and George Goddard they can hardly have thought that the day would come when their own names would be spoken in the same breath – indeed in the same tones of awe – as those of their illustrious mentors, two thirds of the famous scientific triple pillar supporting the School's great – and growing – academic reputation. Both names will recur at frequent intervals during the remainder of this book and any fuller assessment of their careers must be deferred.

As regards the other newcomers referred to above, shortage of space allows little more than the briefest of details. Geoffrey Jewson taught French and David Brand Mathematics for eight years each. Bob Bratcher spent five years teaching French. Terry "Tiger" Lilly spent a similar period in the Geography Department while John King, a Cambridge double first, gave seven years of outstanding scholarship to Classics. Tony Roberts, a chemist, remained at the School until 1968.

Turning to those leaving the staff in the early years of the decade, we find Victor Cullingworth, after 23 years at the School, taking over the Department of Modern Languages at the young Bexley Grammar School, Richard Davies passing on the Geography Department to Brian Cumbers and Alfred Pickard emigrating to New Zealand after six years teaching mainly History. Bob Cole, after fifteen years in Walsh's English

Department, took up a lectureship at nearby Avery Hill College. The following term Eric Side, who had started on the same September day in 1950, moved to the post of Senior Science Master at the Crypt School, Gloucester. Side, a graduate of Emmanuel College, Cambridge, was one of the sharpest minds to have occupied the Common Room where his devastating wit became legendary. He it was, for example, who coined for Pedley the nickname "Moby Dick" on account of his somewhat cetaceous appearance and imposing – some might say pompous – demeanour. The sotto-voce warning "There he blows!" was often to be heard when "the Mobe" was in the offing. Bill McElroy, the first of at least three Americans to teach English at the School, left, after six years, having founded the Junior Dramatic Society and caused much bewilderment to begin with by directing the first full-scale stage productions of plays by writers who, mysteriously, were not called William Shakespeare.

Roland Rahtz's *Hamlet*, performed in the Spring of 1962, must be deemed the School's most ambitious choice of play to date. The title role was taken by the experienced D.J.Ross and the audiences, one gathers, were "large and appreciative". The following term McElroy's group performed *The Lark* by Jean Anouilh and, for no recorded reason, boys took to wearing bathplugs on chains in the top pocket of their blazers, a craze which seems to have ended as suddenly and as inexplicably as it had begun. An almost equally unexpected phenomenon, on a somewhat larger canvas, was the success of the Liberal candidate, Eric Lubbock, in a parliamentary bye-election, giving rise to the term "Orpington Man" and causing great excitement among psephologists. The General Election was still two years off but, here was a straw in the wind. Some remembered, with a twinge of uneasiness, a certain book by Anthony Crosland. At Speech Day, December 1962, the Headmaster took pleasure in the fact that more than half of the School's intake were now continuing on into higher education. He vigorously refuted the charge, however, that such results were achieved at the expense of a balanced programme and called in evidence the impressive array of cups won in various sports, as well as fine achievements by the actors, the musicians and the cadets (among many others).

The Winter of 1963 was exceptionally long and cold, the worst, by far, since 1947. In the further flung reaches of the building boys were in danger of freezing to their desks until, released by the bell, they rushed outside to warm up by pelting each other with snowballs. Portable convection heaters were summoned to outlying rooms and only strenuous efforts by Bill Hamblen and his staff kept the School open at all. Tired of snow-men, half a dozen second-formers completed an igloo one lunch hour, though it was soon demolished by a passing gang of fifth-formers with nothing better to do.

Tony Perry's departure, after eight years, to a post in Bromley brought a year of confusion to an end. To have a Mr Perry and a Mr Berry simulta-neously around one's Chemistry labs required a combination of Professor Higgins style enunciation and Royal Festival Hall style acoustics that was not generally to be found in the building at Lamorbey.

During 1963 a new form christened "Transitus" was launched, con-sisting of a dozen or so boys who were to be accelerated through the exam system to give them an extra year in the Sixth before trying for their uni-versity scholarship. One of its first members, C.Riddle, informs us that the unit was run along nautical lines. A bell was sounded at half hour intervals, as in the Navy, and each member of the form was assigned a rank, from first mate to cabin boy. Since rum was not available a toffee ration was broken open, or "spliced", on occasions for celebration. In the light of all this it comes as no huge surprise to discover that "H.M.S. Transitus" was soon consigned to Davy Jones' Locker.

That Summer came a new sensation. Chips were served in the Dining Hall following the installation of a deep-fat fryer. Nothing like this had ever happened before and boys stared at each other in wild disbelief. Only two things prevented Miss Haye-Forbes from rotating in her grave: first, she weighed around eighteen stone and, secondly, she was still alive.

At Speech Day in December, 1963, the Secretary of State for Education himself, Sir Edward Boyle, appeared as guest of honour. It was not an opportunity to be wasted and Mr Pedley protested that, to abolish schools like his "with their unique concentration of effort on the needs of that small, gifted minority of children on whom so much of the future well-being of our country depends, would be the crassest of follies." Sir Edward, in reply, praised the work of Wally Moat's new Sixth Form Social Services Work Group, which had already given great help, of a practical nature, to elderly and disabled people in the locality. On the burning issues of boundary changes and selection at eleven he said very little.

It was a difficult time. The Christian Union met to discuss the problem of communicating the Gospel to "Teddy Boy types" and stuffy Sidcup fathers worried that their sons were becoming "beatniks" according to one gloomy and anonymous member of 4B. "The Beatles are a plague which no insecticide will stop", wrote A.P.Robshaw of 3A in the *Chronicle*. He must now be in his early fifties and it would be interesting to hear how he has turned out.

The Autumn of 1964 was notable for several reasons. For a start, it marked the tenth anniversary of the School's – and the Headmaster's – arrival in Hurst Road. Despite Mac's dark forebodings it had, in fact, gone from strength to strength. The 152 major awards and state scholarships amassed over the decade overshadowed the 27 achieved in the School's first 23 years of life – though the comparison is, of course, an unfair one in many ways. A month or so into the new term, on October 16th to be precise, Harold Wilson entered 10 Downing Street, the first Labour prime minister since 1951 – though with a wafer thin majority of four seats. Despite his protestation that the grammar schools would be " abolished over [his] dead body", the fact that he chose Anthony Crosland to be his first Secretary of State for Education made it pretty easy to see the way things would go.

By comparison, the decision to abolish the wearing of caps in the Sixth Form (even those with a golden tassel!) might seem trivial to some but there were those among the more senior members of the Common Room who saw in it the thin end of a very substantial wedge and who muttered darkly about where such a decision might lead given the sartorial predilections of modern youth. Before long they would be all turning up in jeans.

On July 12th the following year the skeleton in the cupboard duly rattled. Anthony Crosland published *Secondary Education Circular 10/65*. The document began by declaring the Government's objective "to end selection at eleven plus and to eliminate separatism in secondary education". After a brief explanation of "the need to raise educational standards at all levels" it continued: "The Secretary of State accordingly requests local authorities, if they have not already done so, to prepare and submit to him plans for reorganising secondary education in their areas on comprehensive lines." In conclusion came the reminder that the Government's policy had been "endorsed by the House of Commons in a motion passed on 21st January 1965." It was signed by the Permanent Under-Secretary of State, Herbert Andrew. To make matters worse from Richard Pedley's point of view, 1965 was also the year in which the Greater London Act came into force. The School was cut adrift from Kent after 34 years, depriving it of three quarters of its catchment area, and handed over to the new

London Borough of Bexley – an amalgamation of Erith, Belvedere, Welling, East Thamesmead, Crayford, Bexleyheath, Sidcup and Bexley Village. These districts seemed to Pedley unlikely to provide sufficient numbers of the able, well motivated primary school pupils from "professional", middle-class backgrounds that had, by and large, fed his school before these new lines were slashed across the map.

As though all this were not problem enough, a third factor supervened. The first Bexley Council had a Labour majority and its leading lights were strongly in support of Government policy as far as schooling was concerned. Prominent councillors such as the leader, Ronald Brierly, Dr Audrey Martin and Elgar Handy, the first Chairman of the new Education Committee, ordered plans to be drawn up for the reorganisation of local secondary schools, as quickly as possible, along comprehensive lines.

At the first Speech Day under this new regime the Headmaster thanked Harry Lester for his "far-seeing and inspired support for the School over thirty years" and regretted that the reorganisation of the Governing Body, scheduled for March 31st the following year, had led to his retirement as Chairman. He was at pains to report all the School's extra-curricular and non-academic achievements, of which there were many, in order, yet again, to refute the accusation that the School was "merely a hot-bed for the forced production of examination results." At length, however, he carelessly let slip that the School had, for the second year running, obtained twenty admissions to "Oxbridge". Of these forty successful applicants nineteen had obtained open awards. "The School's aim", Pedley continued, nailing his colours to the mast, "is to encourage the pursuit of individual excellence and to develop the highest potentialities of that minority of children upon whom the health and wealth of the country in the future will depend". Guest of honour W.A.Barker, Head of the Leys School, Cambridge, told the audience not to regard the disappearance of the grammar school as inevitable and he praised Dick Pedley for his resolute stand in its defence.

In September Peter McKenna, a South African graduate who had worked in Nigeria, arrived to teach Physics. He remained just one year but has the distinction of being the first black member of the teaching staff.

The end of the Autumn Term, 1965, was marked by the retirement of George Goddard, first of the three science "giants" to depart. In his twenty years at the School he developed the Chemistry Department into one of the most successful in the country and played a major role in launching numerous pupils on highly successful careers in such fields as medicine, engineering and the pharmaceutical industry. A tough, stocky man, Goddard could quell a difficult class with a slight lift of the chin, though he kept a supply of rubber tubing at hand should more emphatic action be needed. His annual boxing bout in the Gym with Milton Williams was, for many boys, a highlight of the year. He had a great fund of anecdotes about

George Goddard (1944–1966) in retirement.

famous scientists such as Ernest Rutherford whom he had met at the Cavendish Laboratories during his time at Cambridge in the early twenties. Though not Welsh by birth he was married to a Welsh woman, Vera, and had taught in Wales for twenty years hence, perhaps, his passionate devotion to rugby. George Goddard went on to enjoy over thirty years of retirement – much of it playing golf – before his death in 1997 at the age of 94. The Chemistry Department was entrusted to Stanley Darke who would run it for just a year before passing on the Bunsen flame to Martyn Berry.

The School entered 1966 with Councillor John Cronin, a political appointee, on the bridge as its third Chairman of Governors though with Richard Pedley, of course, still very much at the helm. When, on April 1st, Harold Wilson increased Labour's majority from 4 to 96 the outlook for grammar schools looked even grimmer still. Pedley (in a campaign eerily reminiscent of his predecessor's fight to keep the School at Crittall's Corner) now threw all his energies into opposing a scheme to merge Chis and Sid with neighbouring secondary modern, Hurstmere, as an eight form entry, split-site comprehensive. In a letter to parents that Spring he warned that Bexley proposed to terminate the School's existence as a separate entity in three years' time. He drew attention to the School's "unsurpassed national reputation" and said that its elimination would be seriously detrimental to the interests of the children themselves, their successors and the community as a whole.

The staff rallied behind him, passing a unanimous resolution requesting that plans drawn up by Sidcup headteachers should be considered as an alternative. At a meeting held on July 6th 1966 a Parents' Association was formed to fight the proposed changes. Nancy Crust, Jim Preston and Ted Mulberry were prominent among those parents who gave powerful support to the "resistance movement" that was now underway. When Councillor Handy claimed that the Borough's teachers were in favour of Labour's plan a ballot of six staff-rooms organised by Martyn Berry, showed that this was not in fact the case.

There was a considerable turnover of staff in the Summer of 1966. Foremost amongst those departing was undoubtedly Dennis Clarke, one of the few still remaining from pre-war days in Station Road. An appreciation of his career appeared in Chapter Four. Suffice it to add here that "Nobby" Clarke spent thirty years as Head of History, including his wartime service in the Royal Air Force. He went on to enjoy 23 years of retirement (during which wrote a history of Otford) before his death in 1989. Eva Jackson, the Head of Classics and first "permanent" woman teacher at Chis and Sid, retired after 22 years' service, although she continued in a part-time capacity for a further four. Fuller details of her career were given in Chapter Five. After six years in charge of Mathematics Bob Payne moved to Dulwich College and Steve Dunball, the School's first Director of Music, left for Cheshire, after nine years in Sidcup, to take up a lectureship. The last day of that academic year, July 20th 1966, was one of much speech-making, present-giving and bidding of farewells in the Common Room. The boys broke up in good humour, keen to enjoy the closing stages of the World Cup. Ten days later they were celebrating England's victory.

The most prominent new arrival was Miss Dorothy Stephenson to join the English Department. "Steve" – as she always insisted on being called in the Common Room – though in her fifties had graduated only two years before (from Birkbeck College) after a long career as a certificated teacher. Determinedly a "character" from the start, she quickly laid claim to the adjective "redoubtable" and (like Mac and Cedric Morley) is one of that small number who contrived to become, in some sense, School legends while their careers were in full flow. Short, combative, with plaits hauled tautly across her scalp, she took great pride in her spinsterhood and would expatiate upon it at some length to any colleague she could manoeuvre into a corner for the purpose. She came to be regarded, by both staff and boys alike, with an odd mixture of terror and affection.

At what was to prove his final Speech Day at the School, in December

1966, Pedley protested at moves to "restrict the flow of boys from Bromley" which, he declared, would be "an example of parish-pump parochialism at its pettiest." The School's "remarkable academic achievements" had been made possible by the "concentration of academically able staff upon academically able pupils in a bracing atmosphere of intellectual energy and endeavour." Had he cared to do so, Pedley could have enlarged upon this comment by pointing out that Chis and Sid was the top maintained school in the country that year as regards Open Awards at "Oxbridge" (gaining ten) and 22nd in the country over all, being "beaten" by 15 independent schools (headed by Dulwich Collge with 25) and 6 direct grant schools (headed by M.G.S. with 32). In this unofficial league table the School came just below Marlborough and Rugby (11 each) and ahead of such prestigious establishments as Tonbridge, Westminster, Charterhouse, Repton and Tiffin's. There was much activity taking place outside the classroom too, he again reminded his audience, singling out for special mention the remarkable achievement of the two senior rugby sides in going the whole season unbeaten by other schools and praising Stanley Simmonds' directoral debut, a production of *Timon of Athens*, a play rarely performed by amateurs at all, let alone by such a young cast.

The following year, 1967, brought a number of new recruits to the Common Room, several of whom would enjoy notable careers at the School. David Pennycuick arrived to take charge of Mathematics together with Michael Baker, who would inherit the Department from him nine years later. Garth Pinkney took charge of Economics and Robert Ims, a former Head Boy, became the second ex- pupil to join the staff, taking over the Geography Department from Brian Cumbers. David Huke replaced Steve Dunball as Director of Music, though two years later he himself gave place to Ronald Halford who stayed in post until 1974. Sadly, on May 1st came the news that Sydney Grindrod had died following the amputation of his leg. He had completed 25 years at the School, many of them burdened by illness, and his death, by a cruel irony, came on what should have been the first day of his retirement.

On May 15th the D.E.S. accepted the Bexley plan. A fortnight later, following a fruitless round of petitions and deputations (including one to Edward Heath) official notice of closure was posted on the School fence.

Although, given the circumstances, it should not have been a great surprise, Richard Pedley's resignation came, nevertheless, as a very considerable shock at many levels. Edward Palmer described it, at the time, as "a

Bob Ims (Pupil: 1931–38; Staff: 1967–1982).

stunning blow". Despite the record number of "Oxbridge" places that year – twenty-three – he decided to accept the Headship of St Dunstan's College in Catford. In a farewell message he wrote: "I do not suppose I would have taken notice of vacancies if I had been more in sympathy with the proposed future of this School," before adding, with no pretence of false modesty, "There is certainly no maintained school which surpasses our successes."

Among the many tributes to his thirteen years as Head came the observation that at least two thirds of starting boys now entered university seven years later. The Sixth Form was over three times larger on his departure than it had been in the first year in Hurst Road.

Like his predecessor in the job, Dick Pedley was in poor health by this stage. He suffered from diabetes and, at the age of 55, it seems clear, with hindsight, that he should have retired there and then instead of shouldering a new and equally heavy burden. In his *Centenary History of St Dunstan's* Nigel Watson writes: "Sadly, the dynamic and lovable man who first entered College became a shambling shadow of his former self within two years."

Richard Pedley died suddenly on 17th March 1973 at the age of sixty, leaving a widow, Jean, and two grown-up children, Susan and Timothy. His funeral took place, six days later, at St George's Church, Perry Hill.

Back in Hurst Road the next chapter was already two thirds written.

Michael Brown (1967–1976).

CHAPTER EIGHT

The Embattled Years of Michael Brown

THE COMMON ROOM COPY of *The Times Educational Supplement* for Friday, February 17th 1967 was quickly lifted from the pile of newspapers and the "Big Five" – Messrs Palmer, Freeman, Morley, Jenkins and Walsh – huddled around it, studying the long-awaited advertisement. Their worst fears were confirmed. The salient section read as follows: "The proposal for this school in the Authority's plan for the reorganisation of secondary education (on which the Secretary of State's decision is awaited) is that it should be amalgamated with Hurstmere Secondary Modern School. The two schools would form a comprehensive school of eight forms of entry, starting in September 1969 and it is envisaged that the large VI form would be maintained. It is expected, too, that the [successful applicant] would become Headmaster of the comprehensive school in 1969." The salary offered was £3,150 per annum, rising, in stages, to £3,450, to which would be added the London Allowance of £70.

Only those in sympathy with such a plan (one assumes) applied for the post. The successful candidate proved to be Michael Brown, the thirty-nine- year-old Headmaster of Prescot Grammar School, situated between Liverpool and St Helens and founded in 1544. He was born in Bury, Lancashire, on October 29th 1927. His father, a graduate of Bangor and Manchester, was headmaster of the local technical school. Brown attended Bury Grammar School from which he went to Emmanuel College, Cambridge, leaving, in 1948, with a degree in History. After National Service in the R.A.F. he went to St Peter's College, Oxford and took an M.A. in Theology, thus achieving the rare distinction of a degree from both the "ancient" universities. He was a talented footballer and a keen Methodist, becoming a lay-preacher in his early twenties, a calling that he was to follow for the next fifty years.

Michael Brown's first teaching post was at an independent school, Wrekin College, in Shropshire. He moved, next, to the super-selective Reading School and then, in 1957, became Head of History at Wallasey Grammar School. That same year he married Rosemary Johnson, an English graduate from the University of Leeds. Six years later Brown took on the first of his four headships when he moved to Prescot in 1963. Merseyside was well to the left in its educational philosophy and the early sixties saw the abolition of many grammar schools in southern Lancashire as a whole. There was much highly vocal opposition, protest meetings degenerating into near riots on occasion. Commenting on local educational politics, a colleague of Brown's at a neighbouring school remarked: "I knew it would be like wading through treacle but I didn't expect it would be shark-infested treacle." It was an image that Michael Brown would recall in later years when he grappled with a similar situation a couple of hundred miles to the south-east.

The reorganisation scheme for Prescot Grammar, Brown felt, was dreadfully misconceived, entailing, for example, the eventual loss of its Sixth Form. Though sympathetic to the wider aim of a more egalitarian system, the young headmaster became increasingly disillusioned by events and sought a more intelligent plan elsewhere, one that he believed he could wholeheartedly endorse. It was this that drew his attention to the advertisement for the post in Lamorbey. A telephone conversation with Bexley's Chief Education Officer, Dr Semple, elicited the information that the scheme for an amalgamation along comprehensive lines was all but settled and so Michael Brown put in his application. He was, of course, well aware of Chis and Sid's academic reputation and he had acquainted himself with the spacious setting and the proximity of the two schools concerned. To his mind it seemed a plan with a high prospect of success and he felt confident that he had both the experience and the determination to make it work. He could hardly, however, have anticipated the fury of the storm that he would walk into on September 7th. The treacle was soon crashing about his ears and triangular fins coming at him from every side.

To those in the Chis and Sid Common Room, particularly staff of some thirty years standing, the situation, of course, looked very different. Though the new man was, they soon saw, a courteous, modest individual and an excellent listener – qualities that not all would necessarily have attributed to his predecessors in the post – his new colleagues might well have chosen another zoological metaphor to convey their feelings towards him. Despite the very favourable first impression the new Head conveyed on the human level he was, self-evidently, a viper sent by the authorities to entwine his way into the bosom of the School in order to destroy it. The customary courtesies were, of course, given and returned and professional decorum was, by and large, preserved. The education of the boys thus proceeded, in most respects, as before and few noticed much difference in the way the School was run. The staff – or the great majority of it, at least – nevertheless girded their loins for action. The enemy was now within the walls and only drastic action could save the citadel.

A visiting Australian academic, Dr I.V.Hansen of Melbourne University, recorded a wringing of hands among the staff. "I'd be lost in a class of less able boys," was an oft-repeated comment. There was frequent talk of "the need to stretch the brighter students" and great lamenting over what was seen as "an unthinking quest for mediocrity." During the nineteen-sixties Chis and Sid sent approximately 10% of its university entrants to either Oxford or Cambridge, compared with little more than half this proportion at similar institutions such as Alleyn's and Kingston Grammar School. One anonymous Sixth-former complained to Dr Hansen that "The School [was] obsessed with getting boys through exams and keeping up its own reputation" and a School joke, apparently, posited that, in the event of fire, one senior teacher was allocated to the safe evacuation of the boys while another was instructed to stand in the Foyer and hose down the "Oxbridge" honours boards.

Some of the more elderly staff claimed to detect what they called "a dilution of talent" in the new entrants to the School over recent years, particularly since the diminished catchment area was introduced after the separation of Bexley from Bromley in 1965. They even observed such a "dilution" among the staff. Teddy Jenkins was heard to declare: "I went to a humble school in a Welsh valley. Some of the masters may have been a little queer but they were all *scholars*. Where are the scholars now? – coming into schools like this, I mean." This remark, recorded verbatim by Dr Hansen in 1969, reflects a view that was becoming widespread. The rapidly declining pay of young teachers, relative to their fellow graduates, in the nineteen-sixties no doubt accounts in large part for this perception.

The arrival amidst them of Michael Brown clearly presented the Staff with a dilemma. Having lost their great champion of maintained grammar school status to the independent sector they found themselves faced with a personable man from an "Oxbridge" (indeed "Ox" and "bridge") and grammar school background himself who, unaccountably, seemed determined to be the head of a comprehensive school. He had held a commission in the R.A.F. and could not be blamed for having been only seventeen when the Second World War came to an end. He did not rant or rave and, despite "left-of-centre" views and northern vowels, could hardly be described as another Arthur Scargill. He was wont to gaze out of his study window during a lengthy and sometimes heated tirade from a Morley or a Freeman and then, after a period of silent reflection, deliver himself of a calm, considered and irritatingly reasonable response. The quietly spoken words: "I personally favour comprehensive education" would bring many such one-sided confrontations to a close.

Asked by the Staff, early on, to make a statement of his educational philosophy, Brown denied being either, as he put it, "an educational mercantilist" or "an educational Calvinist", going on to explain that he did not hold with the idea that only a limited amount of education was available nor that children were unalterably fixed in a pre-ordained intellectual stratum.

Although the new Head converted few of them to his point of view, his staff quickly came to realise that he was no bigot and that there was much upon which they could all agree. So long as Chis and Sid remained a grammar school Michael Brown was determined to maintain the tradition of pointing the ablest boys towards the most prestigious universities. "Oxbridge" successes continued unabated under his regime. Indeed marginally more students per year gained entrance to Oxford or Cambridge in Brown's time than under Pedley, although it should be borne in mind that, during the former's headship, the over-all Sixth Form numbers increased somewhat. The total of twenty-three places gained in Pedley's final year, 1966–67, was never subsequently exceeded but there were two eighteens and a nineteen under Brown between 1969 and 1973. In all 124 students gained "Oxbridge" places during Brown's nine years compared to the 150 gaining similar success during the thirteen years of Richard Pedley. As regards open awards the statistics are again in Brown's favour, averaging about six a year during his stewardship as compared to about five per annum under his predecessor. There will no doubt be many readers, particularly younger ones, who find such figures tedious and pointless. To an older generation of Sedcopians, however, they are an endless source of fascination and argument. At a time long before the widely-publicised "A" Level league tables, with which we are now familiar, it was the unofficial "Oxbridge" contest which, by general consent in academic circles, placed the relevant institutions in their pecking order for the year in question (it being deemed, with good reason, that where a school's "Oxbridge" statistics led their other examination results would follow). There were, it hardly needs saying, many more boys going on to study at other universities of high repute, notably Imperial College and the great London medical schools.

Michael Brown readily maintained that what happened in the classroom was what really mattered and that this, in the end, was more important than systems or philosophies. On this point he was at one with his staff and he quickly came to recognise and to value those of his colleagues who excelled behind their closed classroom doors and whose pupils' results, year after year, bore testimony to the skill with which they had been taught.

The coming of the new Headmaster in the Summer of 1967 must not deflect our attention from the other arrivals and departures in Hurst Road. Robert Bratcher and D.G.Brook moved on, to Bedford Modern and Alleyn's respectively. The new arrivals included the mathematician Robert ("Bob") Buxton, a graduate of Queen Mary College, London, who had done his teaching practice at the School the previous year. He is, at the time of writing, the longest-serving member of the Staff. David Cole came to teach Geography and Richard Mason, from Exeter College, Oxford, – who once shared a dormitory at Shrewsbury with *Monty Python's* Michael Palin – arrived to join the Classics Department. David Turner, a former pupil, was appointed to teach Mathematics and P.E. and, despite staying for just five years, made a notable mark, particularly as an outstanding cricketer.

A month or so into the new academic year came news of the death of Arthur Parsons, the School's founding Deputy Head and the first in that long line of distinguished science masters – Freeman, Morley, Goddard, Martin, Side, Burgess, Berry, Lewis – who did so much to make Chislehurst and Sidcup Grammar School a famous name in the realms of state sector education.

At Prize-Giving on December 11th guest of honour Chris Chataway (born in the same year as the School) the leader of the I.L.E.A. and famous middle-distance runner, together with Chairman of the Governors John Cronin, heard Michael Brown make his first public speech as Headmaster and praise his predecessor Richard Pedley's "considerable contribution to the educational life of the country."

On January 12th 1968 the new Secretary of State, Patrick Gordon Walker, accepted, in detail, the Bexley reorganisation plan and a few weeks later Michael Brown received from the Education Committee an official invitation, dated February 22nd, to be Headmaster of "the combined Chislehurst and Sidcup Grammar School for Boys and Hurstmere Secondary School for Boys on amalgamation" and " to undertake the necessary forward planning." On April 2nd the appointment was confirmed though, as things transpired, the previous day might have been a more appropriate one for the issuing of this letter since within five weeks the Conservatives swept the board in the local elections, winning every seat in Bexley. It took less than three weeks for the new Schools Sub-Committee to withdraw the plan.

"Confusion now hath made his masterpiece!" Macduff's words sum up well the situation that now obtained in Hurst Road with Harold Wilson's Labour Government firmly established in Whitehall and the triumphant Tories, newly settled in the Crayford education office, busily unscrambling the painstaking work of their predecessors in defiance of declared national policy and with scant regard to the new appointments that had just been made. The embattled Michael Brown, like other local heads, saw the carpet snatched away from beneath his feet. As he sat in his lonely study and contemplated the mess he had inherited he was all too well aware of the ill-concealed delight that radiated from the Common Room along the corridor.

Bexley's withdrawn plan, of course, had to be replaced with another that met the Government's criteria, principally the abolition of selection at eleven. Between June and October the heads and staff representatives of Bexley's secondary schools – known by the acronym "BACOT" – met six times to consider how education in the area might be reorganised. At the end of this concentrated process, on October 23rd, they recommended to the C.E.O., Dr Semple, an interim plan whereby the four secondary modern schools would continue to teach pupils between the ages of eleven and sixteen on an "all-ability-range" basis. At the end of the second year some forty or fifty pupils from each school would, on "guided parental choice", transfer to "the present grammar school" (i.e. Chis and Sid) which would therefore receive between six and eight forms of children at 13+ who would, supposedly at least, be suitable for the type of education on offer there. Others might later transfer into the Sixth Form if appropriate. Chis and Sid would, at the same time, become co-educational.

In order to make this scheme more palatable to the opponents of "comprehensivisation" it was further suggested that up to sixty of the ablest pupils in the Borough should transfer directly into the (ex-) grammar school from their primaries at eleven. The selection process for these children could, in the words of the document, "conveniently be supervised by a consultative committee of head teachers in the area" which would meet the Government's objection to the "Eleven Plus" examination. "Children of special ability are readily noticed by an experienced teacher" remarked the writers of the plan, somewhat disingenuously. All five schools were to be considered as a unit and "would not be identified by any name which indicated difference of status". Michael Brown's signature is appended to the document along with those of J.Sutton, R.Jones, J.Watts and P.Statham, his counterparts at the non-selective schools in the Sidcup area.

As so often with attempts at compromise this plan satisfied neither side in the argument. For those in favour of the status quo, of course, it went much too far while for the zealous egalitarians it did not go far enough. The following year a modified version of it was forwarded to Secretary of State Edward Short who sent it back to Bexley for alteration, describing it as "a two-tier arrangement [that is] not fully comprehensive." It was now 1970 and Labour's six years in Westminster were drawing to a close. On June 18th the Conservatives won the General Election against most people's expectations and the School's own M.P., Edward Heath, found himself in Downing Street. The next day Margaret Thatcher was appointed Secretary of State for Education and, with the Conservatives in control both locally and nationally, the flames of controversy subsided for a few months, though so strongly held were the beliefs on both sides of the argument that they smouldered on, not far beneath the surface. In the Spring of the following year they flared up again with still greater ferocity upon the return of a Labour-controlled Bexley Council.

Important though these issues were there was much else going on in Hurst Road with equal claim to be written into the record. New staff in the Autumn of 1968 included N.M. ("Nick") Pannell to teach Mathematics and Jestyn Lewis to teach Chemistry, the latter beginning a career at the School which would span 24 years, the last ten of them as Head of Department. Among the part-time staff appointed, one name in particular stands out, that of Anne White who joined John Walsh's English Department and served under his successors for 28 years until she took early retirement in 1996.

The production of *As You Like It* which brought 1968 to a close featured Sixth-former Will Hutton as Jaques, perhaps Shakespeare's most incisive social critic – an inspired piece of casting on the part of Roland Rahtz. He could hardly have guessed, however, that Hutton's own critical acumen would earn him an international reputation and a *Who's Who* entry nearly as long as Quentin Blake's. Will Hutton went on to read Social Sciences at Bristol University. After some years in stockbroking he joined the B.B.C., becoming first a senior producer for Radio Four and then, variously, correspondent, director and producer for *The Money Programme and Newsnight*. From 1990 to 1995 he was Economics Editor of *The Guardian* and in 1996 he became Editor of *The Observer*, winning the title of Political Journalist of the Year in 1993. Among his many books *The State We're In* (1995) won the most widespread critical acclaim, being top of the non-fiction bestseller list and reprinted five times in as many weeks. Will Hutton is currently Chief Executive of the Industrial Society, which has over 10,000 member organisations. In a *New Statesman* article he attributed much of his success to the inspirational teaching of his Economics master, Garth Pinkney.

The Spring of 1969 brought major changes to the Governing Body. John Cronin retired after three years as Chairman to be replaced by Douglas Fielding, the Deputy Chairman of the G.L.C., who served in this capacity until he was succeeded by Dr Audrey Martin in 1972. Of the new governors appointed two, C.F.B.Grassby and Cllr. P.K.Talbot were Old Sedcopians. Alderman Alec Higgins, M.B.E.,M.C.,J.P., was another to become a governor at this point, going on to replace Dr Martin as Chairman in 1975.

At Easter 29 boys went on a Classics Department expedition to Italy accompanied by Messrs Wilson, King, Mason and Morris. They stayed in Florence, Rome and Sorrento and enjoyed excursions to Pompeii, Herculaneum and Vesuvius. A highlight of their visit was the Papal Mass in St Peter's Square amidst a crowd of some 300,000 worshippers.

By now it was becoming clear that it would take more than the arrival of a pro-comprehensive headmaster to disrupt the "Oxbridge" conveyor belt that chugged on in Hurst Road much as before, even though change was everywhere in the air. A week into the Summer holiday man walked on the moon for the first time. The United States began its painful with-drawal from Vietnam as Britain began to pour troops into Northern Ireland. Even the Beatles broke up but academic success under Michael Brown's headship remained the equal of that achieved in the latter years of Richard Pedley's. "A" and "O" Level pass-rates maintained their customary high levels and the "Oxbridge" statistics were virtually identical to those achieved over recent years. The Common Room Cassandras had cried woe and wrung their hands but, as the School entered its fifth decade, a time-traveller making the forward hop from 1960 would have found things, in essence, pretty much as he had left them.

There were, of course, some innovations. A performance of Sophocles' *Antigone*, put on by a remarkably enterprising group of Sixth-formers led by I.C.Davies, broke new ground in several respects. Not only was it the first Greek play to be performed at the School but it was also the first occa-sion on which real girls had trod the boards – apart, that is, from the cameo role appearance of McGregor Williams' daughter Norah in *Henry V* back in 1943. It fell to the lot of Julie Smith, Sally Christian and Valerie Simms to breach the walls of the all-male bastion that was Chis and Sid Drama, thus forging a path that many more actresses would follow.

Another "first" was the election of School Governor and Old Sedcopian Raymond Pope to be Mayor of Bexley for 1970–71, a distinc-tion matched by his colleague on the Governing body, Bertha James, who was elected Mayor of Bromley for the same year. Nancy Crust, the vocifer-ous opponent of re-organisation schemes, joined the two mayors as a Governor of the School, shifting the lines of battle to this higher plane.

John King left the Staff to be Sixth Form Classics Master at Rugby, David Brand became Head of Maths at Eltham Green and Henry Foot returned to Southampton after nine years in Hurst Road. The death of Les Stringer the following Easter came as a terrible shock to all who knew him. He had served the School for almost 32 years, most of them as Head of German, having joined the staff a few days before the outbreak of the War. Stringer, who held a first class degree from the University of Leeds, was the author of several books as well as Chief Examiner in German for the Oxford Board. He captained Warren Golf Club and the speed with which he demolished the *Times* crossword was a constant source of amazement to his colleagues in the Common Room.

Hard on the heels of this sad news came a further blow as far as the vast majority of its recipients in Hurst Road were concerned. In the Spring elections of 1971 Labour regained control of the local council and, within a few months, a pamphlet entitled "Secondary Education in Bexley" was published, containing renewed plans for an amalgamation of Chis and Sid with Hurstmere, either as an 11 to18 comprehensive or with Hurstmere taking boys from 11 to 14 and Chis and Sid a mixed intake of 14 to 18 year-olds. In either case the group concerned would be an all-ability one. The second option, the "Revised Handy Plan" as it soon came to be known, sent Michael Brown on a fact-finding visit to Leyton Senior High School, recently "comprehensivised" to take boys aged 14 to 18. He returned with considerable misgivings, as he made clear in a memo to the Governors dated October 27th 1971. "Let it be clearly understood that I will do my best to make a success of whatever plan is decided upon," he wrote before going on to complain that the "present proposals lack idealism." The hypothesis that 14 was an advantageous age for transfer was unproven, he maintained, even though Bexley's "negative" and "uninspiring" plan depended heavily upon it. The School, he felt, was being asked to assimilate a great many changes in a very short space of time. These included coming to terms with an all-ability intake, co-ordinating the syllabus with the junior "branch", learning to teach the new C.S.E. course, managing without junior forms on site and, of course, that unexplored and worrying territory known as "girls". The coincident raising of the leaving age to 16 was another complicating factor, he pointed out. "It is a thousand pities that education in Bexley is a fiercely political issue in an unstable political situation." The further diminution of the School's catchment area that Cllr. Handy's scheme envisaged gave the Headmaster additional cause for concern. "I do not see that [the proposed new school] will have much, if anything, in common with the existing C.S.G.S."

A strongly-worded letter, drafted by Tom Palmer, was sent from the Staff to Margaret Thatcher at the D.E.S. on November 3rd objecting, in vehement terms, to Bexley's proposal to "change the character" of the School and asking her to receive a deputation that could argue their case at greater length. Although most Bexley teachers favoured the abolition of selection at 11+ they were equally against the introduction of 11–14 schools, fearing that staff there would quickly become the "poor relations" of their colleagues in the senior high schools. There were meetings between the Staff and the Governors to discuss "the virtual disappearance of this school as we now know it" contingent upon the arrival of 150 or so "unselected" boys in a year or two if the plan were to go ahead. Palmer,

Pennycuick, Freeman and Burnip were prominent among those who, in their own words, took "the unusual step of placing their views, personally and collectively, before the Governing body." The pupils, too, added their voice, sending a protest letter to Mrs Thatcher in a further attempt to sabotage Bexley's project. Perhaps appropriately it was dated November 5th.

A fortnight later the Heads of Department requested a meeting with Chief Education Officer Sam Semple to discuss "the problems posed by the re-organisation as to the future of this School." The Head was reluctant to endorse their move, pointing out that the Staff's views were already well known in Crayford. They had, he reminded them, refused to have Dr Semple present at their meeting with the Governors even though he had expressed his willingness to attend. In a note to his HoDs Brown wrote: "I regret that we have reached some sort of impasse for the moment." As far as he was concerned the decision was now "entirely a matter for the Secretary of State."

The Headmaster began to arrange meetings between his Chis and Sid colleagues and their "equivalents" at Hurstmere across the grass. If their respective curricula were to be linked in a year or two then detailed planning would need to start right away. "However tactfully it is framed, we are now in effect under orders to carry out the first exercise in consultation and there is great pressure on us to get started. It is, apparently, the clear wish of the elected Education Authority that we should." This memo from Brown to his Staff, dated November 19th 1971, gently reminded his colleagues that a democratic process did, after all, underpin the proposed changes, however unpopular they might be to all those anxious (understandably) to preserve the even tenor of their ways undisturbed by an influx of what they may have deemed "rough" boys from elsewhere. There were plenty of teachers in other local schools who were far better placed to deal with *them*. They had a point, no doubt. What would happen to Chis and Sid's "enviable national reputation as an exceptionally successful school" and to its "distinguished contribution to the community" if the floodgates were opened to the *hoi polloi*? The sixty or so "bright boys", if they materialised, might well be "swamped" by the 180 or so "non-selective" pupils and a viable Sixth Form was unlikely to emerge from the morass.

Meetings duly took place, nevertheless, between pairs of departmental heads at the two neighbouring schools, the first being held, tactfully, on neutral territory at Crayford Town Hall in late November. On another occasion the Hurstmere heads of department came over the field to lunch with their opposite numbers at the purple end of Lamorbey Park.

The following Spring Tom Palmer received an important letter from the Ministry. Dated 10th May 1972 and signed by J.Walmsley on behalf of Mrs Thatcher, it announced that "after careful consideration of all the circumstances, including the objections submitted by your colleagues and yourself, the Secretary of State for Education and Science has decided not to approve these particular proposals under Section 13 (4) of the Education Act, 1944, (as amended)." A week later Michael Brown called his Staff together for a lunchtime meeting and it was agreed that "a non-party-political decision" was needed as to the future role of the School. The principle that the School should be available to children from all parts of the Borough met with no objection and most of those present were happy to support Crayford's proposal for the School to become co-educational provided, of course, that the necessary new buildings were forthcoming.

A letter of 24th May 1972 from Dr Semple to Mr Brown said that provision of places for girls and the enlargement of the premises were to proceed as planned. At the end of the month came a letter signed personally by the Prime Minister, Edward Heath, welcoming Mrs Thatcher's decision to veto the Bexley plan and observing that it would indeed have been "a tragedy to remove from more gifted children all opportunity of the higher grade education of which they [were] capable." There were those, of course, who disputed whether that had, in fact, been the intention but there, for the time being at least, matters were allowed to rest.

These contentious issues formed a constant backdrop to Brown's time upon the Sidcup stage but against it, to extend the metaphor, moved other players, emerging from the wings to criss-cross one another, foregrounded momentarily in pools of light before making, variously, their exits as others drifted on to take their place. That September witnessed five such entrances. Those concerned would all, in their different ways, play important roles in the continuing drama of the School. Tony Dunn, a London M.A., sharp, mischievous, ironic, joined the Classics Department, taking charge of it, briefly, three years later before becoming Senior Master at Tudor Grange School, Solihull, in 1975. Michael Hankinson, a Clare College, Cambridge graduate and an Army major, arrived to teach Mathematics. During the course of his nineteen years at the School Mike, the epitome of an English officer and gentleman, endeared himself to pupils and colleagues alike with his courtesy, easy charm and concern for the underdog. An accomplished cricketer himself and a natural leader, Mike made a great impact on the playing fields as well as in the classroom. Keith Jenkins became the third returning pupil when he joined the French Department of his namesake and former teacher, Teddy Jenkins, filling Geoffrey Jewson's vacated shoes. Like his boss and fellow Welshman, Keith was a great rugby enthusiast as well as an expert at dealing with those recalcitrant boys for whom the mastery of a foreign language did not loom uppermost in their scheme of things. Sadly the younger Jenkins encountered increasing health problems. After 23 years'service he took early retirement, dying in 1995 at the early age of 49, having outlived his illustrious mentor – 36 years his senior – by just five years. Last but far from least of this 1970 quartet was Ian Page, a graduate of Trinity College, Oxford, who joined Jack Burnip's History Department which, four years later, he inherited from him. In 1983 he was promoted to be Head of the Arts Sixth. At the time of writing, Ian is second only to Robert Buxton, among the current staff, in length of service to the School.

Speech Day in December 1970 was enlivened, for the boys at least, by a power cut which plunged the Hall into sudden darkness. The Headmaster resourcefully continued his speech by torchlight (courtesy of the Physics Department) before handing over to the guest of honour, Sports Minister Eldon Griffiths, who declared that "the aim for a school must not be to achieve equality but to excel." His words struck a very different note from those of Sir Gordon Sutherland who, the previous year, had spoken about "the dangers of an educational elite."

Among the many achievements of this school year pride of place belongs, perhaps, to Graham Clinton of LVIM, a former Hurstmere pupil, who toured India with the English Schools team. The M.C.C.'s "most promising young cricketer" of 1971, Clinton went on to play for both Kent and Surrey for many years.

In the July of 1971 Chis and Sid lost another of its near-legendary figures with the retirement of John Walsh after 37 years as a teacher of English, the last 25 of them as Head of Department. Walsh earned a national reputation for his writings on the art of teaching but will best be remembered by his many pupils for his eccentricities. One famous party piece was his trick of circumnavigating the classroom without touching the floor, a feat he achieved by judicious use of desks, sills and ledges, aided, where need be, by a lengthy window-pole. The deeds of Jim Spragg the burglar, an open-ended serial which he effortlessly ad-libbed, enlivened spare moments at the ends of lessons for countless of the smaller boys – provided that their behaviour had earned as much. Many now well into middle age, who might balk at differentiating between a preposition and a pronoun, will unhesitatingly regale you with a vivid moment from the saga – a late flowering, it could be said, of an oral tradition that reaches back to a time well before the invention of writing several thousand years B.C. Unhappily John Walsh, like his first headmaster, enjoyed but a few months' retirement before his death in February 1972.

Walsh was succeeded as Head of English by Robert Solbé, a graduate of Lincoln College, Oxford, and a man not afraid to set the cat among the pigeons. His first priority was to re-energise a Department that had had just two leaders in forty years. Though he stayed only eleven terms (as against Walsh's one hundred and eleven) before taking a deputy headship in Bromley, Solbé gave a new lease of life to Drama at the School with spectacular productions of modern plays such as *The Royal Hunt of the Sun*. His most enduring contribution to Drama, however, was his founding of the Junior Play Festival in the Spring of 1972. This rapidly established itself as one of the most keenly anticipated events in the School calendar and gave thousands of children their first experience of performing on a proper stage. Sadly the pressures of an over-inflated National Curriculum and examination system have led to a drastic scaling down of Solbé's brainchild in recent years.

In the Oxford and Cambridge Entrance Examinations of November 1971 six Open Scholarships were won, a School record that still stands. Ten awards in all were gained, equalling the previous highest total achieved in 1965. A further nine places brought that year's "Oxbridge" tally to nineteen, a total that has never been equalled since, although the following year's fell just one short.

The Staff, in the early seventies, was augmented by Michael Ashby (German and Russian), E.J.F. ("Jim") Reddaway (Biology), Will Scott (Woodwork), Andrew Williams (Geography), David Durban (Physics), Stephen Gooden and Dr Arthur Waters (both Chemistry), Philip Weatherly (History) and – still a rare event then – another female teacher, Mrs M.P. ("Pat") Thompson (French). All of the aforementioned were to remain at the School for at least five years and in some cases a great deal longer, Mike Ashby, at the time of writing, having just completed thirty years in Hurst Road. It is perhaps worth explaining at this juncture that, to avoid turning what purports to be a history into little more than a directory of names and dates, the numerous members of the teaching staff whose length of service was comparatively brief have, generally, not been mentioned. As a rule of thumb the presence, at least, of all those who taught for five years or more at the School has been recorded, though exceptions have been made where it seemed appropriate to make them and for a wide variety of reasons. Nor is it possible to mention more than a very few of the non-teaching staff who have served the School so loyally down the years. As for the most important people of all in the School's story, the pupils themselves, a moment's thought will show the impossibility of mentioning, by name, more than a tiny fraction of all those thousands who have passed, and are still passing, through this gateway to their adult lives. Of the tiny number that are mentioned personally, most are included because of something surprising or remarkable that they did or that was done to them. Others will find their names included in these pages for little reason other than random chance.

One name which does merit another mention at this point is that of Roedean-educated Bertha James who retired from the Governing Body in the Spring of 1972 after over 25 years' service, a total exceeded only by the thirty years of Harry Lester (1936–66). At the same time D.M.Fielding handed on the Chairmanship to Dr Audrey Martin who was to prove a controversial figure in the post since her sympathies were closely identified with the fight to abolish selection in the Borough.

There was much good news in the early months of 1972, the half-way mark, as it proved to be, of Michael Brown's eventful nine year headship. An extensive building programme was getting underway with the prospect of co-education now on the horizon.This crucial development came even quicker than had been anticipated, the girls' arrival lying, in fact, a mere eighteen months ahead. At Whitsun the first "Chis and Sid wedding" took place, David Turner marrying Miss P.A.Kemsley the assistant secretary. The first marriage between two members of the teaching staff was to follow two years later when Janet Marshall married Andy Williams. This same year David Slater won an England rugby cap at Under 15 level. M.J.Callow and M.A.Green, both winners of Open Scholarships to Trinity College, Cambridge, took part in the British Mathematical Olympiad, the former joining the staff four years later in 1976.

Some 150 boys flew to New York at Easter. This bold enterprise, the first time a School group had crossed the Atlantic (or, indeed, left Europe) was organised and led by Bob Ims. A British Caledonian plane was chartered for the purpose and the accompanying staff were taken aback when, shortly after take-off from Gatwick, the stewardesses came round with 150 miniature bottles of whisky courtesy of the airline. An impasse developed when the staff insisted that the boys could not receive them and the stewardesses declared that they belonged now to the School and could not be given back.. Feelings underwent a rapid change, however, when, as a way out of the dilemma, the aforesaid bottles were divided up among the teachers instead and, on arrival, each left the plane with a clinking carrier bag. The party spent three weeks on the East Coast, visiting New York, Niagara Falls, Boston, Montreal and Washington, and staying with American families while in Maine and Philadelphia.

During this temporary lull in the fourteen year long "Battle of Lamorbey" more good news continued to pour in. John Sewell became English Schools' Junior 800 m. Champion. Eric Standidge joined the National Youth Theatre and the Film Society amalgamated with its Beaverwood Girls' counterpart, a development greeted with enthusiasm by all concerned as they settled down together in the darkness to watch *On the Waterfront* and *To Kill a Mockingbird*. Caps were, at long last, abolished for all (six years after their abolition in the Sixth Form). The boys had come to feel that this headgear made them objects of ridicule in the streets of Sidcup and its wearing became impossible to enforce beyond a hundred yards or so from the School gate. Rather than fight an endless losing battle Brown decided the time had come to admit defeat and to let the offending item of uniform quietly pass into history – which, with cheerful alacrity, it did.

New links were established with Marlborough Special School by the Social Service Group, established by Wally Moat but led now by Classics master Tony Dunn. The Gift Fund bought for the Marlborough children two much appreciated trampolines. Even the plague of locusts proved less than a disaster. Lindsey Page of IIIA described the scene in Bill Freeman's lesson one Friday morning when the enterprising insects broke out of their container and swiftly scattered to the four corners of the lab. All were, in due course, recaptured but the class had cause to be grateful to their small allies on two counts. Not only did the locust hunt provide great diversion in itself but, such was the pandemonium, the stern Head of Science, perhaps uniquely, forgot to set the homework for that night.

The Junior Play Festival, referred to earlier, took place for the first time at the end of the Spring Term. Six plays were performed before a large and appreciative audience. The first of them, Form 1/20's production of *The Pie and the Cake* by Hugh Chesterman, was eventually deemed the winner by Dora Williams who adjudicated the competition. Whether she ever realised that the title had been changed from the original *The Pie and the Tart* to spare yet more blushes for the unfortunate boy who, under great peer pressure, had reluctantly agreed to take the female lead, which he duly did in his mother's clothes, is beyond the scope of this history to establish.

The year of course, like all years, had its less than happy side. The School was sad to bid farewell to Roland Rahtz who retired after 26 years, for most of which he was in charge of Drama. During his career at Chis and Sid Rahtz directed seventeen Shakespeare plays for public performance and it seems inconceivable that such a feat will ever be equalled at the School. Dutch Elm Disease struck the Glade and many beautiful trees were cut down and burnt. Speech Day in December brought problems with it too. Such was the resentment of the Staff towards the new Chairman, Audrey Martin, and her openly-expressed opposition to selective education, that they refused to join her on the stage and sat in the Gallery instead. This gesture proved to be the opening salvo of renewed hostilities.

With the Heath Government running into ever greater difficulties, particularly in its relations with the unions, the Labour leadership of Bexley Council apparently felt the time was ripe for a final heave to dislodge their remaining "elitist" schools. Chis and Sid, of course, had long been a thorn in the flesh of the local Labour Party and it was now time for the Trojan Horse within the Governing Body to do its job.

The Education Committee, under the chairmanship of Elgar Handy, announced their intention that the words "secondary", "grammar" and "technical high" should be omitted from the titles of all the county schools in the Borough since they were said to cause resentment and a feeling of inferiority among pupils and staffs in the non-selective sector. Accordingly, on May 14th 1973, the Governors, with their half dozen or so political appointees, led by the Chairman herself, Dr Martin, met to discuss the matter. Before long voices were raised. "We're being foolish – we're going to have a confrontation and trouble. We have to accept that the word "Grammar" is going," she said, according to verbatim notes, and threw her casting vote behind this decision when the first show of hands produced a

6:6 tie. Tempers ran high and, according to the *Kentish Times* report published three days later, there were "stormy scenes" with three Governors, including the volatile Nancy Crust, walking out in protest.

The Education Committee had suggested "Parklands" as an appropriate new name but, after long debate, it was decided to keep "Chislehurst and Sidcup" even, if need be, without its concomitant "Grammar School" appendage. Not only was the name nationally familiar, it was argued, but there were still some sixty or so Bromley boys on roll to give it a veneer of legitimacy in a purely geographic sense. Perhaps surprisingly in the circumstances, the meeting finished with an agreement to defer a final decision on the name until the next Governors' meeting on November 12th.

The *Kentish Times* for May 31st carried a banner headline: "OUTCRY OVER SCHOOL NAME PLANS". Three hundred parents attended a P.A. meeting at which Nancy Crust described the proposed name change as "a back-door way of lowering the standards of the School." A vote of no confidence in the Governors and the Chairman was carried and £500 earmarked as an initial fighting fund to resist the change.

Among Michael Brown's archived papers is a handwritten note, dated October 17th, which records his regret that "this matter has become so complicated and emotional ...because of political motivation and non-rational thinking on all sides." What particularly dismayed him, on a personal level, was "the uneasy sensation of pulling a different way from the staff." In view of the near unanimous wishes of his colleagues he argued that the proposed alteration be postponed until a change in the nature of the School was under consideration. However he refused, no doubt wisely, to "join any campaign the parents might mount", since it seemed to him "that a slanging match could be on." In a letter to the Governors dated November 7th 1973 Brown repeated these views, adding that it would be "highly undesirable" if new recruits, on arrival, learnt that "there was a sharp difference of opinion between the Headmaster and the Staff and that they must choose which side to join."

On November 19th the Common Room passed a resolution which deeply deplored the Governors' decision to remove the word "Grammar" from the School's name despite "the emphatically expressed views of the Staff and the great majority of the parents." Councillor Handy, however, in a letter sent the following week, saw "no justification in asking the Education Committee to recommend that the Council rescinds its policy on this matter." At a meeting of the said Committee at Erith Town Hall on

November 27th the members voted for the new name – Chislehurst and Sidcup School – despite a petition from Staff and parents which had been delivered the previous day by a deputation led by Raymond Pope and Nancy Crust, the latter decked out in purple blazer and scarf. The petition's argument that keeping the existing name would "preserve a famous school for future generations of children" and thus "maintain a proud tradition" had cut no ice. "Grammar" is only one word", declared Cllr.Brierly, ignoring the muttered "So is prat!" from behind him somewhere, and insisting that the change was not a political matter. Alderman Potter, however, believed that it was and reminded him that the majority party had a mandate to abolish the "Eleven Plus". When a resolution to defer the decision until the next meeting of the Committee was carried by 20 votes to 16, Ronald Brierly declared, with some heat, that any further delay would "make a mockery of local government" and insisted that the issue go to full Council, invoking a standing order to that effect. This "rabbit-from-a-hat" solution was instantly deemed ungentlemanly conduct by his opponents and uproar predictably ensued. "TEMPERS FLY IN THE BATTLE OF THE WORD," screamed the *Kentish Times* headline later in the week.. It was left to Audrey Martin to point out that, since the name change would not be effective until September 1974, the Bexley voters could always reject it in the local election to be held in the May of that year.

With the darkening days came the "three day week" as the Tory Government fought Joe Gormley's miners. On February 28th 1974 a General Election was held to answer Edward Heath's question: "Who governs Britain?" Although the reply came back somewhat indistinctly the phrase "not you!" could clearly be discerned and Harold Wilson found himself back in Downing Street again, this time at the head of a minority administration. Any joy in Bexley Labour Party circles proved shortlived, however, since Audrey Martin's earlier invitation to the electorate was accepted and the Conservatives regained control of the Council some ten weeks later. By a nice irony the political situation was thus elegantly reversed. The pressure to abolish selection now lay back in Curzon Street while the resistance movement raised their old bluish-purple flag again to flutter over Crayford. In the light of all these events it is perhaps just as well Michael Brown's joke that the School should be rechristened "The Richard Pedley Comprehensive" remained for many years a private one.

The cost limit of £355,644 set by the D.E.S. for the building work to enlarge the School's capacity from four to six form entry proved to be far

Tom Palmer and Teddy Jenkins at their
retirement celebration, 1973.

too low. It was, in fact, £26,056 lower than the lowest tender submitted for
the job. In consequence drastic economies were necessary, a not unfamiliar story in Hurst Road. "Fair-face" bricks replaced the usual brick and
plaster combination and "wood-wool," not timber, lined the roof of the
Music Block. In the event, again unsurprisingly, the new buildings were
delayed due to "difficulties in the industry."

The year of 1973 was marked by a number of hugely significant
changes on the Staff and by an event which was radically to alter the
nature of the School. This latter point, the arrival of the girls in September,
merits a chapter to itself, however, and our attention turns instead to the
retirement of two men who, between them, gave 81 years of service to
the School.

Tom Palmer, last of the original Station Road five, retired in July after
42 years of full-time teaching and "unswerving devotion to the School", as
the Headmaster put it in his *Chronicle* tribute. No other member of staff
has served the School so long and it is highly improbable that his record
will ever be surpassed. Palmer succeeded Arthur Parsons as Deputy Head
in 1958 and fulfilled this role for fifteen years, running the School for several months during Pedley's spell in Cambridge in 1965. Supported by his

wife, briefly on the Staff herself during the War, he was a tower of strength both in the School and in the local community where he was deeply involved with orchestral music and light opera. Tom Palmer died in 1986. At the time of writing, his widow, Enid, now in her mid-nineties, is still fit and active, living in a pleasant flat close to Wells Cathedral in Somerset.

Teddy Jenkins, or "Jenks" as he was known to his colleagues, retired after 39 years at the School, most of them as Head of French, during which time he led 25 Easter trips to Paris. In 1958 he was made Head of Junior School and, at the end of his career, he became Second Deputy Head, a post created specifically for him. Many former pupils will still remember his rich Welsh voice, his off-the-shoulder gown and the solemn ear-inspections he conducted in his form-room, the boys lined up with their heads tilted to one side. Not content with a mere forty-three years in the classroom, Jenkins taught for several more at Combe Bank School near Sevenoaks and then took a degree in German at the University of Kent, which he completed at the age of 78. He died four years later in 1990.

Into the large gap left by the retirement of this illustrious pair stepped Douglas Hahn and Margaret Harris as the new Deputy Heads. The former was educated at Dulwich College and went on to read Geography at St Edmund Hall, Oxford, where he won his Blue as a sprinter. Hahn taught at two South London comprehensive schools, Thomas Calton and Kingsdale, before spending two years in Uganda. He was Head of Geography at Trinity College, Kampala from 1966 to '68. After five more years back at Kingsdale School, Sydenham Hill, he took up, in September 1973, his first post in the selective sector, despite his firm belief in the merits of the comprehensive system he had left. At last Brown had a substantial ally at his side. Margaret Harris, ten years older than Douglas, was educated at Kettering High School during the difficult years of 1940 to '47. She took a B.A.General degree at Goldsmiths' College in 1951 and began her teaching career at Dartford Girls' Grammar School where she taught from 1951 to '56. studying, while doing so, at Birkbeck College from which she received her B.A. Honours degree in History in 1957. Over the next twelve years Margaret gained extensive experience in schools of different types – secondary modern, comprehensive and grammar, both mixed and single sex. The four schools concerned were: Wellingborough Secondary, Wellington Girls'College, Greenford Grammar and Coborn School for Girls in Bow. Miss Harris then left the state sector, becoming Head of History at Blackheath High School where she taught for four further years before being appointed, in May 1973, to her post at Chis and Sid. She was, of course, the School's first Deputy Headmistress and given the demanding task of integrating sixty eleven year-old girls (and their successors) into what was an overwhelmingly masculine environment, as the next chapter will seek to illustrate.

Other appointments to the Staff in the Autumn of 1973 included Malcolm Rees (T.D.), Mike Sale (P.E.) and Joyce Crust, who arrived to develop the new Girls' P.E. Department. She had trained at Anstey College and had been Head of Department at both Orpington Girls' and Bexley Grammar School so her experience proved invaluable. The distaff side was further augmented by two new members of the English Department, Linda Martin and Diane Southgate, who arrived together. That same September Alastair Wilson became Senior Master, thereby completing, for the first time, a "senior management" quartet in recognition of the School's rapidly increasing roll. Wyn Lewis took over from him the command of the A.T.C. Squadron, 1227.

A difficult year ended on a high note with the selection of Jonathan Hartley and Tony Crust (son of Nancy) for the England Under 19 rugby

Douglas Hahn, Deputy Head
1973–1987.

Margaret Harris, Deputy Head
1973–1989.

Jonathan Hartley and Anthony Crust,
England Under 19 Rugby team, 1973.

team to play against Australia at Twickenham. Famous philosopher Stuart Hampshire was guest of honour at Speech Day in December.

February 1974 saw the School "invaded" by David Dimbleby and a huge television crew, the Hall having been chosen for the General Election count and declaration in the Prime Minister's constituency. Mr Heath would doubtless have been happy, as things turned out, to exchange his Party's fortunes for those of Robert Backhouse, Conservative candidate in the School's own mock election and winner by a huge majority.

The Literary Society that term pulled off its greatest coup when Kenneth Williams addressed them. Despite its being on "The Quest for Truth" rather than his career in the "Carry On" films his lecture attracted a sudden influx of keen new members, the meeting being closed to "outsiders." It should also be recorded that, in 1974, the 1st XI cricket team, captained by David Fowler, won 14 of their 24 matches and drew a further 5, a record that remains unsurpassed. Paul Williams became Great Britain Junior Men's 1500 m. Champion with a time of 3 mins. 59.8 secs. and went on to represent his country against both France and Spain. He still holds three of the School records he set during the early seventies.

Among the Summer's departures the most notable was that of Jack Burnip who retired after a quarter of a century at the School. To the remarks made about him already, in Chapter Six, one might add that he was, beyond doubt, the only member of staff who, in retirement, combined the taking of a degree in Bulgarian with a new career as renovator (and re-seller) of dilapidated property. Stanley Simmonds, who probably had a better grasp of the Italian Renaissance than any of his colleagues, once dubbed Burnip "Machiavellian", using the term as a compliment, he made clear. Brilliant, powerful, alarming – even a witch, or so he insisted more than once – "Pinrub", as the boys called him, ranks as one of the strangest people to have taught at Chis and Sid, a title to which quite a few others have laid a claim.

The arrival, in September 1974, of three more female teachers brought the number of women on the Staff into double figures. Anne Fuller and Jenny Mills came as modern linguists and Edna Jamieson, a Northern Ireland hockey international, joined what would soon become, if only briefly, an all-female English Department – an odd situation to arise so soon in a School that was still heavily male-biased. Lawrence Hickey (Classics) and Clive Wederell (History) joined the Staff at the same time, the latter going on to become Head of First Year (later known as Year Seven). At the time of writing, Clive, another talented hockey player, has completed 28 years in Hurst Road.

In October came the second General Election of 1974, producing this time a much reduced Tory majority in the School's mock election and, in what some insisted was the real thing, a Labour majority of just three seats. It was the term in which Chis and Sid "won" the *Kentish Times'* "Top of the Form" general knowledge competition for schools in Bexley and Bromley, though the trophy had to be shared with Beaverwood after four tie-break questions failed to produce an outright winner. The team consisted of the captain, Ian Lynch, Craig Norris, Richard Tolliday and a very young and somewhat nervous Helen Taylor, last heard of as Professor of English Literature at a leading American university. Frank Tomlinson retired at Christmas after a quarter of a century at the School, the last to leave of the English Department triumvirate – the others, of course, being Walsh and Rahtz – that stretched back to the War years and mustered, in total, eighty-eight years of service to Chis and Sid.

At the start of 1975 Philip Geen, who taught French at the School from 1957 to 1961,became Chief Education Officer for Bexley. A few months later Bob Solbé resigned the Headship of the English Department and left, after less than four years, to become Deputy Head of Ravenswood School in Bromley. That same Easter a second tour of the U.S.A. took place, ranging even further afield to the Pacific Coast, including visits to the Yosemite National Park and San Francisco. This time there were a dozen girls in the party. In April Alec Higgins took over from Audrey Martin as Chairman of the Governors, a position he held with distinction until 1982.

The death of Susan McGregor Williams on June 12th severed a link with the School stretching back 44 years to its foundation in 1931. For over twenty years, after her husband's death in 1954, she had maintained a keen interest in goings on at Lamorbey and possessed an encyclopaedic memory of faces and events, indeed of all things "purple" – the colour for which the School was indebted to her, as was explained in Chapter Two.

This was the Summer in which the New Building was officially opened. "Comparing it with the old building I find it rather impersonal. The desks have hardly any messages or amusing phrase on them," lamented an anonymous voice from Year Three. Within a couple of terms the stairs had twice undergone repair and a door had been broken. "It went up slowly but it seems to be falling down fairly quickly," observed another occupant of the block. Interestingly, the building was designed "the wrong way round", that is to say with its main entrance facing the Glade rather than towards the rest of the School. This, apparently, was so that it could, if need be, at some point in the future form part of a separate, though neighbouring, school which affords an insight into the thought processes of the administrators and politicians at Crayford who were still manoeuvring for position behind the scenes.

In September 1975 Charles Wells (the present writer) arrived as Head of English. He was, like his predecessor but one, John Walsh, a graduate of University College, London and, like the Headmaster, a native of Bury in Lancashire. He moved to Chis and Sid after teaching for twelve years at Parmiter's School in Bethnal Green. To join him as number two in the Department and as Director of Drama came Andrew Stafford who had studied under the celebrated F.R.Leavis at Bangor and gone on to teach at Kingston Grammar School. Other arrivals at the start of this academic year included Stuart Cunningham, from the University of Dundee, to teach Mathematics, Cynthia Curry (later Smith), an American, to join the Art

Department and, by strange coincidence, another Linda Martin (Domestic Science) to join her namesake mentioned above.

During rebuilding work on the main corridor the Staff decamped, for the Autumn Term, up to the Conference Room overlooking the Hall in which, on December 9th, Edward Heath was the guest of honour at Speech Day. He was still, of course, the local M.P. though no longer Prime Minister or even Leader of the Opposition – a role that had fallen to Margaret Thatcher, soon to be the first (and so far the only) one of the twenty-two secretaries of state for education since the Second World War to go on to become Prime Minister. Proceedings started at the untimely hour of 6.30 p.m. since Mr Heath had to be in the House later that evening. He urged his audience to do two things: to continue the struggle to preserve the grammar schools and to purchase a copy of his new book on sailing. In his final Prize-giving speech Michael Brown commented on the previous year's disappointing "Oxbridge" performance in which just two candidates were successful – the lowest total for 22 years – but pointed out that the group concerned were from the first "non-accelerated" year since 1957. "O" Level results, on the other hand, were, he said, quite outstanding with a pass-rate of over 76%.

Three other events deserving of mention occurred in the last few days of term. Andrew Stafford's first School production – *Hadrian VII* by Peter Luke – was performed to great acclaim. Ian Lynch took the title role and Sharon Woodall of 3B1 became the first "home-grown" girl to take a major part in a main School production. Another member of the cast was Nick Starr, who went on to gain an Oxford first in English and subsequently became Executive Director of the Almeida Theatre. News came that Alison Barrett had won a place to read Natural Sciences at Sidney Sussex College, Cambridge, becoming the first girl from the School to succeed at this high level. David Pennycuick, after ten years as Head of Mathematics, departed to teach in Papua New Guinea where he was one of the first Europeans to live in the remote village of Kerowagi, at an altitude of 6,000 feet. Inter-tribal fights, with bows and arrows, were still common in the area but, having been involved for a decade with inter-tribal warfare in Bexley, he found himself able to take them in his stride.

Michael Baker was promoted take charge of Mathematics, a post in which he continued until 1987 when he left teaching to run a sub-post office in Burton-upon-Trent – another "first", seemingly, in the annals of the School. At Easter the following year, 1976, David Chandler, a graduate of Trinity College, Cambridge and joint author of the new Cambridge Latin Course, arrived from Queen Anne's School in Reading, to be Head of Classics.

The last links with the nineteen-thirties were finally broken in July when the two renowned Chis and Sid scientists, Bill Freeman and Cedric Morley, retired after a combined total of 79 years at the School, the Biologist having arrived at 27, Station Road in 1936, a year ahead of his colleague and great friend the Physicist. Much has been written about them already, in Chapter Four and elsewhere, but space should be found here for some additional thoughts about their massive contribution to the success of Chis and Sid.

Martyn Berry has calculated that, during the nineteen-sixties and seventies, when the School's academic reputation reached national proportions, Chis and Sid provided something like one five-hundredth of the scientists entering British universities. Given that there were around five thousand schools with sixth forms at that time it can be demonstrated that its contribution in this area was, crudely put, about ten times greater than that of its averagely-performing counterparts elsewhere. Under the joint tutelage of Morley and Freeman some two hundred students gained admission to Oxford or Cambridge, about half of them winning awards in the process. Many others went on to such high-powered institutions as Imperial College, U.C.L., Bristol, Manchester, Durham and the London medical schools, though here the precise figures are not so readily available. At the gathering held on July 16th to bid the pair farewell, distinguished surgeons and consultants rubbed shoulders with eminent engineers and with professors from leading academic establishments both in this country and abroad.

Around Cedric Morley, in particular, has accumulated a greater stock of anecdotes than around any other member of staff with the exception of Dr McGregor Williams. Shortage of space precludes mention of all but a handful, unfortunately. It is said, for example, that when a friend called on him unexpectedly one evening, Morley ushered him into the living room, remarking as he did so: "You could have had a cup of tea only the wife's gone to bed." Those who knew Cedric may remember his habit, in the Common Room, of prefacing any remark with an attention-grabbing "Here!" (or, more accurately, " 'ere!") followed by the surname – Morley did not believe in forenames – of the colleague he was addressing. He had an unnerving habit of breaking off without warning in the middle of a

Cedric Morley, 1937–1976.

Bill Freeman, 1936–1976.

sentence. Just when one felt it safe to attempt a reply – though many of his utterances left one floundering in their wake – he would suddenly resume from where he had left off, usually with an "And another thing…." The young physicist David Durban, on his first day at the School, plucked up the courage to ask his Head of Department for some guidance as to what he was expected to teach, some notes perhaps, or even a syllabus. Cedric, by way of an answer, put an arm around his shoulder, opened a laboratory door and steered him gently in. "This is Durban," he announced to the class in his inimitable manner. "Don't muck him about!" With that he left, closing the door behind him as he went. He once famously complained of a particular Fifth Form group that they would not have bothered to pay attention even if a strip-tease artiste had been performing at the front of the classroom, adding, after his characteristic pause, "Well, most of them, anyway." Although what he said was often quite amusing in itself, the way he said it somehow made it ten times more so.

Michael Brown, in his *Chronicle* tribute to Freeman and Morley, wrote: "For nearly forty years they have struck intellectual and humorous sparks off each other in a remarkable partnership of scientific scholarship."

Bill Freeman, on his retirement, threw himself with great zeal into the recruitment of new members for the Old Sedcopians of which he was the honorary secretary. In this activity he enjoyed considerable success but, sadly, he soon fell ill. He died in July 1980, leaving his wife, Beryl, to pick up and carry on the task he had set himself.

Cedric Morley taught on a part-time basis for a while before moving, with his wife, Hilda, to Great Shelford, near Cambridge, where his son, Colin, was a paediatric consultant and lecturer. He died in the Spring of 1990, outliving his friend by almost a decade.

Michael Brown announced his own impending departure almost casually to his Staff at the end of a routine Monday breaktime meeting in the Common Room. There was a stunned silence. For all the not infrequent disagreements, almost everyone was sad to see him go. At their meeting on May 18th 1976 the Governors said that they deeply regretted his resignation. In his *Chronicle* tribute Alastair Wilson spoke of the Headmaster's "diplomacy and endless patience", describing him as "a kindly man who never entertained delusions of vainglory, a man of sympathy for the underdog whose breezy manner concealed a genuine concern for all his pupils." Brown himself later described his headship as "an endless round of seeing politicians and producing paperwork." The School, he said, had provided him with " a rich and complicated pattern of experiences." The last of these was his leaving party on the evening of July 20th when Governors, Staff, Old Boys and Bexley functionaries arrived at the School to find the corridors and the Dining Hall awash with several inches of water as the result of a violent summer storm. Clearly this must have been intended as a sign. Like a more famous flood it may have been sent to punish wickedness – perhaps that of those whose motives, during the struggles of the previous nine years, had been less than entirely altruistic. Brown, like Noah, sailed serenely off, grounding in Framlingham, Suffolk, however, rather than on Mount Ararat. Here the dove with the olive leaf duly appeared in the form of a comprehensive scheme that, at last, made sense and had general support.

After running Framlingham Modern School for two years Brown created the new Thomas Mills High School. Finally he was in charge of the comprehensive that he so long had sought. He left in 1985, accompanied by his wife, Rosemary, on a teacher exchange to Connecticut and found himself teaching "Supply" full-time in the same school. They then taught in a Presbyterian High School in Cameroon for two years. He retired for good in 1991, since when he has lived contentedly, with Rosemary, in the quiet village of Cretingham, occupying himself with foreign travel and the three "g"s of gardening, golf and grandchildren, of whom they now have twelve.

CHAPTER NINE

The Arrival of the Girls

THE BOUNDARY CHANGES BROUGHT about by the Greater London Act of 1963 left a total imbalance between boys and girls in the provision of secondary education for the academically gifted in the new London Borough of Bexley, which came into existence two years later. Bromley, of which Chislehurst, of course, had now become a part, found itself in possession of five girls' grammar schools whereas Bexley had only a half of one such school – the co-educational Bexley Grammar, founded in 1955. Scores of "bright" Bexley girls were, in consequence, allowed to cross the boundary – essentially the line of the A20 – into Bromley for their schooling.

Though welcoming these able students, Bromley soon came to realise that the additional financial burden they brought with them was already considerable and would steadily increase, particularly as there was no commensurate flow of boys in the opposite direction. Their Education Committee therefore announced a "cut-off" date of 1973 beyond which these grammar places would cease to be available to Bexley girls. Crayford was forced to address the problem and it soon became clear that sending some of these "academic" girls to Chis and Sid was a viable option. The Lamorbey site had plenty of room for expansion and this strategy, of course, would be much cheaper than building an entire new school from scratch.

The idea held some appeal for Tom Palmer and his colleagues since an influx of intelligent girls would, it was felt, stem the lowering of standards that they feared – and that was already taking place according to some. If the "worst" happened (as they saw it) and the School was forced to become comprehensive then the acceptance of girls would at least help to ensure that "the quality of the intake fell less far." For once the Chis and Sid Staff and the L.E.A. were of one mind, and the idea also appealed to parents locally, who were keen to avoid lengthy journeys for daughters approaching the end of their time at primary school. The various re-organisation schemes proposed (and abandoned) in the late sixties and early seventies all, therefore, envisaged co-education at Chis and Sid under one guise or another.

The final decision was not announced until 1972 when a letter from Dr Semple to Michael Brown, dated May 24th, instructed him to proceed with the enlargement of the School from four to six forms of entry, the extra forms to provide sixty places for girls. The School had less than sixteen months in which to organise such a major step and it is hardly surprising that everything was very rushed. Margaret Harris, the new Deputy Headmistress, on whom a great deal of the responsibility of planning for the girls' arrival would necessarily fall, was not appointed until the following May, little more than three months before the deadline in early September. The situation was made even worse by the economic crisis which followed hard on the heels of Britain's joining the Common Market. The building trade was badly affected and it seemed difficult to believe that the necessary extensions would be completed in time.

By the following August, panic was setting in, with no facilities for the girls yet in place. The mobile classrooms promised had not arrived. The new gymnasium had not even been started, nor were there any changing rooms completed. Men worked through the night on lavatories and washbasins in a desperate attempt to get at least these basics in place for the start of term.

On the morning of Tuesday September 4th 1973 – a momentous date in the history of the School – clusters of small girls were to be seen making their way, with some trepidation, along Hurst Road. Forty-two years after the foundation of Sidcup County School for Boys, the doors had finally opened to admit the fairer sex. Again, as in 1931, sixty apprehensive pioneers stood on the threshold of a new era, ready to blaze a trail for the thousands who would follow on behind. It was the feast day of St Marinus, a fourth century stonemason who fled to a hermit's cell to escape the unwelcome attentions of a woman. There were more than a few amongst both Staff and boys who might have wished that they could do the same. In the absence of much in the way of convenient hermits' cells in the Lamorbey area they would, given half a chance, have borrowed the Saint's masonry tools and built a high wall to keep the marauders out. "The female invasion is outrageous! I've got two sisters at home as it is!" lamented one young misogynist in the *Chronicle*.

The opposite sex, of course, were not total strangers to that fortress of masculinity, Chis and Sid. A few had already scaled the ramparts, some on brief visits, like the "guest actresses" mentioned earlier. Kathryn Price, from Newstead Woods, for instance, had made an impressive Isabella in Eric Standidge's modern dress *Measure for Measure* at the end of the Summer Term just a few weeks back. There had even been School Dances in McGregor Williams' day, when girls from the sister school (Beaverwood, as it later became) had fluttered into the Glasshouse in their party frocks, though their spotty hosts had all too often cowered against the wall, admiring the slinky creatures from afar until dragged forth, red faced, to trample on their toes. There had also been a more permanent female presence, notably the various assistant secretaries, kitchen staff, caretakers' daughters and the like – such as Ann Baynham, Joan Partridge and a Pauline whose surname is unrecorded – who, in the quaint forties phrase of Roger Dracup, were "much ogled after" by hordes of adolescent boys in the immediate post-War years. There had even, in those days, been a few young women on the teaching staff. "Diamond Lil" Cunningham aroused a new interest in Biology and the Titian-haired Ann Nex, it will be recalled, had a huge coterie of male admirers, as did Barbara Osbiston who taught English for a few months in 1968 before suddenly vanishing with one of her Sixth Form students, whom she eventually married – or so it is said.

When the girls ventured inside on that warm September morning, however, there were just seven full-time women teachers to greet them on a staff of more than six times that number. Even ten years later, in 1983, women teachers made up barely a quarter of the total full-time staff, and of that small number very few were in positions of seniority. Just three of the smaller departments (Art, Music and Girls' P.E.) were run by women. Eleven year-old girls, who had been used, in many cases, to female teachers throughout infant and junior school, now found that virtually all their lessons were taught by men, many of them still clad in their traditional – and somewhat alarming – black, academic gowns.

Were they overawed? Far from it. The pioneering sixty were a breed apart. They had all been specially recommended by their primary heads

First Year Netball Team, 1973–74. (Back, L to R: Mrs J.Crust, Sue Crook, Jane Abbott, Susan Ives, Diane Harwood, Suzanne Maxfield. Front: Janice Holt, Carole Bewsey, Deborah Purkiss).

who were well briefed as to the situation the chosen few would be entering. These were girls with the highest V.R. scores in the Borough. They were also, in Michael Brown's words, "those with appetite and stamina, girls who were both clever and tough." Nor should one forget the example set by the older girls who entered the Sixth Form on the same day. Though a mere four in number – Alison Barrett, Mary Ryan and the Shaw sisters, Ruth and Susan – they acted, to a degree, as mother figures and gave great assistance to Margaret Harris and the thin pink line, as one might call it, of her half-dozen female colleagues who endeavoured to shield their new charges from the more uncouth males as they roistered on staircases and rampaged along corridors, at least until they had had a chance to find their feet and settle in. In this task, to be fair, they were amply supported by the vast majority of the men, some of whom seemed to regard the girls as items of Dresden china. The boys had been warned in advance to treat the new-comers "carefully, as they were girls." They soon discovered that they "were not as delicate as the teachers made out," to quote from an article written later by one of the celebrated sixty and published in the pages of the *Chronicle*. In fact "they were spoilt rotten," Miss Harris recalled. "It was the boys who tended to need protecting."

Anne White, a veteran of five years' standing by this stage, remembers with amusement the reactions of some of her male colleagues when the great day came. "Overnight a bevy of ladies arrived. Some of the male staff felt very threatened; their world was falling apart." She has a vivid recollection of the staff meeting held at the start of term. A "distinctly pink" Mr Brown announced that the ladies' lavatories would not be arriving for a month or so. There was an awkward silence in the Common Room until Pat Thompson chimed in: "Well girls, we'll just have to keep our legs crossed." At least the laughter came as a relief.

Plumbing – and the drainage that went with it – had been a major headache for the planners. Term began with what Brown, in a nice turn of phrase, referred to as "peripatetic lavatories" and Mike Ashby remembers gazing out of the Dining Hall window during a Junior Assembly conducted by Miss Stephenson to see a "Portaloo" swing down out of the sky, the crane-arm from which it dangled being invisible from inside the room. The girls were thus "lavatorially disadvantaged", as Anne White later put it.

Another problem for those planning to receive the first intake of girls was to agree upon a suitable uniform for them to wear. This was very much Margaret Harris territory and, after consultation with colleagues, she opted for a grey pinafore dress intending that, in the Third Year, the top should be cut off and the garment thus transformed into a skirt, the surplus material being used to make the waistband. Though few, if any, girls actually carried out this transformation two years later, the idea is wonderful testimony to Miss Harris' notions of domestic economy, formed amid the wartime austerity of her schooldays in Kettering. Blouses were lilac, in cotton or nylon, and a grey cardigan was prescribed. A mauve roll-neck sweater was an option for Winter wear.

Not until well into the 1980s was the famous purple blazer worn by girls, a fact which, in retrospect, could be said to have hindered, unnecessarily, early attempts to integrate the sexes and make them feel equally a part of one great whole. In Summer the girls wore cotton dresses made to a McCall's pattern in grey, white and purple check. Some of the boys objected that they, too, should have been allowed to change into cool Summer uniform but, when it was suggested that they wear the same gingham frocks as their classmates their complaints quickly died away. In an odd reversal of this situation an attempt was made, many years later, to put the girls into white shirts and school ties. A few welcomed the idea and paraded proudly in their new attire but there was such a storm of protest from the majority, staff and parents included – many of whom argued that there had been no consultation process beforehand – that the idea was soon abandoned.

Eric Thomas Ltd., the School's outfitters in Station Road, had little time in which to meet the new demands placed upon them. Pauline Matkins, one of the original sixty girls and the first of them to later join the Staff, recalls that they soon ran out of the full uniform but had a plentiful supply of grey, regulation knickers, though few girls in fact wore them, according to her. One such garment, nevertheless, mysteriously found its way onto the School shield high above the stage, from a corner of which it dangled for a remarkable lengthy period of time.

Sport was another area that called for important decisions to be made. Since their changing room was not ready, a temporary screen was provided to preserve the girls' modesty while they were getting ready for P.E. Miss Harris, years later, would still smile at the memory of a horrified Milton Williams hammering on her door. He insisted she come immediately. Her first thought was that there had been a dreadful accident but it was far worse than that. The girls were throwing off their clothes in amongst the boys because it was what they had always done at junior school. It was thereafter decreed that they change in the Weight Training Room. Sharing a gym was also a problem, the girls' own facility not being completed until 1976.

In her article entitled *Twenty Years of Girls' P. E.*, published in the anniversary issue of the *Chronicle*, 1993, Joyce Crust recalls a line of girls in grey shorts and white "Aertex" blouses walking to Waring Park for a games lesson, accompanied by Margaret Harris and Michael Brown, the latter staggering under the weight of the hockey sticks. Girls who had earned six "A"s for deportment were allowed to wear a purple stripe down the side of their shorts. Deportment grades were introduced by Mrs Crust in an effort to improve the girls' posture and prevent them slouching and slumping their way around the School. Every term, marks were totted up and ranking lists published outside the Gym. Awards were occasionally made during Assembly when, embarrassingly, it was incumbent upon the recipients to walk across stage in an exaggeratedly elegant manner to the accompaniment of rapturous applause from the largely male audience.

Under 15 six-a-side Cricket Squad, 1977. (Back, L to R: Penny Cottee,
Sue Crook, Carol Edison, Diane Harwood, Debbie Purkiss, Brian Burgess.
Front: JoAnna Wilson, Janice Holt, Judith Beresford).

Embarrassment was a fact of life the girls had to cope with as, now
entering their forties, they readily tell a researcher seeking information on
those early days. Practising netball or tennis on the playground at
lunchtime in the overwhelmingly male public gaze was one such situation
that many recall. "Watching this new phenomenon was the boys'
lunchtime entertainment." The girls' skimpy grey shorts were later
replaced by more comfortable ones, "like knickers" as Joyce Crust later
described them. These too, however, proved highly unpopular with many
of the wearers and the purple wrap-over games skirt did not necessarily
help, particularly when vigorous movement, or a gust of wind, lifted it to
the all too obvious delectation of prurient boys who, inevitably, happened
by at that particular moment or, worse still, leered and gesticulated
through a nearby classroom window. Many years later this problem was
solved by the adoption of conventional "unisex-style" purple shorts that
even the most fevered male could hardly find erotic.

The girls were, of course, joining a school with a great sporting tradition and it was not long before they opened a new chapter and began

forging notable achievements of their own. The netball team, for example, captained by Diane Harwood, won all five of their matches in their first season, scoring 57 goals to their opponents' 13. A sporting landmark in the annals of the School was their first match, appropriately against Beaverwood, since the fortunes of the two schools had been intertwined for so long. This was the first time a representative Chis and Sid girls' team had taken the field – or, more accurately the court in this particular case – and it was recorded for posterity by a *Kentish Times* photographer. As the girls moved up the School it became difficult to find sufficient opposition locally and so, in 1977, it was decided to join the Whiteoak adult league based in Swanley.In the Summer of 1974 Brian Burgess launched a girls' cricket team which, under the captaincy of Janice Holt, showed great enthusiasm and commitment, though lack of experience contributed to their defeat in the only inter-school match they played that season, against an older Ravensbourne XI. The single wicket competition, at the end of term, was won by Deborah Purkiss. The team later went on to achieve considerable success, for example by winning the Kent Girls' Six-a-Side Senior Championships three times in the early eighties.

Within a couple of years a girls' hockey team was up and running, coached by Janet Williams and captained by Jackie Patrick, winning seven matches out of twelve in season 1975/6. That same Winter Chis and Sid girls won the North West Kent Junior Cross Country Championship.

Before long girls' games were going from strength to strength at the School, under the experienced eye of Joyce Crust, herself a netball international. Swimming, tennis, rounders and athletics were added to the list already mentioned and gymnastics and dance proved very popular. Michelle Cooney gained junior international honours in athletics while Samantha Finch and Nia Davies were selected for the Synchronised Swimming training squad. Among those gaining full international honours in succeeding years were Wendy MacDonald (athletics for Scotland), and Jackie Empson, who went on to play over fifty games for the England hockey team, including the final of the 1998 Commonwealth Games tournament against Australia. Jackie's fifty caps are, not surprisingly, a record for any Chis and Sid athlete, of either sex in any sport, and one that is likely to remain unequalled for very many years.

Despite all this success it always seemed to be the boys' sports results that were read out first in assembly and, as Judith Beresford pointed out in her *Chronicle* reminiscences, "although not allowed to play on the 1st XI's

Jackie Empson (R) in action for England against Australia.

wicket the girls were given the privilege of making tea for them." The "for Boys" had, of course, been dropped from the School's name but there were constant reminders, in the early years, that this was still, essentially, a male bastion. "All over the site were sticky patches of recent paint and hastily made notices of change of gender," Judith recalls. Indeed as late as the 1990s, according to Kate Trodd, books still turned up in the Library bearing the official School stamp with a "for Boys" appended to the end. These were minor details, perhaps, and maybe inevitable given forty-two years of androcracy, but these constant reminders of what the School had been rather than what it had become could nevertheless be a source of irritation to the girls and did not help the process of integration that was underway.

Some of the older (male) staff seemed to "treat the girls softly as though they were long-term guests," wrote one anonymous representative of that first female intake, some years later. What was perceived as "favouritism" did, in fact, cause some resentment among the younger boys. It was, for example, agreed from the start that girls would be addressed by their christian (or fore) names and most of the Staff, even the old stick-in-the-muds, managed to remember to do this, even if it went against the grain. There were limits, however, and those who had spent the best part of a lifetime in all-male classrooms found it impossible to do the same in the case of the boys. For several years, therefore, a dual standard tended to operate, whereby girls were "Gillian" or "Jennifer" but the boys in the row behind were "Johnson" or "Jones".

Punishment was another sore point, so to speak. Caning was still quite common for a dozen or so years to come. On the evidence of the "Punishment Book" lodged in the Bexley Borough Archives, a caning took place, on average, at least once a week. Nor was the unofficial "clip round the ear" at all uncommon. No "School Clip-round-the-ear Book" appears to have survived in any archive, however, so precise numbers give way to subjective recollection. "Are you allowed to slap them?" asked Anne White, who had taught in two rather tough boys' schools and was encountering girls in her classroom for the first time. It was decreed from the outset, however, that girls were exempt from all forms of physical chastisement (perhaps they were Dresden china!) and many – not exclusively the males, either – felt it unfair that, for a similar offence, very different punishments might be meted out, determined solely by the gender of the malefactor concerned. A system known as "fatigues" had to be devised for the girls, as soon, that is, as they became old enough for serious breaches of the rules. Whereas a boy caught smoking, for example, might expect two or three strokes of the cane on his backside (administered, most probably, by the athletic Douglas Hahn) a girl similarly apprehended would be subjected to a special "smokers' punishment programme" devised by Margaret Harris which lasted a week and included running round the field, writing an essay and copying out a gruesome account of lung cancer and its effects. It could be that some girls, on reflection, might actually have preferred to be caned!

These were, after all, young ladies however and Miss Harris was at pains to teach them how to sit at a desk with their knees together, their ankles crossed and their feet tucked neatly beneath their chair, as Pauline Matkins remembers in her "anniversary" article, though she could not resist adding that Miss Stephenson set a fine example of how not to do it every morning as she sat on the platform in Junior Assembly with her knees akimbo.

In the School Hall the increased numbers led to the abandonment of chairs and children stood packed tightly together for Morning Assembly, with a spate of faintings as the predictable result, though it has to be said that, in defiance of tradition, the girls seemed no more prone than the boys to hit the floor. One stereotype that was fulfilled, one might say, was the formation – by Jane Watkins and Catherine Young – of the Needlework Club which met in Room 21 on Wednesday lunchtimes, though its avowed object was primarily to afford its members an all-female space in which to chat rather than, specifically, to sew. Several prior expectations, however, remained unmet. The new typewriters in the so-called "Commerce Room" remained in their boxes, for example. Home Economics (or Domestic Science – it seemed to answer happily to either name) was introduced, initially, for girls only but soon boys too were allowed to participate. The first lesson was on "making a sandwich" since the ovens had yet to be installed. "Boys are really pathetic, honestly. They can't even boil water without burning it!" observed one young lady, tartly, and back into one's mind swims the tale of Morley's unexpected evening guest. Mention of Cedric prompts recollection of one early September morning when his plaintive voice rang out across the Common Room: "'ere, Burgess, what do you do with girls?"

It was perhaps an ally of his, though some fifty years younger, who opined: "We should not have to tolerate the girls. They don't play football at break. All they do is stand in little groups and chatter to each other – and beg food from the boys. They just sit and giggle in class – and yet they still manage to come top in lots of subjects!" This gem, happily preserved in the columns of the *Chronicle*, was certainly true as far as the latter point, at least, was concerned. Hopes that the academic quality of the intake would be boosted by the advent of the girls proved amply justified in the event. To begin with they were evenly distributed ten to a form and, when marks were tabulated during the year and after the Summer examinations, it was their names that almost invariably occupied the first few places in each list.

Alison Barrett, as mentioned earlier, led the way, academically, with an engineering degree from Cambridge at a time when this subject was an almost exclusively male preserve. Soon afterwards, in 1983, while working as a volunteer on a project to bring fresh water to Korem, a town in a remote part of Ethiopia, she was taken hostage by the Tigray People's Liberation Front and made international headlines for several months, an experience she graphically described as guest of honour at Speech Day after her release.

Many of the 1973 girls duly followed in her footsteps through university in the early eighties. Some, such as Susan Ives (the School's first Head Girl) and the Anne Boleyn look-alike, Cheryl Wallis, went into teaching, the latter marrying Paul Johnson who had been two years above her at the School. This was one of the first Chis and Sid pupil marriages though that between Diane Harwood and Roger Crook may well have beaten them to it. Judith Beresford, referred to earlier, after gaining an Oxford degree in English, became an investment analyst and spent some time working in New York. The academic career of her friend Helen Taylor, who read English at Durham, was mentioned in the previous chapter.

Pride of place, in a sense, belongs to the tall and athletic Jane Abbott in that she will always have the cachet of being the first girl ever to be registered as a student at the School. Although her number in the Admissions Register is 5,202, this distinction makes her, it could be said, the female counterpart to Michael Carreck who was, readers may remember, the very first pupil of all back in 1931.

By the nineteen-eighties the contingent of girls on roll had grown so rapidly that, to the consternation of Noel Horrobin and his rugby coaches, they actually outnumbered the boys for several years before the balance tilted back again the other way. Mixed P.E. was introduced at this time in Years One and Five. It was always largely mixed in the Sixth Form.

When the first year of girls came to an end in July 1974 there were very few, if indeed any, at the School, either staff or students, who would not have agreed that their arrival had been a shot in the arm. The School was undeniably enriched and strengthened in a variety of different ways. As we approach the thirtieth anniversary of their advent it becomes increasingly hard to remember – or, in the case of younger Sedcopians, to imagine – how things were before they came. There are those who will be taken aback to discover that, at the time of writing, there are only three members of staff remaining – Messrs Buxton, Page and Ashby – who taught at the Chislehurst and Sidcup Grammar School for Boys.

John Sennett (1977–1994).

CHAPTER TEN

Sennett Centre Stage

THE ADVERTISEMENT TO FIND a successor to Michael Brown was very different from that which had appeared, nine years before, on the resignation of Richard Pedley. With the Conservatives firmly in control in Bexley this time, it contained no suggestion that the School would change its character, despite Labour's 1976 Education Act which required local authorities to prepare proposals for the reorganisation of education in their areas so that children "may be admitted to secondary schools without reference to ability or aptitude." This time the advert spoke of "a progressive grammar school with a fine reputation whose hallmark is academic success." There was no mention of amalgamation and the contentious word "comprehensive" was nowhere to be seen.

September 1976 arrived, however, without an appointment having been made. The post was readvertised and the most promising interviewee from the previous "round", John Sennett, invited to reapply. Douglas Hahn was asked to fill the breach and he duly served as Acting Headmaster, with his customary efficiency, until Easter 1977.

In the meantime several important appointments were made. Peter Wiles took over the Biology Department from Bill Freeman – an awesome act to follow, of course, but, assisted by his pet chameleon, Angus, he settled quickly into his laboratory and the subject flourished much as before. Michael Callow, an old boy of the School, arrived from Trinity College, Cambridge, to add lustre to the Mathematics Department and to make a major contribution on the cricket field. Noel Horrobin replaced Mike Sale in the P.E. Department and, four years later, succeeded Milton Williams as its Head. Maggie Goodman took charge of Religious Education and Patricia Thornton joined the English Department, inheriting the editorship of the *Chronicle* from Diane Southgate. Linda Williams, a Warwick graduate and the fourth of that illustrious surname to serve the School, added further strength to Mathematics. Later she would play a pivotal administrative role as Examinations Officer and as provider of cover for absent colleagues amongst much else. The following January this group was augmented by the arrival of the bearded mountaineer, John Temple, to teach Geography and Ian Windeatt to join the Chemistry Department.

The start of this school year saw other important changes. Martyn Berry became Head of the Science Sixth, Brian Burgess took over Cedric Morley's Physics Department and Robert Buxton was put in charge of the Fifth Year. Among those leaving during this same period mention should be made of Nick Pannell, Arthur Waters and another of the aforesaid Williamses, in this case Andrew, who moved to be Head of Geography at Charterhouse School in Orpington.

The chairmanship of Bexley's Education Committee passed to Councillor Brian Sams, an outspoken defender of the Borough's selective schools and the father of two pupils at Chis and Sid. Supported by his Old Sedcopian deputy, Raymond Pope, who chaired the Schools Sub-Committee, Sams answered Shirley Williams' demands for change by insisting that no action could be contemplated until "the facilities available at every school are, in the opinion of the Education Committee, suitable for the provision of a curriculum adapted to the needs of pupils of all abilities." It was proposed to retain a selection procedure pending the "provision of the full range of facilities at each school." Bexley declared itself flatly opposed to Sixth Form Colleges and to split-site amalgamations. Any significant re-organisation along the lines envisaged in Labour's renewed legislation would therefore have necessitated expensive new buildings and, since Bexley was perennially short of money, it soon became clear that Sams and his colleagues proposed to sit tight and wait for the next Conservative government, a not unreasonable policy, from their point of view, given that Callaghan boasted a majority of just three seats. A letter of February 10th 1977 declares, with heavy significance, that if any changes along comprehensive lines were forced upon Bexley they would be "planned on the principle of ease of reversibility."

A staff resolution passed in response to Sams' development plan (such as it was) strikes a very different tone from those promulgated at the end of Pedley's regime and under that of his successor, Michael Brown. It reminded the politicians that any developments would require a great deal of money to be spent if they were to be acceptable and that any such change should be implemented "gradually", the choice of adverb, of course, being one dear to Brian Sams' heart.

Nothing short of imprisonment in the Tower of London was going to make the Bexley Tories abolish their grammar schools and the situation was therefore far less fraught, as far as the vast majority of those connected with Chis and Sid were concerned, than it had been a few years earlier when Labour had held the reins both in Crayford and in Whitehall. The advent of Margaret Thatcher's government in May 1979 removed any further threat to Chis and Sid's grammar school status and, apart from a brief wobble at the start of David Blunkett's period in office towards the end of the nineties, this situation has stayed unchanged right up to the present day, although Labour's victory in the local election of May 2002 could yet re-open old wounds. For nearly half a century, since Anthony Crosland's famous (or notorious) promise to "close every .... grammar school in the country", Chis and Sid, against all the odds, has retained its selective intake while still remaining firmly inside the state sector. Fewer than 150 other schools, nationwide, can make a similar claim.

After a couple of months or so a further round of interviews took place and John Sennett emerged as the new Headmaster. He had, apparently, succeeded this time in persuading Bexley's Senior Advisor, Dr Black, that he did not wish to turn Chis and Sid into a carbon copy of Manchester Grammar School, regarded in Pedley's day, by some at least, as the main rival or northern counterpart. An unnamed governor on the interview panel, it is said, had raised objections over the candidate's pacifist leanings, worrying about the effect that this might have upon the School's celebrated Air Training Corps. His misgivings, too, must have been allayed when the panel reconvened.

John Sennett was born in Plymouth in 1934. His father who, remarkably, was almost seventy when his son was born, had served in the Royal Navy for forty years. The family moved to Weston-super-Mare in 1937 and Sennett began at the local grammar school in 1945, following his father's death the previous year. Eight years later he went up to Sidney Sussex, Cambridge, emerging with a first class degree in History.

Early thoughts of pursuing his father's naval career had been dashed by poor eyesight. Later, strong Christian conviction led him to refuse National Service in the forces. Instead he joined the Society of Friends (Quaker) Ambulance Unit and went on to work as a porter and ward orderly in Malvern and in Homerton Hospital, Hackney.

In 1958 John Sennett married Alice Haworth, whom he had met through the Methodist Church while they were fellow students in Cambridge. His teaching career began at Latymer Upper, Hammersmith, the following year. In 1963 he joined the prestigious Manchester Grammar School, founded in 1515 and drawing in the ablest boys from as far away as Stoke-on-Trent. In 1970 he was promoted to Head of History and was soon running the Arts Sixth with responsibility for the pastoral work of 17 form-masters. Some idea of what this post entailed may be gleaned from the fact that the Sixth Form at M.G.S. contained over five hundred students and that, in a typical year, some seventy of them – getting on for a third of leavers – went on to study at either Oxford or Cambridge.

The Sennetts' two children, Karen and Paul, were born in 1960 and 1962. Karen was to join her father in Hurst Road, spending two years in the Sixth Form before going to medical school.

Although the new Head was appointed during the Autumn Term, and in time to attend Speech Day on December 8th, he was not free to take up his post until Easter the following year. It therefore fell to Douglas Hahn to continue as Acting Head for a few more months. In this task he was greatly assisted by Head of School Ian Lynch, an outstanding actor and classicist and one of the most notable holders of the post in modern times. It was Hahn's avowed objective to hand over the School to the new incumbent in the best possible order and this he achieved. John Sennett later compared him to one of Oliver Cromwell's officers in the New Model Army – "a plain russet-coated captain that knows what he fights for and loves what he knows."

It did not take the new Head long to sum up his first impressions of the Hurst Road set-up as he found it upon beginning work in April 1977. In a report to the Governing Body dated May 23rd he praises the teaching staff – "strong, well-qualified, resourceful" – but finds fault with the premises, describing them as "tatty, uncared for and in urgent need of redecoration and modernisation." Only the boiler-house escaped his criticism. "I am told it is a masterpiece which people come from great distances to inspect." The office and catering staff he describes as "outstanding", singling out for particular mention the "incomparable" Mrs Butler and the "highly professional" Mrs Buckingham. Bryan Hales, the groundsman, is described as "a devoted and knowledgeable enthusiast." As for the pupils, they seemed to him "well turned out, well disciplined and keen to do well." It was important, he felt, to even up the intake of girls and boys as soon as possible, moving to 90 of each from the ratio of 60:120 that he had inherited.

What of the School's first impressions of *him*? Tall, balding, bespectacled, Sennett possessed a carrying voice and a booming laugh, features commented upon by several former M.G.S. pupils encountered before his arrival in Sidcup. Conscientious, hard-working and genial, he nevertheless took time to settle into his new role, which is unsurprising given that he is the only one of the School's five headmasters with no prior experience of such a post. For all his initial awkwardness, however, no one doubted that he was a fully committed grammar school man, unlike his predecessor, and that in itself was sufficient for many of his more senior colleagues who now felt confident that they could see out their remaining years in the calmer waters of the selective system. Any satisfaction gained from this new sense of security, however, was often tinged with resentment when acquaintances in the secondary moderns and comprehensives teased Chis and Sid counterparts about their good fortune in spending their days in what was perceived, from the outside, to be an oasis of punctilious rectitude and tranquil, scholarly contemplation. Those who actually taught there, though, felt that they had their fair share of "difficult" children ("bright" troublemakers tending to be more ingenious at disrupting lessons than their less intelligent fellows) and would have argued that, in any case, they paid for benefits bestowed by (generally) high standards of classroom behaviour in the extra hours they were called upon to work in consequence of their heavy marking load and their often considerable extra-curricular commitments.

At the end of the Summer Term, Edgar Martin retired after thirty years at the School. Following wartime service as a meteorologist in the R.A.F. he had arrived at Crittall's Corner in 1947 to join Cedric Morley as the School's second physicist. Before the days of the full-time specialist, Martin, an accomplished church organist and choir master, was responsible for music in the School and generations of students will recall his playing of the piano in assembly.

September 1977 witnessed the official handing over of the new Sixth Form Centre after prodigious labours by volunteers from the Parents' Association under its chairman, John French, assisted by a number of the teaching staff. A sizeable building was purchased from the Borough of Greenwich for £5,000, dismantled, transported in sections to Hurst Road and re-erected during the Summer by a team led by Don Paddon. It was positioned some distance from the main building between the cricket pavilion and the caretaker's house.

For the first time Sixth-formers had purpose-built facilities of their own for both study and recreation. For all its manifest benefits, the tension between these two very different – not to say conflicting – functions was to cause a number of problems over succeeding years, culminating in the events of Christmas 1982 which will be considered in some detail later in this chapter. The Head, in a Report to Governors dated February 10th 1978, observed that what he termed "horseplay" had taken place within weeks of the Centre's opening and some minor damage had already been caused.

Three new members of staff began their Chis and Sid careers at the start of the Autumn Term, 1977. Two posts, those of designated Careers Master and Librarian, had been newly created by the incoming Headmaster, straining his staffing budget almost to breaking point. The former was taken by Patrick Taylor, who also taught some Classics, and the latter by Kenneth Tricker who, additionally, taught some English. Previously this Library work had been carried out by staff on virtually full teaching timetables and fitted into whatever odd moments they could make available for it. Mary Davies became Director of Music in succession to Jim Rowland.

Those pioneering girls who had begun their careers at the School in 1973 had now, of course, reached the Fifth Form and this placed an additional burden on already less than adequate facilities, particularly as far as examinations were concerned. The Hall was not large enough to accommodate, simultaneously, 180 "O" Level and well over a hundred "A" Level candidates and so the Gymnasium had to be pressed into use as well, much to the displeasure of the P.E.Department. They were only slightly mollified by the purchase of a canvas floor-covering with a very odd smell which came in bulky rolls known, in the trade, as "druggets."

John Sennett's first Speech Day guest of honour, on December 5th, was Samuel Gorley Putt, the Senior Tutor of Christ's College, Cambridge. Just two days earlier the stage had been occupied by Andrew Stafford's production of *The School for Scandal*, in which Morag White, Fiona Levey and Timothy Crossley figured prominently. Ian Lynch, as Snake, made his final appearance in a School production after many dazzling performances over the years, going on to Gorley Putt's college to read Classics the following Autumn. Term ended with farewell tributes to Dorothy

Stephenson, known universally as "Steve." Having survived the Coventry blitz as a fire-watcher she was, it seemed, indestructible and once strode out onto the field, single-handed and waving a chair-leg above her head, to confront – and quell – an angry mob of Hurstmere boys bent upon avenging some perceived slight from their purple-clad neighbours to the west. Steve was a law unto herself and nobody taught by her will ever forget the experience.

One of these former pupils, Stephen Anderson, took her place in the English Department at the start of the following term. Nearly a quarter of a century later he still has vivid memories of her unique teaching style, particularly her Chaucer lessons with the Sixth. Other new appointees during 1978 included Bob Green (P.E.), Hilary Taggart (Geography) and Mohindra Handa (Economics) who had lectured at the University of Nairobi.

The "Oxbridge" successes announced in January totalled twelve and represented the best performance for five years at this top academic level. Particular mention should be made of three candidates, Mark Buckingham, Colin Dean and Trevor Monk, who each achieved four "A" grades at "A" Level, having already been awarded Open Scholarships. Jane Crust, in gaining a place to read English at New Hall, followed in the footsteps of Alison Barrett, two years earlier, becoming the School's second female student to gain an "Oxbridge" place.

It would not be long (three years in point of fact) before the girls would outperform the boys for the first time in what was jocularly termed by some the "Oxbridge Stakes." The results achieved by the first intake of girls when they took their "O" Levels in June 1978 justified the confidence that had been placed in them when they arrived in 1973. Thirty-eight (63%) of the original sixty gained eight or more passes as compared with sixty-one (51%) of the 120 boys who sat the exam. Mark Stubberfield achieved "A" grades in every one of his nine subjects.

With the number of secondary pupils in Bexley predicted to drop sharply over the next decade (coming down from a peak of around 20,000 in 1981 to about 16,500 by 1990) it was proposed that the Borough be divided into five areas for the purposes of planning and development. Area 5, the southernmost sector – Sidcup and Bexley Village – would constitute the School's new catchment area, thus narrowing it still further with a consequent loss of incoming students at the higher end of the ability range. In these circumstances it is hardly surprising that Sennett was anxious to see the number of places for girls increased as soon as possible. A big step forward in this direction was taken in 1981 when, for the first time, an approximately equal number of girls and boys entered the First Year. During the next few years the balance slowly tipped towards the girls and for a brief period in the mid-eighties they were actually in the numerical ascendancy. Academic performance was significantly higher at this period than would – in all likelihood – otherwise have been the case and there was, predictably enough, a shift towards arts subjects in the upper years at the expense of the sciences which had, by and large, carried off the major honours at the top level throughout most of the School's history, and certainly during the headships of Pedley and Brown. Although there was, in due course, some swing back of the pendulum the other way, the hegemony established by the sciences under Freeman, Morley and Goddard was never to be re-established and henceforth departments competed for the academic accolades on a far more even footing. In John Sennett's time, for example, some two dozen or so students gained admission to Oxford or Cambridge to read English (with commensurate numbers going to other prestigious establishments such as Durham, Bristol, U.C.L. and Edinburgh) – a far cry from the situation that had obtained previously when, with the partial exception of Classics, arts admissions at the top level were few and far between, as the most cursory glance at the honours boards will confirm.

A great deal happened in 1979/80 and coverage of these events must necessarily be sketchy, much as one would like to dwell longer on certain topics.

As far as arrivals and departures are concerned, mention should first be made of Nick Forsdick, who arrived in January to teach Geography and quickly established himself as one of the most popular members of staff with his lively wit and his ability to engage a young classroom audience. His undying devotion to Norwich City F.C. provided an endless source of good humoured banter for all concerned. He was later joined by Valerie Perryman who brought energy, skill and charm to a French Department which, in time, she would inherit from Terry Maylam. Valerie, a graduate of Royal Holloway College, came to Chis and Sid from Tiffin Girls' School, Kingston-upon-Thames. Visits to France increased markedly with her arrival and one of the more traditionally minded departments began to take on a new lease of life. Another new arrival noted for an abundance of energy was Bob Carlysle who taught History and English and threw himself wholeheartedly into numerous aspects of School life, making a particular impact (like Pat Taylor) on the hockey field. Doctor Brian Hellyer joined the staff to teach Maths and Physics and he too, by force of personality, quickly established himself as one of the most welcome faces around the School.

The most notable departure at this time was that of Stanley Simmonds, Head of Art, who retired after thirty years at the School. At the time of writing he is living in Cornwall and still painting, an exhibition of his recent work being held in Plymouth in 2002. Into his shoes stepped Mrs C.L.Smith who, as Miss Curry, had joined the Department in 1975. The School was much the poorer for the loss of the Scot, Anne Fuller, who endeared herself to students and colleagues alike during her six years teaching German, a period in which she involved herself deeply in charitable and social service work.

This was a period of considerable change among the non-teaching staff. The Office, having lost one of its greatest characters in Nola de Lury, a few months earlier, saw the retirement, in May 1979, of Eileen Butler after twenty years as School Secretary. "The School's debt to her is beyond words," wrote John Sennett in the *Chronicle* and Alastair Wilson went even further, describing her departure as "a catastrophe." Mrs Butler served three headmasters with great distinction and her formidable grasp of the complex detail behind educational matters was legendary in the Borough and beyond. Rita Hawkins arrived to take her place, together with – by odd coincidence – an unrelated namesake, Maureen Hawkins, as her assistant. Sadly Rita Hawkins' tenure of the post proved very brief as she died within a year of her appointment. Her successor as School Secretary was Jennifer Breen who went on to rival Eileen Butler in indispensability. Another important figure in the life of the School, Dorothy Buckingham, retired the same term after sixteen years in charge of catering. Her place was taken by Maureen Doyle, who introduced a new, cafeteria-style lunch which offered a much wider choice than hitherto. Next in this line of succession was Jenny Collins and then, most recently, Julie Ferguson, who began as a kitchen assistant in 1980 and became Catering Manager ten years later. Lastly, in this connection, mention must be made of Bill Hamblen whose career as Caretaker came to an end in 1981 after 27 years of sterling service to the School which he joined when the new building opened in Hurst Road. For much of this time he kept wicket for the staff cricket team. He was succeeded in the post by Peter Tuppen and behind the stumps by Bob Buxton.

The Mikado, 1979 (L to R: John Butterworth, David Pope, Barry Howard, Judith Beresford).

Notable events at the turn of the decade included the School's first Gilbert and Sullivan in the Spring of 1979. *The Mikado* starred David Lidiard, Barry Howard, Audrey Dean, Sharon Coutts, David Pope and Judith Beresford. Brian Burgess designed the set, Mary Davies directed the music and Terry Maylam took overall charge of the production which was universally acclaimed as a great success. Two "theatre of the absurd" productions, directed, respectively, by Andrew Stafford and Charles Wells – *The Man in the Bowler Hat* by A.A.Milne and Eugene Ionesco's *The Bald Prima Donna* – were followed by the Sixth Form's production of Terence Rattigan's *The Winslow Boy* in which Michael Rose excelled in the leading role.

The new Junior Science Laboratory was completed at the end of April and, a few months later, more hutted classrooms (known as "mobiles," though you could watch them for ages and they never seemed to move) were put on the West Field making four in all and reflecting the steady increase in the School roll which, within two years, would exceed twelve hundred.

On May 3rd 1979 Timothy Crossley, supported by a lunchtime speech from no less a personage than Edward Heath, won the School's mock election for the Conservatives with a massive majority of 313, a harbinger of Margaret Thatcher's famous victory the following day. In December Crossley enjoyed another triumph when his Shylock was adjudged one of the best performances on the School stage in the memories of even the most seasoned members of the audience. It was a part that McGregor Williams had made very much his own but it is doubtful whether even the redoubtable Doctor surpassed Crossley's interpretation of the role in power or subtlety. Fiona Levey (Portia) and Mark Smith (Bassanio) shared the honours with him in a lavish production.

Another name that deserves mention in this chapter is that of Steve Hill who captained the 1st XV in his final year, besides representing both Kent and London Counties and making the England trials at Under 19 level. After a serious shoulder injury he devoted the latter part of the season to coaching junior players, an experience which stood him in good stead in later years since he is, at the time of writing, in charge of rugby at Oxford University and one of the best known figures in the game. The following season Mark Detnon played for the England Under 16 team against both Holland and Wales. The 1st XI's 275 against Lamorbey C.C. in 1979 remains the highest total ever scored by a Chis and Sid cricket team.

Among the more unusual visits around this time was a climb up the spire of Salisbury Cathedral (on the inside, fortunately) organised by the English Department for "A"Level students studying the novel by William Golding that tells of its construction. One of the climbers that day was Susan Ives who would shortly climb to another pinnacle by becoming Chis and Sid's first Head Girl. Twelve students gained admission to "Oxbridge" in 1979, the last time the School would achieve a double figure score in this most esoteric of competitions.

The School entered the sixth decade of its existence amid much excitement since it stood poised to achieve one of its greatest ever successes and to make a rare appearance in the national spotlight. On January 30th 1980 Chis and Sid defeated Peterhead Academy by 74 points to 68 in the final of Radio Four's celebrated *Top of the Form* general knowledge competition. In a previous round they had achieved the highest ever score (82

The winning *Top of the Form* team, 1980. (L to R: Ruth Westgate, Jane Kidd, Fergus Brunning, Timothy Crossley).

points) in the thirty year history of the programme. The team consisted of Ruth Westgate, Jane Kidd, Fergus Brunning and, as captain, Timothy Crossley. Cecil the Snake, in his Chis and Sid scarf, proved a lucky mascot. The trophy was presented at Broadcasting House by the Head of Radio Four on March 5th.

That same Spring Cllr. Brian Sams joined the Governing Body though he was to remain a member for just two years before being replaced by Cllr. Peggy Flint. On July 21st the School's first Junior Speech Day was held, principally in order to enable younger pupils to participate in an important occasion which, in recent years, with increasing numbers and limited accommodation in the Hall, had been restricted to Sixth-formers and prize-winners only. First Guest of Honour was Bill Cowmeadow, who had given enormous help to School rugby over many years. It was the Head's sad duty, in his speech, to report the death of Bill Freeman some three weeks earlier. As Membership Secretary of the Old Sedcopians Bill had, through unremitting effort, seen numbers rise to around the six hundred mark for the first time, a fitting memorial to his 44 year association with the School. His widow, Beryl, took over this role and threw herself into the work with similar enthusiasm. Indeed, her meticulous record-keeping in a wide range of matters pertaining to the School has proved to be of great value in the compiling of this history.

Issue number 83 of *The Chronicle*, published in the Summer of 1980, was the first to be edited by Ken Tricker, who went on to produce nine further magazines before handing over the task to William Husband. The year finished with a spectacular production of *Macbeth* featuring David Ellis in the title role and Susanna Berry as his wife. In all, five public performances were given if one includes a half-price final dress rehearsal attended by groups from several local schools. It was a fitting swan song for director Andrew Stafford, who left at the end of the Autumn Term to become Head of English at Sir William Borlase's School in Marlow. He was replaced by John Hazelgrove, who had studied under Germaine Greer at Warwick.

There were other important staff changes at about this time. John Churchill arrived to join the Maths Department and Andrew Alford succeeded Maggie Goodman as Head of R.E. Jim Reddaway left for Dulwich College, Phil Weatherly moved to Cheshire and Linda Martin became Head of English at the Ursuline School in Greenwich. The latter pair were replaced by Rosemary Carey and Adele Radelat, respectively, while Adrian Pitts arrived to add his considerable presence to the Music Department. The most conspicuous departure, however, was that of Milton Williams who, in July 1981, retired after 35 years' devoted service to the School. He was the last surviving member of staff from Crittall's Corner days and the last, therefore, to have served under the School's first headmaster, his namesake and fellow-Welshman Doctor McGregor Williams. Milton was largely responsible for making Chis and Sid a respected name on sports grounds throughout the Southern Home Counties and beyond. Four headmasters and countless sportsmen had good cause to be grateful to him for his organisational skills and his ability to inspire others with his own boundless enthusiasm.

April 1981 saw the start of the School's Golden Jubilee year – or, more accurately, eighteen months since the final event, the sponsored walk, had to be postponed until September 1982. To mark the beginning of this fiftieth anniversary celebration a group of 98 pupils and 9 accompanying staff, led by Bob Ims, left for Florida on Sunday April 12th. Disney World, the Kennedy Space Centre, the Everglades and the Miami "Seaquarium" were all visited and the alligator-wrestling display proved highly entertaining for all those present, with the possible exception of the reptile concerned.

First of the Jubilee productions was *Iolanthe*, another Davies/Maylam/ Burgess enterprise, which played to packed houses and involved over a hundred students of whom about half appeared on stage. Nancy French sang the title role and was ably supported by Matthew Beetschen, David Pope, Julian McDonough, Gareth Stubberfield, Katherine Bundell and Sian Miller, to mention but a few.

Another major musical event to celebrate the Jubilee was the concert held at the Queen Elizabeth Hall on July 19th 1981. The School Orchestra and two choirs entertained a near capacity audience. Highlights of the evening included Brahms' Sonata for Violin and Piano in A, played by Alexa Wilson and Matthew Beetschen; Haydn's Mass to St Nicholas featuring Audrey Dean and Michelle Spinks and Bach's taxing Magnificat in B.

On the sporting front the Jubilee Winter's Day was a great success. The Bill Freeman Cup – in fact a magnificently engraved glass vase – was presented for the first time at this event. Later in the year two hockey tours took place – to Bristol and to Birmingham – and an Under 16 rugby squad played three matches in Edinburgh. Three ski-ing holidays were organised (to Norway, Italy and Switzerland) and the History Department took a group to Florence and Venice, the latter city being visited during Carnival, an experience described as "being caught up in a foreign film" and "like an extract from Dante's *Inferno*." This second reference might equally well be applied to the narrow-boat holiday on the Grand Union Canal that Autumn – not the ideal situation to be in perhaps, when half the group went down with a severe stomach bug. T.M.C.Smith recalls dragging the walking wounded up the infamous Hatton Flight (twenty-one locks in rapid succession). Under the leadership of their "Admiral", Miss McDonnell, they somehow survived the experience.

On September 30th a Service of Rededication was held to mark the fiftieth anniversary of the School's opening. It was conducted by the Reverend Brian Simmons with the Bishop of Rochester as guest preacher. The Old Sedcopians' Jubilee Dinner took place on October 31st. Female guests were now conspicuous by their presence and it was pointed out during the course of the evening that the Old Sedcopian Netball Club was up and running under the direction of Diane Harwood.

Mention should be made of several other happenings during the crowded days of 1981. A team consisting of Keith Mason, Jeffrey Bronks, Anthony Barker and their captain, Ian Birchall, reached the semi-final of the London Schools Mathematics Competition, beating Dulwich College en route before losing, narrowly, to the Headmaster's former school, Latymer Upper. A sign of changing times was the setting up, by Brian Hellyer and Mary Monks, of the School Computer Club which met at lunchtimes,in the hut known as "B1," to use the new RML380Z machine. To Lorraine Wild and Judith Beresford, who started at Hurst Road in 1973, fell the distinction of being the first "home-grown" Chis and Sid girls to gain admission to "Oxbridge", both going up to St Edmund Hall, Oxford, to read, respectively, Geography and English.

At the end of term the Golden Jubilee Drama Production, *The Government Inspector* by Nikolai Gogol, went ahead despite heavy snow. It marked John Hazelgrove's directorial debut at the School and was voted a resounding success. The central roles were taken by Andrew Reeve and Roger Meredith, the latter, as always, coming to life in front of an actual audience and giving a brilliant performance despite being unable to remember his lines in the dress rehearsal earlier in the week. Term ended with the revival of the traditional Old People's Christmas Party, thanks, in large part, to the inspiration and hard work of Sharon Carter.

The following year earns its place in School history primarily on the strength of what took place (or what supposedly took place) on the final day of the Autumn Term. Other matters, however, must be written into the annals and detain us, briefly, before we can turn our attentions to the events of Christmas 1982.

On April 2nd Argentinian troops captured the Falkland Islands and, three days later, a British task-force set sail from Portsmouth bound for the South Atlantic. On the 7th the motion that "This House believes the Falklands are not worth fighting for" was overwhelmingly defeated at a crowded Debating Society meeting. The following month Alec Higgins retired as Chairman of the Governors and was replaced by Old Sedcopian Raymond Pope, the first (and, so far, only) former pupil to hold this position. The Jubilee Recital Evening at the end of the Summer Term was adjudicated by Edward Heath. Violinist Alexa Wilson won the Junior Solo Class with a sensitive performance of Beethoven's Second Romance, Op.50, and went on to perform with the National Youth Orchestra at the Albert Hall and the Barbican. The Senior Solo Class was won by pianist Julia Sked with an evocative interpretation of Debussy's First Arabesque. More than ninety pupils participated and Mr Heath praised the high standard of performance over all.

The Jubilee Edition of The *Chronicle, number 85*, came out that same week sporting a bold cover design by David Warren in vibrant shades of royal blue, green and yellow, the first in fifty years to thus burst into full colour. Three Old Sedcopians – Raymond Pope, Geoffrey Pullum and Stanley Linton – contributed their reminiscences to the publication.

The final event of the extended celebrations was the Jubilee Walk which was eventually held in September, having been postponed the previous year. Virtually the entire School and Staff took part, the idea being to walk past both of the previous sites, the original one in Station Road, now the Music Centre, and the "Glasshouse" at Crittall's Corner, vacated in 1954 and subsequently Kemnal Manor School. Planning was meticulous and everyone completed the circuit without mishap, raising over £3,000 in sponsorship money. In all over the Jubilee period a total surpassing £13,000 was amassed for the Library Appeal, most of it from the events already mentioned but some from other sources, such as the sale of the attractive Jubilee mugs. Much of this sum went to equipping the new extension which was completed in January 1983, thereby doubling the Library's original capacity. The stock of books reached 10,000 for the first time and the Library became the envy of the Borough.

Peter Wiles left to become a Head of Sixth Form in Sutton, the Biology Department passing into the charge of Gerwyn Lewis. Assistant Caretaker David Kearney, who had helped to build the School in 1954, retired after many years and everyone missed his cheerful smile and familiar Irish tones. Kevin Colwell arrived to join the Physics Department and Sister Beryl Honour joined as School Nurse with responsibility for some 1300 bodies on site, the School roll itself having passed the twelve hundred mark during the Autumn Term.

A magnificent *As You Like It*, directed by John Hazelgrove, was, by popular consent, the best Shakespeare production for many years and deservedly won the Bexley Arts Trophy for play of the year, an outstanding achievement given that it was competing against the work of adult drama groups in the Borough. Corinne Blatch was a lively and engaging Rosalind. She was well supported by a strong cast in which Neil Cleghorn, Louise Wheeler and Martin Knight excelled.

The year ended on a sad note with the death, on December 28th, of Bob Ims, Head of Geography and the Arts Sixth. He was a pupil of Tom Palmer's in the 1930s and eventually took over from him in 1967. It is extraordinary to think that, for over fifty years, the Geography Department had been in the charge of just these two men. At the time of writing, his successor, Paul Avery, still holds the reins after almost twenty years more. Bob Ims, who came from Norwegian stock, joined the School as a pupil in 1933 and was Head Boy at the start of the War. His association with Chis and Sid stretched back, therefore, almost to the very start and was, of course, far greater than that of any other serving member of staff. He was much respected by colleagues and pupils alike and with his passing the last direct link with the School's pre-War days was finally broken. Such continuity is remarkable. Like Geography, several other subjects – French, Physics, History and Boys' P.E. – have had just three heads of departments in over seventy years. Biology has had four to date. English and Classics have had five. Chemistry and Mathematics, with six each, have been run by fly-by-nights, comparatively speaking, their leaders averaging a mere dozen years or so as against a figure (for the ten largest departments at least) that averages about seventeen. This middle-management – as it tends to be called nowadays – provides, so to speak, the engine room of a school and the stability of this crucial area, no less than the leadership from the bridge, must account in no small measure for the success Chis and Sid has enjoyed over so many years.

The fifty-second year of the School's existence was on the point of taking its place, unremarked, on the end of the line formed, invisibly, by the previous fifty-one when an extraordinary sequence of events flung Chis and Sid suddenly into the national – indeed international – headlines for the first, and quite possibly the last, time in its history. "Crisis Christmas," as Steve Anderson later memorably dubbed it, began on the final day of the Autumn Term, Friday, December 17th, 1982, an unusually early finish to the year. For some weeks the Sixth Form had been planning to hold a party in their Centre to celebrate the end of term. Around £25 had been raised by the Social Committee, under the chairmanship of "Warden" Steve Gooden, with which to decorate the Centre and purchase food. Disco equipment was brought in and loud music soon issued forth. Because of the building's isolated position near the main gate, little disturbance was caused to the rest of the School. Indeed the "party", if such it can be called, developed during the course of the morning largely ignored by the Staff, the vast majority of whom, of course, were busy in the main building or the New Block well out of earshot, though several put their heads around the Centre door at various points and found little to concern them apart from the decibel level which, on a number of occasions, they turned down, only for it to rise again when they had retreated back to the main body of the School where lessons were continuing as normal – or, at least, as normally as can be expected just before children break up for the Christmas holiday. The Lower School soon headed off for a carol service at Holy Trinity, accompanied by many staff, including the Headmaster.

Some senior teachers, among them Douglas Hahn, had expressed misgivings about Sixth-formers socialising with minimal supervision in what had originally been designated the "Study Centre" and, in the five years of its existence, the "hut" – which, despite its considerable size, is effectively all it was – had been closed on several occasions following episodes of misbehaviour and minor damage. The Head, however, having checked with Steve Gooden, decided, not unreasonably, that to close the Centre early on this occasion might well lead to a mass exodus of Sixth-formers for an extended lunchtime during which some might have drifted into local pubs and come back the worse for wear. There is a certain irony, therefore, in the fact that, unknown to the Staff, "a quite considerable amount of alcohol" (as the Head later put it in a letter to parents) had already been smuggled into the Centre – not a difficult undertaking given its solitary location near Hurst Road.

By late morning the Centre was packed with exuberant teenagers, the numbers no doubt swollen by the fact of the Library's closure, that day, for repairs. The inevitable happened. Some Sixth-formers – though relatively few – had too much to drink and, at lunchtime, Gooden called an ambulance to deal with one student who had fallen over and injured his head. Later that day another Sixth-former was found slumped in a lavatory cubicle in the main building. He was clearly drunk and his father was summoned to take him home. By 1.40 p.m., however, the Centre was empty and the final assembly for the term took place as normal shortly afterwards in the Hall. Some cans and a few bottles were later removed by a cleaner from the Sixth-form Centre. The ambulance-borne student's injuries proved superficial and the hospital quickly discharged him with nothing worse than a rather unpleasant headache as a souvenir of the occasion.

It is highly probable that a similar scenario was played out in sixth-forms up and down the country that day and there matters would doubtless have rested but for several additional factors which, in unfortunate combination, were soon to set the cat among the pigeons.

During the course of the unusually long Christmas holiday the Headmaster turned over and over in his mind the conduct of his senior pupils on that final day. He felt that the breaches of discipline were too serious for a Nelsonian eye and, after telephoning various senior colleagues, he decided that, on the first day back, an investigation would have to be held and "ringleaders" identified and punished. This was the first of those factors alluded to above. Sennett, in his own words, was "not prepared to let it go" simply because nearly three weeks had elapsed since the misbehaviour had taken place.

Spring Term, 1983, began on Thursday January 6th and at the end of school the following day the entire Sixth Form was assembled in the Hall where the Headmaster addressed them. He announced the suspension, for five days, of seven students all of whom had admitted drinking "a number of glasses" at the end of term. This was the second in the series of critical decisions taken and again, in itself, it should not have proved problematical. The Head, however, was not content to let matters rest there, which, with the benefit of hindsight, he might have chosen to do. He ended the meeting by instructing all those who had drunk alcohol on the 17th to report to him at 9.30 a.m. the following Monday with their written "confessions". He told them that, in fairness to their suspended colleagues, they should expect a one day suspension as reward for their honesty. The students went off for the weekend with time to mull things over and talk amongst themselves.

Two days later, on January 10th, some 160 or so students duly presented themselves and were addressed in the Hall by Douglas Hahn and the Head. Sennett told them he wanted to know precise details of who had drunk what and it now appeared that differentiated suspensions were to be handed out in proportion to how much alcohol each admitted to having consumed. Some felt (rightly or wrongly) that goalposts had been moved. Sheets of paper were handed out and the students were now told, it seems, that unless everybody signed up to his or her own particular "quota" then the entire group would be suspended for one day.

This may not have been altogether wise, seen in retrospect, although the Head had taken the precaution of phoning Raymond Pope the previous day and getting approval for this course of action, despite warning him that "there could be press coverage" – the understatement of all understatements as it transpired. Before long a two-way question and answer session developed with voices from the floor insisting that there should be no discrimination between those who had had "quite a few drinks" and those who had "simply had the odd glass."

It was then, it could be argued, that another error of judgement was made. The animated Sixth-formers were, at their own request, left to themselves in the Hall for half an hour or so to decide upon their response. The result, predictably, was a decision to stick together and declare their collective, generalised guilt. There would be no "victimisation", as they saw it. The Head was left, therefore, with little choice but to carry out his threat, painted into a corner as he was, and 157 students received a token suspension of just one day. In one sense it was an extreme reaction yet in another the "punishment" was really very mild. Honour, it seemed, had been satisfied on all sides and here the matter (which had already taken up far more time than it perhaps warranted) would have been allowed to rest. In all probability the outcome would have been, at worst, a paragraph somewhere in the middle of the local newspaper had it not been for two further pieces of bad luck.

Someone telephoned *The Sun*. Opinions differ as to who this was. Some blame a suspended pupil with a grudge and others the irate father of a suspended offspring. It may have been both of them, independently, but it matters little. In the normal course of events any coverage would have been buried somewhere like the foot of page 17, assuming that it was deemed worthy of even that much attention amid the competing claims of the innumerable "stories" that land on a sub-editor's desk. Here the final element comes into play – the only one that no course of action on the part of anybody connected with Chis and Sid could have avoided.

Wednesday January 12th 1983 was, by unfortunate chance, one of those rare occasions dreaded by editors of national newspapers – an almost totally "non-news" day. The best *The Telegraph*, for example, could come up with for its front-page headlines were a reference to "a late rise in bank rates bringing relief to the pound" and a proposal for compulsory ballots in the election of trade union leaders. Neither story, needless to say, was calculated to cut much ice with the tabloid readership. Had the suspensions been announced a week later, on the day that Klaus Barbie, Hitler's infamous "S.S. Butcher" was arrested, then the Sidcup story, if story it was, might have merited half a dozen lines at most. Herr Barbie, however, having successfully remained in hiding for some 14,000 days, contrived to evade his captors for a further seven and, in consequence, a bombshell exploded in Hurst Road that, metaphorically at least, was the equal of any of those Nazi rockets that his Führer sent to fall on Crittall's Corner and, some might claim, did even more damage to the School than they had done.

"SCHOOL BAN 157 BOOZING PUPILS" screamed *The Sun*'s main front-page headline. Journalist Robert Bolton then went on to describe what he called "an amazing drinking orgy which led to five pupils being taken to hospital." The article also claimed that "others smoked pot." The assertions became more ludicrous as Bolton got into his stride. "One boy downed a bottle of brandy in 1 minute 50 seconds," he alleged. "Everyone started just after nine and within half an hour dozens and dozens were paralytic."

Not to be outdone *The Star*, that same morning, blazed the following nonsense across the top of its front page: "SIXTH FORM BANNED AFTER BRANDY ORGY." Reporter Joe Clancy added: "A furious head-master suspended his entire sixth form yesterday after a wild drinking spree put five in hospital." Of this sentence only the reference to the Headmaster's fury has any basis in fact and even this was an exaggeration

A selection of headlines, January 1983.

since John Sennett's feelings, by the New Year, could better have been described as indignation coupled with a determination to act firmly but fairly towards all those involved. The Express chose the slightly more temperate headline: "The Day my Sixth Form went Wild." Even the staid *Telegraph* ran the story. Its headline: "160 Pupils Suspended after Party" was the plain, unvarnished truth and the two inches on the back page were the most such an incident deserved.

It later emerged that six reporters and a photographer had virtually besieged the Headmaster's study, refusing to leave until he had answered their questions. They then stopped and questioned pupils at the School gates, apparently giving £5 notes to those prepared to provide sufficiently lurid accounts of what had taken place. Not surprisingly the more imaginative children seized their chance with a poetic licence of which, in different circumstances, their English teachers might well have been proud.

That evening the story made B.B.C. Television's local news and, within a surprisingly short time, clips of a Sennett interview were being shown as far afield as New Zealand. The next day *The Sun* followed up its story with the now famous – or notorious – Franklin cartoon. Two roistering teachers, in gowns and mortar-boards, are seen raising their glasses beneath a sign saying "Sozzlehurst & Hiccup Grammar School." Sprawled on the floor in front of them are a couple of dozen inebriated boys and girls, lying in pools of spilt drink, their faces suffused with imbecilic smiles. The caption reads: "Greatest number of pass-outs we've had for years, Headmaster!"

There was, not surprisingly, much amusement in staff rooms in Bexley and beyond, especially, one imagines, in the non-selective sector. *The Star* embellished its previous piece with an account, the next day, of what it called "Bacchanalian revels," claiming that "some of the babies in the First Year were pie-eyed by 9.30." A measure of the absurdity of such reporting can be gauged by the account, in the same article, of "Sixth-formers smuggling in drink in their satchels." Satchels had disappeared in the 1950s and, even then, of course, no self-respecting schoolboy above the age of about thirteen would have been seen dead carrying one.

It was then the turn of the local press. At first *The Sidcup Times* (Thursday January 13th issue) appeared to be trying to outdo The Sun and *The Star*. "ORGY OF DRINK" ran its main headline across the front page, adding that "The big thing was to see who could get drunk first," though it

"GREATEST NUMBER OF PASS-OUTS WE'VE HAD FOR YEARS, HEADMASTER!"

The famous Sun cartoon, January 13th 1983.

did have the grace to add: "one eye-witness allegedly said," which is more than the tabloids had done. Reporter Alastair Irvine then went on to give a much more calm and moderate account of events, quoting extensively from the denials and disclaimers that were swiftly issued by those connected with the School. The following week a cool and fairly accurate summing up was given under the headline: "What Really Happened at Party." It had been, according to Chairman of the Governors, Raymond Pope, "a storm in a sherry glass." John Sennett, the paper reported, had received "stacks" of sympathetic letters and phone calls supporting his actions and very few that were critical of them. Raymond Green, Chairman of the Parents' Association, declared: "You could not have a more caring man than Mr Sennett" and the Head himself lamented: "I am just very sad that people have tried to blacken the School's excellent reputation." He added: "This remains a very fine school and I am happy to rest my case on its record."

Once the media frenzy had subsided, the internal investigation began. Interviews were conducted with anyone who might, conceivably, have been able to shed light upon the matter. Steve Gooden, for example, claimed to have lost track of the number of times he was "hauled out of class for a series of inquests" as he put it, much later, when reminiscing about those difficult days. Meetings were held and reports duly written and submitted, some of them supplying quotations that have been used over the last few pages. Nobody resigned and nobody was dismissed but lessons were undoubtedly learnt. For the next few years alcohol was allowed in School only under the strictest supervision and, even then, only at official functions with a heavy adult presence. Inevitably, however, damage had been done. Although sensible people, particularly those in the education world, realised that the press reports were grotesquely sensationalised the School became, for a time, something of a laughing stock. Some Sixth-formers were discomfited by jokes made at their university entrance interviews and – whether coincidentally or not – applications for admission the following September were considerably down on the previous year.

Twenty years, almost, have now passed since "Crisis Christmas" and recollections have, inevitably, dimmed. Many at the School today will not even have heard of "Sozzlehurst and Hiccup." For others, however, the episode remains burned deep in the memory, though whether what happened is recalled with a shudder or with amusement depends very much, of course, upon where one was on that fateful day. Everyone, so the saying goes, is famous for fifteen minutes. How sad, though, that, despite its numerous successes and the many achievements of which it has good cause to be proud, the School's one undeniable moment of national fame, lit up, albeit briefly, in the spotlight of the nation's collective gaze, should have been occasioned by such a tawdry and inconsequential non-event.

CHAPTER ELEVEN
All Change

THE REMAINING YEARS OF John Sennett's headship, 1983–1994, may be best characterised as a period of rapid and disorienting transition. Staff came and went with increasing frequency and these changes of personnel in themselves, featuring, as they did, so many major figures and so many key positions, together with all the readjustments they brought with them, might have been more than sufficient for staff and students to absorb even had educational policy maintained a steady, unruffled course across these years as it had tended to do in earlier decades. The period in question, however, was turbulent in the extreme and far more disruption was caused to established patterns than by anything that took place during the struggle against "comprehensivisation" which occupied so much of the previous twenty years.

Mark Carlisle, first of the seven education secretaries to serve during the Conservatives' eighteen years in power, was a cautious, uncontroversial figure but when his successor, Keith Joseph, took over the role in 1981, a furious onslaught was launched upon the so-called "educational establishment" and crackpot schemes came tumbling out of Curzon Street with bewildering, not to say chaotic, rapidity. These measures, which appeared hot on each other's heels during the eighties and nineties, often contradicted their predecessors of a few months earlier, to the frustration and eventual fury of the school staffs called upon to put them into practice.

Among the "new initiatives" that landed on John Sennett's desk during these years were: the G.C.S.E.; the "Baker Contract" with its laughable 1265 hours; A/S Levels; the National Curriculum with its Key Stages and Attainment Targets; Local Financial Management of Schools; Records of

Achievement; Grant Maintained Status; the S.A.T. examinations; OFSTED inspections; staff appraisal; coursework examinations; a new "Oxbridge" entrance system and the proliferation of examination league tables in the newspapers. The list is far from exhaustive though the changes the legislation imposed – invariably with inadequate consultation and far too little breathing space afforded in which to implement them effectively – left the nation's teachers in a state of exhaustion. Worse still, they became demoralised and bitter as their professionalism was all too often disregarded or, it seemed, treated with contempt by the politicians. With the exception of the War years, it is doubtful whether Chis and Sid has ever undergone a period so fraught with difficulties as the second half of Sennett's time in charge. Works to rule and withdrawals of good will were rife across the nation's schools during the 1980s in protest against the ill-thought-out diktats of Messrs Joseph, Baker, Clarke and Patten, each seemingly bent upon outdoing, in terms of intransigence and unreasonableness, the previous holder of his office.

For all their professionalism, the staff of Chis and Sid were, inevitably, caught up in the disruption. Unsurprisingly, the number taking early retirement or leaving the profession altogether to make a less stressful (and often more lucrative) living in other fields was never higher and certainly ran well into double figures during these troubled years. After this broad-brush picture of that era, for the finer detail we must return to 1983, a year in which there was much to celebrate, despite its unfortunate beginning.

As Winter gave way, reluctantly, to Spring, the events of "Crisis Christmas" began to loom less large in people's minds and soon attention turned to other matters. On the sporting front there were two notable successes. The Rugby Club won the Askeans' Floodlit Competition and Steven Garrett became English Schools Champion at 400 metres.

Ian Page was made Head of the Arts Sixth in succession to Bob Ims, combining this demanding task with the running of the History Department, the latter function one that he had been carrying out for the previous nine years. Paul Avery arrived to be Head of Geography, together with Birgit Kuypers and Shirley Beck (later Puxty) – both Biologists – and a Classicist, Rosemary Farrant. Edna Jamieson took on the role of School Counsellor in addition to her responsibilities in the English Department. The "Jubilee" Library Extension was officially opened on the evening of April 25th.

ALL CHANGE

On July 9th the School's traditional Mock Election was won for the Conservatives by Matthew Clowry who achieved just over 50% of the vote. Ian Garrett, for the Liberal/S.D.P. Alliance, gained 28.8% forcing Martin King, the Labour Candidate, into third place with a derisory 13.6%, precisely the figure, coincidentally, that his predecessor, Susan Ives, had achieved in 1979. Again this outcome proved a reliable predictor of the real General Election result later that same day, a victory for Margaret Thatcher with a massive majority of 143 seats, the largest since Attlee's triumph of 1945.

This memorable year ended on a vibrant note (or succession of notes) with a concert held at the Purcell Room on the South Bank. Mary Davies and Adrian Pitts presented a lively programme of music which included Bach's Second Brandenberg Concerto, Schubert's String Quartet in C and Khatchaturian's frenetic Sabre Dance. The most unusual offering of the evening was Walton's *Façade*, a setting of Edith Sitwell's weird poetry to music, which produced a masterful recitation from Corinne Blatch. Mark Bennett, Helen Burton and Ian Turvill stood out among the many accomplished young musicians to be heard.

For the first time in its history the School had not been oversubscribed when applications were put in for selective places in the Borough of Bexley following the publication of the results of the "Eleven Plus" examinations in the Spring. This disturbing development was attributable in part simply to falling numbers in the primaries but also (it was generally presumed) to the unfavourable coverage in the tabloid press back in January. The First Year cohort that began their School careers in September 1983, therefore, were regarded with wary anxiety by their teachers. It was as though they wore the word "unchosen" stamped invisibly on their foreheads. What an odd twist of fate it was, then, which decreed that it should fall to this particular year-group to pioneer the new G.C.S.E. exam in 1988, especially given that the "O" Level examination had been in existence since 1951.

At Half Term the English Department staged its "Shakespeare Marathon", a non-stop dramatised reading of all 37 plays. Fifty Sixth-formers and ten members of staff, working in four teams to a complicated shift system, began with *Henry VIth Part One* at 3 p.m. on Friday October 21st in the Prefects' Room at the end of the "A" huts. Members of John Hazelgrove's team began *Richard III* at 4.30 the following morning and are unlikely ever to forget their re-enactment of the Battle of Bosworth as dawn was breaking over the rugby pitches. Without a break the performances continued, morning, noon and night, until, some 103 hours later, the last play, *Henry VIII*, reached its end at 10.25 on Tuesday evening. To Alistair Harwood fell the longest role, Hamlet, and when Lady Macbeth (Teresa Jones) sleep-walked people understood how she felt. This unique event was enjoyed by all participants and raised over £1200 in sponsorship money for the Save the Children Fund. Press coverage, this time, was universally positive, giving the lie to much of the nonsense that had been written earlier in the year. Two months later some of the "Marathon" participants, led by Ian Garrett, Louise Wheeler and Corinne Blatch, reassembled for Anouilh's *Ring Round the Moon*.

The first event of note in the Orwellian year, 1984, occurred at the end of January with the landing of a Wessex helicopter on the School Field as part of a recruitment drive by the Royal Navy. At Easter the School's fourth trip to America took place, led this time by Brian Burgess. Some fifty pupils, accompanied by six members of staff, flew to San Francisco on April 12th. The holiday included visits to the Yosemite National Park, to Universal Studios in Hollywood and to Disneyland as well as a stay with local families in Modesto and a brief visit to Tijuana, across the border in Mexico.

In the Summer John Weston retired after nearly thirty years at the School. Following seven years in the Army, during which he took part in the D-Day landings, Weston graduated from St Edmund Hall, Oxford and worked for some years with the Inter-Varsity Christian Fellowship before joining the Staff in 1955. He took over from Leslie Stringer as Head of German in 1971. John's tall, upright figure on his huge bicycle was a familiar sight to generations of pupils in the streets of Sidcup. In addition to the running of various Christian organisations, John Weston played a leading role in the School's Social Service Work Group and, in his younger days, ran the 1st Rugby XV and the Table Tennis Club. He was replaced as Head of German by Henning Fischer.

Colin Parker became the School's seventh junior international rugby player when he was capped for the England Under 18 XV against France, Scotland and Wales.

In his notes for the 1984 edition of the *Sedcopian* the Headmaster referred to changes in the School's catchment area, reminding his readers that Richard Pedley recruited from much of North West Kent rather than merely the southern part of Bexley, Greater London's smallest borough. Though the academic quality of pupils coming in remained high, "the ablest, certainly, are less numerous than ten or twenty years ago." This undeniable fact, together with what he called "professional disquiet" between employers and teaching staff, with the consequent withdrawal of good will and other forms of so-called "industrial action" that characterised the mid-eighties, led to increasing stresses and pressures. High inflation put a huge strain on School finances, a fact recognised by Oxford University which, in November, set its traditional Seventh Term Entrance Examination for the last time. Cambridge would soon follow suit, with the consequent demise of the School's prestigious Third Year Sixth after some forty years of high-powered teaching of the most academically able students. At its peak, in the mid sixties and early seventies, this elite group of eighteen and nineteen year-olds had sometimes numbered two dozen or more. Nearly 400 young men (and a few young women) passed through the Third Year Sixth on their way to either Oxford or Cambridge and its disappearance was mourned by many.

It is rare in the history books that the reservists step forward into the limelight but the rugby season 1983/84 was remarkable for the performance of the Second XV. Coached by Keith Jenkins and captained by Brian Meehan, an inspired leader behind the forwards, the team won all fifteen of its matches, scoring 427 points against a mere 40 conceded.

The year ended with a vigorous production of *The Merry Wives of Windsor*, directed by John Hazelgrove. There were memorable performances from Matthew Ansell as Falstaff and from Louise Wheeler and Tara Harrison as the Wives themselves, ably supported by William Gallop, Alex Lester, Juliet Prew and David Chappell among others. The ambitious set with its mobile half-timbered houses provided a suitably Tudor context to the play.

In 1985 the School's first mini-bus arrived thanks to the fund-raising efforts of the Parents' Association under its energetic Chairman, Ray Green, who also found the money to erect a sizeable storage building on the West Field. At Easter *The Pirates of Penzance* was staged. Again the team of Davies, Maylam and Burgess combined their talents to excellent effect. Adrian Pitts of the Music Department sang the Pirate King and, soon afterwards, moved up into Mary Davies' position on her departure to a deputy headship at Townley Grammar School. In a strong ensemble, mention should be made of Katherine Bundell, Adam Corrigan, Heidi Moulinie, Nicola Rehling, Christopher Walledge and Ian Turvill. The Recital Evening on July 23rd was adjudicated by Dr Meredith Davies,

Principal of Trinity College of Music. Winners included Heidi Moulinie (piano), Alexa Wilson (violin), Tara Harrison (soprano) and Sarah Larkins (clarinet). Another musical highlight of this year was the debut in August at the Tramshed, in Woolwich, of Adrian Pitts' new jazz group, Fascinatin' Rhythm, made up of former pupils of the School.

The Summer of 1985 saw the departure of Dianna Rimmer from the French Department and the arrival of Eluned (Lynne) Hughes to take her place. Barbara Hamblen, wife of former School Caretaker Bill, retired after more than twenty years of invaluable service as a laboratory technician. Sadly, the withdrawal of staff good will, resulting from the appalling treatment of teachers by Secretary of State Keith Joseph – widely considered to be at least slightly mad – led to the curtailment of many extra-curricular activities, notably the cancellation of a scheduled production of *One-Way Pendulum*. For the first time for fifteen years – and only the second time since the War – there was no School Play at Christmas.

When Kenneth Baker took over the Education Department from Keith Joseph in 1986 any hopes harboured by the teaching profession that things would improve were quickly dashed. Baker's aim seemed to be to make as many changes as he could in the shortest possible time and then move on rapidly to a different sphere – as was his wont – leaving his successor to cope with the mess that he had left behind him.

For the second time, Douglas Hahn stepped into the breach, taking over the day-to-day running of the School during the Head's sabbatical term at the University of Sussex in the Spring, a period he spent studying aspects of appraisal and staff development. Staff morale, already low, sank still further under Baker's ill-judged and ill-informed criticisms of the profession. Recruitment also plummeted in certain subjects, particularly Physics. There were already early indications that Hahn was far from well and, with the benefit of hindsight, it seems likely that the additional stresses of these few months accelerated the deterioration of his health.

By no means all, however, was doom and gloom. Michelle Cooney won the English Schools Senior 400 metres hurdles title in the record time of 59.3 seconds and an even greater feat of endurance was achieved by Old Sedcopians Andrew Grubb and Gary Simmons who walked from Land's End to John O'Groats to raise a large sum for Leukaemia Research. The School's own sponsored walk that year, a somewhat less demanding saunter around Danson Park Lake, raised over £3,000 for various good causes. Other sporting achievements in 1986 included Matthew

Brimson's selection for the Young England cricket team, Steven Willis' victory in the national 1500 metres Freestyle and a remarkable season for the girls' 1st XI hockey team who were undefeated, scoring fourteen goals and conceding only one in their seven matches. The talented violinist Alexa Wilson won scholarships to both the Royal College of Music and the Royal Academy of Music as well as becoming co-leader of the National Youth Orchestra.

The year is also memorable for seeing the official abolition of corporal punishment in state schools. The dubious privilege of being the last ever pupil to be caned at Chis and Sid fell to Stuart Doxey of 4G2 who, on February 24th, received "one stroke on seat" for "snowballing on play-ground against instructions." An analysis of the last Punishment Book, now in Bexley's Local History Archive, reveals that between September 1973 and February 1986 about 400 canings took place, which averages out at something like one for every term-time week.

On the staffing front Barbara Brown stood in for Charles Wells during his absence on a Fellowship at St John's College, Cambridge and, soon afterwards, joined the English Department full-time, going on to become a popular and successful member of it for the next sixteen years. Departures that year included those of Dr Brian Hellyer, Michael Davies, Bob Carlysle, Ian Windeatt, Kevin Colwell and Hilary Taggart. Amongst the new people to arrive in September were Carol Tipper (Chemistry), Tony Tipping (P.E.), Brian Seve, David Bartlett and Valerie George (all Physics).

A major development was the advent of the new G.C.S.E. examination which was intended to combine the existing "O" Level and C.S.E., since the current set-up was believed by many to separate children unfairly into sheep and goats. The Fourth Form began work on it in September while their teachers grappled with unfamiliar approaches such as the 100% coursework examination system in English. The installation of the School's first administrative computer, once the teething troubles had been overcome, offered the prospect of much greater efficiency, particu-larly as far as record-keeping was concerned.

The School was saddened to learn of the death of Tom Palmer, youngest of the original Station Road five, the second of the School's Deputy Heads (1958–73) and holder of the record for length of service with forty-two unbroken years of full-time teaching on three different sites. A rousing production of *Oh What a Lovely War* brought 1986 to a satisfying close. Led by John Hazelgrove and Adrian Pitts, the English and Music Departments combined their resources to good effect: for the second time, Chis and Sid won the coveted Bexley Arts Council award for the best production of the year at all levels. In an accomplished cast Alan Nathan, Ben Ackland, Debbie Jones, Angela Spinks and Nicola Rehling stood out. Andrew Clarke, the Head of School, made a splendidly gruff Field Marshal Hague and Joanna Willis got the biggest round of applause when she made a sortie into the audience, in her black stockings and suspenders, to perch seductively upon the Headmaster's lap.

Although Douglas Hahn had been seriously ill with cancer for some months, a stunned silence fell over the Common Room when news of his premature death, aged just 48, was announced before the start of lessons on the morning of Thursday January 22nd 1987. Tributes flooded in, generous and sincere. Quoting Roger Ascham, Tutor to Queen Elizabeth the First, John Sennett observed that Douglas "delighted rather to discover and call forth the talents of others than to make display of his own." The School's loss, he added, was "irreparable and beyond measure." Michael Brown described Douglas Hahn as "a family man, a man's man, a man of integrity and culture, who took genuine delight in the success of others." He declared: "You will never come into contact with anyone in education for whom professionalism was more important." Lorraine Wild, a former pupil, writing from Hahn's old college, St Edmund Hall, concentrated on his qualities as a classroom teacher: "We always knew that he had our interests at heart and it was for this, above all, that he gained our respect and affection."

The funeral took place at Shoreham Parish Church in Kent amidst the deepest snow for many years. Mourners making their way along the country lanes found it piled above head height on either side as they drove through. The School Choir sang at the service and Chairman of the Governors, Raymond Pope, gave the address. Many colleagues and pupils joined Douglas' widow, Janice, his three children, family and friends at the graveside for the interment, their dark clothes etched against the brilliant white of the churchyard in a scene that might have been taken from *Wuthering Heights*. A memorial service was held on March 3rd at St John's Church in Sidcup. This time the address was delivered by the Reverend Brian Simmons. Music was provided by Matthew Beetschen, Alexa Wilson and Angela Spinks. Andrew Clarke read the lesson. A cedar tree was later planted in memory of the Deputy Head during a simple but moving ceremony attended by one pupil from every form. Sixteen years later the tree, between the Biology wing and the Sixth Form Centre, is sturdy and strong, as Douglas himself was before disease so cruelly cut him down.

The search began for a replacement and Ian Page stepped up, temporarily, to fill the vacancy caused by Hahn's death. It was hardly the ideal timing, therefore, for a full-scale L.E.A. Inspection but it went ahead, nevertheless, between February 9th and 20th. The report however, when it eventually arrived, was favourable. It is worth noting, as the Inspectorate did, that the teaching staff at this point numbered 68 (excluding the Head) of whom 63 were full-time. Despite the fact that 1987 was the fifteenth year of co-education at the School, the ratio of female staff to male was still only 19 : 45, an imbalance that was to disappear over the next decade or so and indeed, recently, tilt the other way for the first time. The Inspectors described the Staff as "extremely conscientious" and anxious to maintain the School's "tradition of excellence". The standard in exam results remained high, they noted, but they felt "a more cross-curricular approach" was needed, with more in-service training and some modernisation of teaching styles. The Headmaster was described as "a man of energy and ability". He was, they declared, "a man of conviction who is not afraid to express his views in forthright terms both within the School and outside." Forthright views, of course, were very much called for during Kenneth Baker's period at the helm.

The Easter Concert at St Martin's-in-the-Fields may be taken as marking the tenth anniversary of John Sennett's arrival in Hurst Road. The large church was crowded and the acoustics good. Adrian Pitts conducted a programme that involved some 200 musicians and included works by Mozart, Bartok, Kurt Weill, Dvorak, Lloyd-Webber and Mendelssohn before concluding with part of Beethoven's Piano Concerto No.3 featuring Heidi Moulinie at her sparkling best. Other notable contributors were Louise Hennessy (clarinet), Sarah Railton (violin), Scott Gladwell (trumpet) and sopranos Angela Spinks and Kathy Bundell. A lively rendition of "Rock Around the Clock" may well have recorded a "first" in the 260 year history of James Gibbs' elegant building. What a pity, as Martyn Berry observed in his *Chronicle* report of the event, that so few of the participants were male.

On June 11th the School's Mock Election, won by G.J.Lee for the Conservatives by a 28% margin, yet again proved an accurate predictor of the real thing, Margaret Thatcher sweeping back to Downing Street with a majority of 102.

That Summer "O" Level examinations were held for the last time. When the results appeared in August it transpired that the pass-rate of 86.5% represented the School's best performance since 1969 when a figure of 90.3% was achieved. This latter percentage, in the early days of Michael Brown's regime, was itself surpassed only once when, two years earlier, in Richard Pedley's final year, a success rate of 90.5% was recorded. "O" Level, it may be recalled, was, unlike the new G.C.S.E. examination that replaced it, originally intended for the top 40% or so of the ability range.

Among those members of staff leaving in the Summer of 1987 particular mention should be made of Michael Baker, Head of Mathematics, who, after 21 years at the School, quit teaching altogether. The premature loss to the profession of such a gifted teacher and respected departmental head was symptomatic of the disillusionment felt by so many in the eighties in response to a plethora of misguided policies by a succession of Tory ministers who appeared rarely to have set foot in an actual school since they left (in the first three cases) Radley, Harrow or St Paul's.

Richard Mason was another to abandon the British teaching scene after twenty years at Chis and Sid. A great debt was owed to him, not just for his work in the Classics Department but also for the enormous amount of time he devoted to cricket in all its aspects at the School. He will perhaps, additionally, be remembered for keeping alight, in various sneaky ways, albeit flickeringly, the flame of association football which many wrongly supposed to have been extinguished when the School officially swapped codes in 1955. Richard settled in Bergamo, Northern Italy, where he taught English (and cricket) to the natives and transferred his support from West Ham to Atalanta.

New arrivals in September included former pupil Pauline Matkins, together with Christine Head-Rapson, to teach Physics and Mathematics, and Samuel Pam to teach French. Other staff changes saw Bob Buxton become Head of the Mathematics Department, Valerie Perryman take over from Terry Maylam as Head of French and Joyce Crust become the Head of Year Five just in time to deal with the problems created by the new G.C.S.E. exam. The post of Head of Girls' P.E. was taken by Pippa Rust, her diminutive in terms both of surname and physical stature.

During the night of 16th October 1987 came the Great Storm, the worst to batter Southern England within living memory. Although the School buildings themselves suffered little damage, many beautiful trees

192

Graham Lightwood, Deputy Head (1988-2006).

were flattened in the Glade. On the preceding afternoon, as the gale set in, there was an uplifting moment which caused one senior member of staff to regret her brave decision to cross the car park, encouraged enthusiastically by those crowding the windows up above.

John Hazelgrove's production of *A Midsummer Night's Dream* in December was notable for a strong performance by Alan Nathan as Bottom. Shelley Paterson, Richard Sexton, Ben Ackland, Robert Claggett, Nicola Strange and Elizabeth Bell all distinguished themselves in a fine ensemble cast, as did the lighting team led by Rick Wickes whose ambitious effects made a huge contribution to the play's success.

New Year 1988 was marked by the arrival of Graham Lightwood as Deputy Headmaster. This post had remained vacant for a year since the death of Douglas Hahn. It took four advertisements before a suitable candidate emerged, almost certainly a record in the history of staff recruitment at Chis and Sid. Graham Lightwood hailed from Walsall where he had attended Queen Mary's Grammar School (founded 1554), becoming Head Boy before going up to London University to read French and German. He began his teaching career at the Royal Grammar School in Guildford and was promoted to Head of Modern Languages and Senior House Master. At Guildford he commanded the School Cadet Force, achieving the rank of Major in the Territorial Army, attached to the Queen's Regiment, before moving to Rippon Grammar School as Head of Modern Languages in 1984. Stocky, forceful, determined, he quickly settled into his new role, an important aspect of which was the maintenance of good discipline among the boys. Having been the Sergeant Major of his school cadet force, Lightwood did not need the Headmaster's inches when it came to making his voice heard, particularly if dealing with recalcitrant young men who had been "benched" outside his office. He was soon teaching both French and German. Later he would be called upon to add Latin to his classroom repertoire and, in due course, he was to find himself specialising in this subject area.

The start of term was marred by the sad news that Jenny Peirse, a Fourth Year pupil, had been killed on New Year's Day by a car which mounted the pavement and ran over her when the driver was taken ill at the wheel. Through a bizarre and ghastly quirk of fate the vehicle was driven by a retired member of the School staff.

During the Spring, publishers Sidgwick and Jackson brought out *Page After Page*, the illustrated autobiography of Tim Page, arguably the most celebrated photographer of the Vietnam War. Page was a pupil at Chis and Sid from 1955 to 1961 where he achieved the unusual distinction of being expelled in what was to have been, in any case, his final week at school, for refusing to accept what he felt to be an unjust caning at the hands of Richard Pedley. Tim Page was severely wounded when a large piece of shrapnel lodged in his head. Film buffs may be interested to know that the character played by Dennis Hopper in the famous Vietnam War film *Apocalypse* Now is based on Old Sedcopian Tim Page.

On February 5th the School participated in the first "Red Nose Day" to raise money for Comic Relief. Both staff and pupils went about their business with bulbous plastic appendages attached to their faces, Martyn Berry and Joyce Crust gamely conducting the morning assembly thus embellished. Much fun was had by all to begin with, though the novelty soon palled. Steve Anderson's comic revue, "My Love is Like a Red, Red Nose", contributed further to the week's entertainment. An impressive total approaching £6,000, raised for the suffering children of Ethiopia, made the enterprise well worth all the effort that had been put into it.

It would be a daunting, nigh impossible, task to calculate the sum raised for innumerable charities and other good causes throughout the School's existence but such a figure must be huge indeed and is testimony to the generosity, ingenuity, determination and compassion shown by many thousands of pupils, staff and their families across the years.

Farewells were said in 1988 to Alec Higgins, retiring after 19 years on the Governing Body; to John Temple, after 12 years, who took early retirement following an injury; to Edna Jamieson, who left after 14 years to take up a new career as a counsellor and to David Durban, after 16 years, who became Deputy Head at the Mathematical School in Rochester. The latter's role as Head of Years One and Two was taken over by Clive Wederell, assisted by Lynne Hughes. Linda Williams, assisted by Bob Green, took charge of Years Three and Four. The year saw the return to the History Department of Rosemary de la Bedoyère (née Carey). The lively Amanda Naylor joined the English Department and Michael Hardyman – at six feet seven inches almost certainly the tallest ever member of staff – joined the Physicists. Diane Hill (Geography) began the first of her two spells at the School.

The Rugby Club enjoyed its best ever season of modern times in 1988/89, Noel Horrobin's 1st XV, captained by Neil Baker, winning 18 of their 21 matches and losing only twice. Particularly satisfying were victories over old rivals such as Reigate, Guildford Royal, St Joseph's Ipswich and Campion. The team scored 309 points, conceding just 85. Other sides too did well. Of 54 games played by the three senior teams only 9 resulted in defeat, a success rate of almost 84%. Andrew Baker was capped for the England Under 16 XV against Italy. The season was also notable for the first ever fifteen-a-side Chis and Sid girls' rugby team to take the field. Led by Samantha Newell the girls drew 0–0 with Eltham College, raising £700 for charity in the process. Other sporting achievements in 1988 included Matthew Brimson's cap for the England Under 17 cricket team against Sri Lanka. He later went on to play for Leicestershire and featured in their Championship-winning sides of 1997 and '98. Daniel Sargent became the British Under 19 Judo Champion and Lorraine Brackpool added the English Girls' Golf Challenge Trophy to the Kent Junior Open Championship she had already won.

In the Summer the first G.C.S.E. examinations were sat by the Fifth Year students. The "unchosen" of September 1983 vindicated their selective places by achieving a very creditable "pass" rate (i.e. grades A–C) of 87.4%.

Alan Nathan had his third starring role in December, this time in *Yonkers*, an adaptation of *The Matchmaker* by Thornton Wilder. This production, the first at the School to be staged "in the round", was notable also for the New York accents which the cast successfully sustained throughout performance. Elizabeth Cannon, Geoffrey Warwick, Elizabeth Mobey and Anthony Murray were singled out for particular praise by the critics.

The last year of the 1980s brought with it a number of innovations. The National Curriculum came into force in September, initially applicable just to Maths and Science and in the junior years only which would, henceforth, be known as "Key Stage Three." English followed a year later. At the same time the School moved from a 35 to a 40 periods-a-week timetable. The main corridor and staircases were redecorated properly for the first time in twenty years. Six students gained admission to Cambridge, a figure surpassed by only two other maintained schools nationwide. A memorable visit to Berlin took place in October, just three weeks before the Wall came down on November 9th. The group, led by Henning Fischer, crossed into the Eastern Sector on the very day that Communist leader Erich Honecker resigned amid huge excitement among the local population on both sides.

Computer training began for the Staff, there being now over fifty of the devices in the School. Another "first" in Chis and Sid's history was the selection of Samantha Finch for the English Synchronised Swimming Squad. Jackie Empson began her illustrious international hockey career with selection for the England Under 16 squad to tour Belgium. Another major sporting achievement in 1989 was the victory of the Staff cricket team over the School 1st XI, their first success in this fixture for 46 years – and the only defeat suffered by the School that season, remarkably.

A School "newspaper" with a strongly satirical slant – *The Chis* – ran to several subversive issues before succumbing to the weight of examination pressures. The *Chronicle* of 1989 was the last of the ten to be edited by Ken Tricker. He handed it over, very much as a going concern, to his successor William Husband, the entertaining and popular new member of the Classics Department. Willy had been Head Boy of Cheltenham College and had featured in Lindsay Anderson's famous film *If* before going up to Peterhouse. Unfortunately he moved on again within two years.

Three men who played crucial roles in the history of the School died in 1989. They were: James Banfield, the mathematician, last survivor of the original Station Road five; Dennis Clarke, the historian, who served the School for thirty years from 1936 to 1966 and Harry Lester, the

School's second Chairman, successor to Francis Edlmann. The Summer saw the departure of four key members of staff. Adrian Pitts and Andrew Alford left the Music and R.S. Departments, having contributed much to the well-being of the School. Mike Hankinson retired after 19 years in the Mathematics Department and on the playing field. Some remarks about his career appeared in Chapter Eight.

Margaret Harris, who had done so much to establish the girls in what had been, hitherto, a virtually all-male environment, retired after 14 years as Deputy Headmistress. A great deal was written about her in Chapters Eight and Nine but one should add here that, despite health problems in her last few years, Margaret struggled bravely to cope with the increasing burden of administrative chores that threatened to drown the senior staff in paper during the eighties. Not only did she set and maintain high standards of appearance and conduct for the girls but she also devoted huge amounts of time to the thankless (and often pointless) tasks imposed upon the School by educational bureaucracies both local and national. Increasingly frustrated by the oppressive weight of countless "new initiatives" and by the inadequacy of resources with which to deal with them, she was glad to rest from her labours. During her well earned retirement she spent much time with friends in New Zealand and it was appropriate that a lament sung, hauntingly, in the Maori language by an elderly lady, who stepped unannounced from amidst the mourners to stand by the coffin, should have featured memorably in her funeral at Eltham Crematorium in 2000. In those compelling moments, as the congregation sat transfixed by the plangent, keening, unaccompanied voice, more than one mind, one imagines, ranged back across 13 years to that icy churchyard in the Darent Valley.

Among September's new recruits to the Common Room was Kevin Moody, who joined the History Department and took charge of cricket. An accomplished player himself, he spent innumerable hours in the umpire's long white coat and contributed greatly both in and out of the classroom during his seven years at the School. David Grubb, an Old Sedcopian, replaced Adrian Pitts as Head of Music, bringing to the task his own unique brand of exuberance and panache. Brendan Murphy, a Liverpudlian, arrived to teach Geography and David Taylor took over as Head of Religious Studies. Michael Rushton, a powerfully built fast bowler from the Potteries, forsook a career as a scientist with the National Coal Board to teach Chemistry at Chis and Sid where he rose swiftly through

Sheila Ford, Deputy Head (1989-2007).

the ranks to become, in turn, Careers Master, Head of Year and, in 2001, to join the so-called "Senior Management Team" as an Assistant Deputy Head. Paul Anning, a former pupil at local rival school St Olave's, joined the Mathematics Department and before long took charge of stage lighting besides involving himself in many sporting activities.

The most important of the new appointments in the Autumn of 1989 was that of Sheila Ford who replaced Margaret Harris as Deputy Head with special responsibility for girls. She was educated at The Ursuline Grammar School, Ilford, going on to study at both Digby Stewart and Birkbeck Colleges before completing her B.Sc. in Mathematics with the Open University. She came to Chis and Sid with considerable teaching experience gained in a variety of schools in such places as Barking, Barnet and Somers Town, a tough area hemmed in by railway lines and sidings behind Euston, St Pancras and King's Cross. Her most recent post had been at St Francis Xavier's Sixth Form College in Clapham. Sheila Ford's computing skills proved invaluable in modernising the School's administrative structures and her experience with disadvantaged children and her extensive travel in the Far East and elsewhere equipped her well for the counselling aspect of her role which seems to have grown in importance over recent years. She still recalls, with rueful amusement, that one element of her original job description put her in charge of the School's stock of sherry glasses.

The nineteen-eighties ended, as far as Chis and Sid was concerned, with a rousing Christmas Concert under the baton of the new Director of Music, David Grubb (the programme ranging from Rossini and Strauss to Buddy Holly and the world première of a Grubb composition) and with a stylish production of Sheridan's elegant comedy *The Critic*. This was Steve Anderson's debut as director of a major show. The Warwick twins, David and Geoffrey, featured prominently. Elizabeth Cannon, Anthony Murray, Alex Giles and Colin Fairweather were others to catch the eye.

The new decade was just a few days old when news came that Raymond Pope, Chairman of the Governors, had resigned in protest at Bexley's refusal to accept the School's decision to exclude a disruptive pupil. After eight years in the chair, Pope felt his position was no longer tenable without the support of the Authority over what he saw as an issue of principle. The Governors elected Allan Frost in his place with, as his deputy, Glynis Smith who would herself succeed to the chair in 1993. Another future Chairman, Graham Holland, (1996–2002) joined the Governing Body at the same time.

It was a year of changes on the Staff as well. Bob Green, who had done so much for cricket during his twelve years at the School, left to take over the P.E. Department at Simon Langton School in Canterbury. Other teaching staff to move on in 1990 included David Kennedy, Mike Callow, Rick Wickes, Brian Seve and Willy Husband, the latter passing the editorship of the *Chronicle* to Cindy Smith. New appointees included Felix Aubel, latest in the line of spirited Welshmen (and, indeed, Welsh women, since Mary Davies and Lynne Hughes must, of course, be included) that stretched right back to McGregor Williams and Teddy Jenkins in the early thirties and was now well into double figures. Felix was a disciplinarian of the old school and the merest intimation of his approach along a corridor or up a staircase was calculated to silence the noisiest of classes. After just seven terms at the School he returned to Wales to train for the Baptist ministry. News later came that his Chapel sermons were famous for miles around. Linda Martin and Julie Fentiman (both Home Economics), Angela O'Rourke (Head of Girls' P.E.), Ian Wessels (History) and Richard Blyghton (Mathematics) were others to arrive that year. They were joined by another mathematician, David Morgan who, like his Head of Department, had begun his career as a student teacher at the School. Will Michael, the well-known jazz pianist, added his Aberdonian verve to David Grubb's Department and those with long memories recalled Eddie Harvey, a pupil during the War years at Crittall's Corner, who went on to be a founder member of the Dankworth Seven, playing with such immortals as Woody Herman, before becoming Head of Jazz Studies at the London College of Music. Naoufel Ben Fredj, a Tunisian, arrived to teach French and the Common Room's increasingly cosmopolitan character was further enhanced by the august figure of Clarence Trotz, a graduate of Selwyn College, Cambridge, who joined Brian Burgess' Physics Department. In his earlier career he had been the headmaster (or principal) of two schools in Guyana and a third in Montserrat. No other member of staff has been able to claim such a distinction. Arthur Parsons (1931–1957), it may be recalled, had been head of just one school before coming to Chis and Sid.

This year, 1990, saw several more "firsts" in the lengthening history of the School. Geoffrey and David Warwick became the first twins to serve, jointly, as School Captains and in May the first Sixth Form Leavers' Ball was held, organised by a committee led by Ali Reza, the youngest of seven brothers who attended Chis and Sid between 1968 and 1990 which is, itself, another record. On December 14th the first "Non-Uniform Day" took place. Pupils came in wearing their "civvies" (almost invariably their weekend "uniform" of jeans, ironically) and some of the Staff wore school uniform in a neat reversal of the normal order of things. Everyone contributed 50 pence for the "privilege" of dressing differently but the same and a large sum was raised for Elmdene, a charity supporting alcoholics. The idea proved to be such a straightforward and painless way of raising money that it is strange that nobody had thought of it before. Old-timers might have turned in their graves but dire predictions of anarchy proved unfounded. No riots were observed and in fact – as with "Red Noses Day" – pupils' behaviour, once the early excitement had abated, was little different from what was experienced on a normal "purple" day. The event quickly became a regular institution, held once a term or so in support of various worthwhile causes.

Another innovation of 1990 was the "dis-banding" of Year Two with effect from September, although setting was allowed to continue in Maths and French. One of the principal motives underlying this change was the desire to remove any stigma attached to the less academic classes "I" and "U". Some years earlier the labelling had changed from the traditional "A", "B" and "C" to a more devious system based on the letters of the word "SIDCUP", the two ablest groups, for example, being known, arbitrarily, as "S" and "D" but the move, predictably, fooled nobody for very long. Now, with six "mixed ability" groups (within, needless to say, the pre-selected intake) no child had cause to feel a failure after just one year in the School. This new system was extended to the Third Form the following year with the effect that, after almost sixty years, streaming finally came to an end in September 1991.

The first year of the new decade was notable for some outstanding achievements by the cricketers. Particular mention should be made of Andrew Baker's selection to tour New Zealand with Kent Schoolboys and, furthermore, his subsequent winning of the award for the outstanding member of the squad. Neil Mobey broke the record for the highest number of runs in a season, previously held by Graham Clinton (773) who went on to open the batting for both Kent and Surrey. Mobey's total of 826 included five centuries and he finished the season with the stupendous average of 165. Another record was achieved by Alec Brand of the Under 15 XI who took five wickets in five balls against Rochester Mathematical School. High-jumper Wendy McDonald was selected for the Scottish Athletics Team.

On the non-sporting front it should be recorded that the new subject of "I.T." (Information Technology) was now flourishing under the aegis of Stuart Cunningham (its first Head of Department) and that the Air Training Corps won the Canberra Trophy, competing against 57 other teams.

The deaths of former staff members Cedric Morley, Teddy Jenkins and Mary Monks were announced during the year. A great deal has been written in these pages about the two men but tribute must be paid here to Mary Monks who, although never full-time at the School, served the Maths Department loyally for many years. With her husband, Ted, Mary worked tirelessly for charities such as Oxfam and her enthusiastic support for so many good causes aroused the admiration of all who knew her, as did the courage with which she endured the affliction of the motor-neurone disease that confined her to a wheel-chair and brought about her premature death. Bill Cowmeadow, a generous benefactor, who devoted so much of his time to the service of School rugby, also died in 1990.

It seems appropriate at this point to recognise the enormous amount of work put in by the modern linguists and others, year in year out, in the organising and leading of innumerable trips abroad. Shortage of space has precluded the mentioning, in these pages, of all but the most spectacular or unusual of these, for instance those to such far-flung places as California or the notorious "swastika" tour of Germany described in Chapter Two. By 1990 it was quite normal for as many as eight foreign visits to take place annually. In that particular year, for instance, there were French Department journeys to Saumur, Champagnole and Le Portel (organised by Valerie Perryman and Lynne Hughes) and German Department journeys to Berlin and the Black Forest (organised by Henning Fischer and Graham Lightwood). There were, in addition, two ski-ing holidays, to Austria and to the French Alps, led by Stuart Cunningham, and a pony trekking holiday in South Wales led by Val George and Jenny Breen. There was also an "Activity Week" in Dorset, led by Diane Hill, and numerous day trips, notably a First Year visit to Bodiam Castle and Battle Abbey, featuring a battle between the Saxons and the Normans in which all took part with great enthusiasm. Field Courses – organised by the Geographers and the Biologists -, theatre visits and sports tours contributed, collectively, a huge number of additional hours to the total. 1990 was in no sense exceptional and is cited merely to represent all those other years, before and since, in which, largely untrumpeted, just such events took place. The generosity of so many dozens of members of staff in giving up so many thousands of hours of their otherwise free time to such academically valuable (and enjoyable) activities says much not only about the individuals concerned but also about the sense of duty, loyalty and purpose engendered by Chis and Sid as a corporate institution over nearly three quarters of a century.

In July, fifteen Lower Sixth-formers attended the first Bexley Shakespeare Summer School, held at Rose Bruford College of Drama across the lake in Lamorbey Park. This was to become an annual event and many "A" Level English students, from Chis and Sid and elsewhere, have experienced this week of lectures, seminars, theatre visits and drama workshops, gaining a much enhanced understanding of Shakespeare and a valuable foretaste of the university life which most of them subsequently went on to enjoy.

The final weeks of this unexceptional year were memorable not just for the dramatic resignation of Margaret Thatcher on November 22nd but also, on the local scene, for an article in *The Leader* claiming a drastic deterioration in the School's examination performance. "Inspectors ask why G.C.S.E. standards are falling," was the headline and the piece referred to fears that "the Borough's prize school" was in decline. Results had apparently "dropped by 13%." The smear on the School's reputation may not have been on the scale of the "Crisis Christmas" press onslaught of 1983 but it caused considerable anger nevertheless. In a letter to parents, dated December 4th, the Headmaster set out to refute the allegations. He explained that his report to the Directorate of Education had been clearly labelled "strictly confidential" and raised the likelihood of a complaint to the Press Council. It turned out that the alleged "13% drop" was, in fact, a decline on the previous year's figures of about 4% at G.C.S.E. and about 1% as far as "A" Level was concerned. The latter figure, put into context, proved to be 1% higher than the average achieved over the previous ten years. Although somewhat disappointing, the statistics in no way justified the hysterical and distorted treatment they received at the hands of the journalist concerned. Apart from being yet another reminder of the damage that could be caused to the School by inaccurate, sensation-seeking press stories, the episode did draw attention to the changing nature of the intake. The proportion of the Borough's children deemed "selective" was now creeping up towards 30% while, at the same time, a new policy was being implemented, not unreasonably, to even up the level of entry across the four selective schools. These factors, coupled with the much reduced catchment area previously remarked upon, meant that, inevitably, there was some lowering of standards and this, of course, was bound to be reflected in the examination results of what had, hitherto, been generally regarded as the Borough's "flagship" school. Those who compared, unfavourably, the academic performance of Chis and Sid children in the 1990s with that of their predecessors in earlier decades did so unfairly since a few moments' reflection would have shown them that they were not comparing like with like. Such comments were nevertheless to be heard in some quarters and were made worse by the "double-bind" which meant that, even when a much improved set of results came in, they were glibly dismissed on the grounds that modern exams were much easier than they had been formerly or were marked far more leniently than had previously been the case.

Musical highlights of 1990 included a thrilling performance of Mozart's *Vespers*, given by the Choral Society; Brahms' First Symphony, played by an orchestra now numbering some seventy instrumentalists and, at Christmas, Gershwin's *An American in Paris* with David Pack playing the taxi horns to great effect. Steve Anderson directed a superb *Under Milk Wood*, the cast sustaining the Welsh accents as successfully as their predecessors had the Bronx accents two years before. In a taut ensemble performance Colin Fairweather, Geoff Warwick, Zoë Godfrey and Liz Cannon all caught the ear.

The following year, 1991, marked the beginning of Local Financial Management of Schools, the Head and the (unpaid) Governors now becoming responsible for an annual budget of just over two million pounds. The Debating Society voted against war with Iraq – unlike their predecessors, nineteen years earlier, who had favoured fighting the Argentinians and their still more distant forerunners of 1937 who had, by a narrow majority, accepted the need to prepare for conflict with Germany. The Gulf War, however, went ahead, even without endorsement from Hurst Road.

Among the staff changes that Summer should be recorded the departure of the popular Nick Forsdick who contributed greatly in such areas as voluntary service and cricket – quite apart, of course, from his classroom achievements – during his thirteen years at Chis and Sid. He moved to a well merited promotion as Head of Geography at Judd School in Tonbridge. Others to leave were Amanda Naylor and Adele Radelat, the latter having organised innumerable theatre visits during her decade in the English Department. Birgit Kuypers relinquished her teaching role but continued, part-time, as School Counsellor. The new arrivals who replaced them in September included Colin Simpson and Carol Geren (English), Carol Jenkins (Geography), Paul Wilsdon (Classics), Lynn Connell (Biology) and Marilyn Stevens (R.S.). Andrew Fraser also arrived that Autumn, initially as cover for Messrs Scott and Rees in the Technology Department (as it was now called), both of whom were on long-term sick leave.

The fact that it was now sixty years since the opening of the School in Station Road did not, of course, escape attention. In recognition of the Diamond Jubilee the guest of honour at Senior Speech Day was (again) Sir Edward Heath. For the first time, Sixth Form numbers topped three hundred and it is worth noting that, since each student at this level "carried" £2,250 on his or her head, the combined contribution to the School's annual budget amounted to a staggering £686,250 which represented more than a third of total income.

Much Ado, 1991 (L to R: Sarah Wheeler, Dominic Corrigan, Mark Williams, Zoë Godfrey).

Only two students – Andrew Mace (English) and Rebecca Ackland (Modern Languages) – gained admission to "Oxbridge" this year, the lowest number since 1975, which was itself the lowest since 1952. The year ended on an optimistic note, however, with Steve Anderson's lively production of *Much Ado* which featured an exceptionally strong cast headed by Zoë Godfrey and Anthony Murray as Beatrice and Benedick, ably supported by Alex Giles, Richard Marriner, Dominic Corrigan and Sarah Wheeler among many others.

The question of Grant Maintained Status arose in the Spring of 1992 and meetings were held to present the options to parents, since the matter would be decided by their majority vote. The proposal was to sever links with the London Borough of Bexley and for the School to be run directly from Whitehall. The School would take control of its own admissions policy as well as benefiting from a "transitional grant" which, in the first year at least, would have brought in an additional sum of around £200,000. On June 12th 1992 Chairman of Governors Allan Frost sent a letter to parents urging them to vote in favour of this new status, explaining that his colleagues saw G.M.S. as a means of improving academic standards at the

School. Under the proposed new system, admission would be by written tests administered (and marked) by the School itself rather than by the Borough.

Councillor Sams sent a strongly worded letter to parents in response, presenting the case for Chis and Sid remaining an L.E.A. school. One of his most telling arguments was that, in view of the famous "Greenwich Judgement" of two years earlier, which enabled children to cross boundaries far more easily than hitherto, Bexley rate-payers would lose out since many of the School's places would be snapped up by applicants from neighbouring boroughs. This would, he suggested, be deeply ironic since Bexley parents had repeatedly voted to keep (and to pay for) their own selective schools whereas Greenwich, for example, had chosen not to do so. Nevertheless, Greenwich parents would have an equal right to a Chis and Sid place and, in fact, in view of the School's position close to the boundary, they might even have an advantage in many cases. Bright children from outside the Borough, in other words, would be snapped up by a "grant maintained" Chis and Sid, Sams claimed, at the expense of pupils in Bexley itself, thereby – and this proved to be his clinching argument – denying places to the younger siblings of children already at the School.

At a packed public meeting held in the School Hall that Summer Term, Sams insisted on addressing the parents even though, strictly speaking, he had no right to do so. Just as Brutus made a fatal error by generously allowing Mark Antony to speak at Caesar's funeral, only to find that the orator's powers of persuasion had turned the crowd against him, so Allan Frost was persuaded to allow Sams to state his case. The Chairman's earlier call for a "yes" vote was swept aside by Sams' passionate speech urging parents to preserve the status quo. To the surprise and dismay of the Governing Body, and a slender majority of the Staff (many of whom had misgivings about the proposed change), when the vote was held in July, Grant Maintained Status was rejected by 713 votes to 632, a majority of just 6%. The "turnout" was 68% of those entitled to vote. The following year a similar vote was held and again the opponents of change prevailed, this time by the much wider margin of some 20%.

In sport there were some notable achievements during 1992. Susan Pendrich of 8S finished second in the National Junior Cross-Country Championships over a demanding 2,950 metres course. A year later she finished sixth out of 610 runners in the National Cross-Country Championships despite a gashed leg (inflicted by the spikes of a fellow runner) and despite being two years younger than most of her rivals. Lisa Potrac, another Second Year pupil, finished third out of 250 competitors in the A.D.T. mini marathon, run over the last three miles of the London Marathon course. Not to be outdone, Wendy McDonald of the Upper Sixth won the Senior High Jump at the English Schools Championship in Stoke with a leap of 1.74m. which, for the benefit of older readers, is 5ft.8½ inches, more than the height of the average Sixth Form girl. Fifth Former Hayley Smith was selected for the England Under 16 Schools' Netball Squad and finished on the winning side against both Wales and Northern Ireland. All these achievements, of course, reflected great credit on the Head of Girls' P.E., Angela O'Rourke.

The special Diamond Jubilee issue of the *Chronicle* (the 95th) contained some interesting retrospective articles, including Roger McGregor Williams' reminiscences of his father, the first Head. In the centre were some old photographs printed in a faded sepia tint which had the bizarre effect of making them less distinct than the originals from which they were taken. Mac might well have been less than amused at being labelled "Mr. R.Pedley" in one of the captions had he been able to look down from some vantage point in that headmasterly Elysium presided over, one supposes, by the shade of another Doctor, Thomas Arnold.

Now that the National Curriculum was in full swing, though frequently amended, to the frustration of those whose job it was to teach or administer it, year groups had to be renumbered to fit in with the new system that envisaged a school career as a seamless garment that one donned in infant school and discarded at the end of the Upper Sixth. Instead of Years One to Five, Chis and Sid pupils henceforth were categorised as belonging to Years Seven to Eleven. Most adjusted to the new terminology quickly enough, though "Years 12 and 13" had considerable difficulty in elbowing out the time-honoured "Lower and Upper Sixth". New Seventh Year pupils thus found, to their mystification, that the awesome elders, in their smart suits, that barred their way into the building at lunchtime, were in fact "Sixth-formers", a status they themselves had outgrown, they thought, when they had left primary school.

But times were changing. Gowns, for example, were no longer worn except at Speech Day. The "Common Room" had now become, as far as most were concerned, the "Staff Room" and "Masters and Mistresses" were now diminished into "teachers" as what some might term egalitarianism and others "political correctness" took hold. Blackboards, too, were rapidly becoming extinct as shiny, clinical whiteboards began to take their place and "dry- markers" superseded the chalk which, since time immemorial, had squeaked and skidded its wavering track from side to side, sending, as it did so, skeins of fine dust to throng the slanted light and settle thinly on ledges and on sills. The traditional wooden desk with its hinged lid, pen groove and rear-facing surface beloved of graffiti-ists was giving way to the bland anonymity of plastic-topped tables from whose sole, horizontal surface offensive comment could be instantly expunged with a squirt of some magic liquid and a quick swipe of a cloth. No more the grate of sandpaper at each term's end.

Another sign of changing times was the victory achieved by a team of Year Nine pupils, led by Rohan Kuruppu, in a "build your own personal computer" competition held at Olympia.

Three long-serving members of staff took early retirement on health grounds in 1992. Malcolm Rees, the Head of Technology and a noted sportsman in his time left after 19 years following a serious car accident. His departmental colleague Will Scott, famous, among other things, for his ceremonial cakes which graced many a School celebration, retired after 21 years in Hurst Road. Jestyn Lewis, another, like Malcolm Rees, in that great "Chis and Sid Welsh" tradition referred to earlier, – in looks, indeed, the quintessential Celt with his dark, wild hair and craggy profile – opted for a farming life among his native mountains after 24 years at the School, yet another victim, the Head later pointed out, of the insane pressures heaped on the profession by so-called Government initiatives which "continue to descend upon the heads of staff and pupils alike with bewildering and exhausting rapidity." Colin Simpson, Diane Hill and Martin Franklin were others who moved on during 1992, though in their cases for reasons of promotion. Incoming members of staff at this time included Dr Marianne Ruffer-Turner, a German biologist, Daniel Keep, who took charge of the rapidly expanding Technology empire and Dominic Russan, who arrived to assist him in his task.

In July came the dreadful news that Year Eleven pupil Rohit Duggal had been stabbed to death in the middle of Eltham on his way home from a party. Many of his school-friends gave evidence at the Old Bailey six months later and the murderer was duly convicted. A tree in Rohit's memory was planted outside the Dining Hall. Brian Sams' was another unexpected death to be announced as Autumn turned into Winter. Not all who knew him numbered themselves among his admirers but none could deny that, over many years, he had been a staunch supporter of Chis and Sid. Towards the end of December the School learnt of the passing of one of its greatest servants, Milton Williams, who had joined the P.E. staff in 1946. He would have been 76 on Christmas Day, a birthday which, by an odd coincidence, he shared with Noel Horrobin his successor.

The production of *Romeo and Juliet*, directed by Charles Wells, sold out so quickly that a fourth performance was hastily arranged and that, too, was sold out before the opening night. The title roles were taken by Richard Marriner and Zoë Godfrey. Jane Gibson played the Nurse, continuing bravely on despite illness and Juliet's parents were portrayed by Sarah Wheeler and Dominic Corrigan, with Richard Judd a flamboyant Mercutio and Tom Dibble a warm, rich-voiced Friar Lawrence. Sumptuous National Theatre costumes and imaginative lighting by Paul Anning's crew gave the production a strong visual impact, as did the furious fight sequences organised by Colin Simpson. It brought the year to a satisfying close.

A great deal happened in 1993, John Sennett's last full year in charge. In February the School lost two long-serving and greatly valued members of its non-teaching staff. Bryan Hales, the groundsman, a big, blond Viking of a man, whose cricket pitches were unequalled among Kent schools, died with horrifying suddenness of a brain-tumour. Jenny Breen, School Secretary since 1980, merely moved a few hundred yards to the Music Centre at 27 Station Road, the building that had housed the fledgling Chis and Sid, but she too was sorely missed. Like Eileen Butler before her she had made herself nigh on indispensable with her astonishing grasp of the multitudinous threads that wove the tapestry of School life. The ever-increasing weight of financial administration had become particularly burdensome in recent years but she shouldered it heroically along with soothing the fevered brows or staunching the bleeding wounds of all those sick or wounded children sent to the Office as to a first-aid post. Jenny's sunny nature and natural charm won the affections of everybody at the School, young and old, in the fifteen years she spent at the hub of events in Hurst Road. The position of School Secretary passed to Brenda Allen, the sixth in a line stretching back to Mary Burnell. She too, over the last nine years, has proved a worthy inheritor of that tradition. Her sister, Margaret Adams, joined her in the School Office in 1993.

The year's major departure, though, was that of Alastair Wilson who had joined the Staff as a young Bristol classics graduate in 1957. He

Alastair Wilson, 1957–1997.

recalled starting on a salary of £43 per month, when a semi-detached house in Hurst Road cost all of £1900. As he looked back over his 36 years of full-time teaching at the School (a total, incidentally, surpassed only by Palmer, Jenkins, Walsh, Morley and Freeman – the latter pair with their war service included) he took particular satisfaction from his thirteen years in command of the A.T.C.Squadron. He recalled with pleasure his term as a schoolmaster fellow at Christ's College, Cambridge in 1970, his trips to Italy with the Classicists and his long association with School music, taking especial pride here in the achievements of his talented daughter Alexa. He continued to teach Latin on a part-time basis until his "ultimate" retirement in 1997 after a forty year association with the school – a length of service exceeded only by that of Tom Palmer, his predecessor as Senior Master (or Deputy Head). Having arrived at the School just as it was approaching what has been called its "golden age", from 1963 to 1973, under first Pedley and then Brown, during which period "Oxbridge" successes averaged over eighteen per year, with other academic achievements commensurately impressive, Wilson was frequently heard to lament the subsequent decline in academic standards at the highest level, though he accepted, of course, that changed admission policies meant that such a pinnacle was no longer reachable. A complex, unpredictable man, caustic or genial as the mood took him, he may not have been easy to get close to but his fierce loyalty to the School remained without question and his going marked the end of an era in the annals of Chis and Sid.

Another important figure to retire was Joyce Crust, who gave up full-time teaching after 16 years as, first, Head of Girls' P.E., then Head of Fifth Year and, finally, Head of Years 10 and 11. Her Chis and Sid career began in 1973 with the arrival of the girls, though for the first four years she taught on a part-time basis, in which capacity, indeed, she was to continue beyond "retirement" to complete 22 years at the School. Having played for the England team at the end of the 1950s (despite being Scottish) Joyce was a tower of strength where schools netball was concerned as coach, umpire and administrator, being involved in the game's organisation at the highest level. Her contribution in other sporting fields such as hockey, tennis, athletics, gymnastics and dance was also invaluable and played a huge part in helping the new girls to feel a sense of achievement and thus to gain confidence in their overwhelmingly male environment. Before long they were winning as many plaudits as the boys and sometimes more. Her role at the sharp end of the G.C.S.E. initiative was another of her major successes during those years.

There were, naturally, new arrivals on the Staff to balance the departures. James Rees, who had lived in China, joined the Geography Department; Gary Janks, a South African, came to teach English and Geoffrey Rishman, formerly of Judd, and a keen aviator, took over as Head of Chemistry from Jestyn Lewis. Chis and Sid was now, reputedly, the largest mixed maintained grammar school in England and, with its budget approaching £2.5m., Commander Roger Paine was brought in to be the School's first Finance and Premises Manager. Chosen from 160 applicants for the post, Paine had seen many years' service in the Royal Navy, including a spell on aircraft carriers, before returning to civilian life as Director of Administration at the National Maritime Museum in Greenwich. His teasing, slow left-arm deliveries were to prove a deadly new weapon in the armoury of the Staff Cricket Team.

Last of the personnel changes of 1993 saw Allan Frost stand down as Chairman of the Governors to be replaced by Glynis Smith. The year also witnessed the first Key Stage 3 tests for Year Nine and the appointment of National Curriculum Co-ordinators for such areas as Environmental Awareness, Equal Opportunities and Citizenship. The examination performance "league tables" that were brought in at about this time were regarded, to begin with, as something of a joke but, before long, their pernicious influence was to become far from a laughing matter. The removal of the "A" Hut, outside the Dining Hall, enabled the quadrangle, with its beautiful flowering cherry tree, to be turfed over to make a pleasant new picnic area for the warmer months. The installation of security cameras at various points around the site brought about a sharp decline in the vandalism that had become a real problem over recent years.

A triumph for the 1st XI cricketers in July was a rare victory against a strong M.C.C.XI, to the delight of Kevin Moody who saw all his hard work bear fruit. The *Chronicle* for Summer 1993 took the form of a special issue to commemorate twenty years of girls at Chis and Sid.

Early in September John Sennett's last Speech Day was held with, as guest of honour, Howard Davies, Director General of the C.B.I. and a former pupil of the Head's at Manchester Grammar. In his final speech Sennett attacked new Secretary of State John Patten for ignoring the advice of the professionals and persisting with a National Curriculum that was "too narrow and too heavy a burden on both pupils and staff." The process of testing hundreds of so-called "attainment targets" was, he added, "impossibly unwieldy."

A few weeks later the Headmaster was lucky to escape with just "a bruised hip and a few aches and pains" after his Peugeot 405 was struck by a speeding police car as he pulled out of the School gates into Hurst Road. That same October two new laboratories were opened, giving long overdue relief to the existing accommodation which had become totally inadequate for the number of pupils studying science. The year ended with a stirring performance of Beethoven's Second Symphony by the School Orchestra and an entertainment by the Dramatic Society entitled *The Seven Ages of Man*.

In January 1994 Maggie Lloyd began work as Accounts Officer, located on the ground floor of the New Building next to Commander Paine's office. In May Sir Edward Heath gave an amusing and informative speech to the Lower Sixth on the art of diplomacy. Speaking entirely without notes he recalled his encounters with many famous – and notorious – figures, including leading Nazis such as Himmler in Nuremburg shortly before the outbreak of the War.

July saw the retirement of Wyn Lewis, the Head of Biology, after a Chis and Sid career spanning 35 years. Appointed by Richard Pedley in 1959,

Quentin Blake's *Chronicle* cover, 1994 (retirement of John Sennett).

he learnt his trade under the illustrious Bill Freeman before diversifying into such areas as the A.T.C., which he commanded for some years, and the demanding pastoral role known as Head of Middle School. He was much involved with sport, in particular rugby, cricket and golf, besides being a key member of that powerful sub-sect of the Common Room referred to by some (though not unkindly) as the "Tafia". Another important figure to leave in the Summer of 1994 was Kenneth Tricker, School Librarian, English teacher and editor of the *Chronicle* since 1977. By training a classicist, Ken succeeded the famous Miss Stephenson in the former role and set about the demanding – and long overdue – task of updating and expanding the Library. The work included making the switch from the somewhat quaint "Cheltenham Ladies' College" classification method to the standard Dewey Decimal System. The impressive Library Ken Tricker left behind him stands as a permanent memorial to his labours. He was a quiet, modest, unfailingly courteous man and all were very sad to see him go. Mohindra Handa, the Economist, who retired after 16 years at the School, was born in India but moved to East Africa, becoming a lecturer at the University of Nairobi. During the persecutions of 1977 he brought his family to England. From 1978 to 1994 he made the daily trek to Sidcup from the Southall area, a prodigious achievement in itself given the many thousands of miles he must have covered by public transport. He, like Ken Tricker, was never one to push himself forward but his quiet dignity and self evident wisdom where anything financial was concerned gave him a unique cachet among his colleagues and earned the respect of those he taught. Among other staff to leave that Summer were Ian Wessels, Mike Hardyman and Angela O'Rourke.

July's issue of the *Chronicle* was distinguished for several reasons, principally the splendid cover illustration by Quentin Blake which featured a headmaster tripping gaily towards a setting sun, gown fluttering out behind him, discarded books and papers scattering in every direction. It also contained a piece by another famous Sedcopian, Will Hutton (at that time Economics Editor of the *Guardian*), in which he recalled his memories of Dick Pedley. This edition of the magazine, the 98th, was the last to be edited by Head of Art Cindy Smith.

By far the most important School event of 1994, of course, was the retirement of John Sennett after just over seventeen years as Headmaster, almost twice as long as his predecessor, Michael Brown. In his *Chronicle* tribute Graham Lightwood referred to the Head's "immense hard work" and "indefatigable support of the School," describing him as "a man of vision and high ideals … intensely caring, supportive and compassionate." Above all else, added the Deputy Head, "he has steered Chis and Sid through a long period of change the like of which secondary education in this country has never before experienced."

In his own valedictory remarks John Sennett wrote: "For every member of the School it is rather like being a runner in a never-ending relay race. One runs one's laps and hopes to hand the baton on, leaving those who will follow in a better position than when one started." When interviewed much later, he considered that his greatest satisfaction had been in pastoral work, helping, as he put it, "to sort out other people's problems behind the scenes," as well as "being able to help people to make things happen." Among his regrets was his failure to bring in the International Baccalaureate examination in place of "A" Level.

Unlike Brown's farewell party, Sennett's was held on a warm, sunny evening and the many guests spilled out onto the lawns at the front of the School, drinks in hand, before speeches began in the Hall. Speakers included Graham Lightwood, who compèred the proceedings, Les Pearson (representing Bexley's Education Department), Glynis Smith (Chairman of the Governors) and Martin Peacock (Chairman of the Parents' Association). Charles Wells, in lighter vein, expressed the feelings of the Staff, pointing out, among much else, that the Head had timed his departure very neatly with the School's first OFSTED inspection scheduled for October. The ominous date was just six weeks into the new term and new regime.

James Rouncefield (1994-2005)

CHAPTER TWELVE

Rouncefield and Renewal

THE ADVERTISEMENT FOR THE vacant headship that appeared in the *Times Educational Supplement* the previous September declared that the Governors were looking for someone who would "enhance the School's fine reputation." The successful candidate would be "a person with proven teaching and management skills" who would be given "an exceptional opportunity … to develop further a progressive grammar school whose hallmark is academic success and which also develops cultural and sporting talents to a high level."

The successful applicant for the post proved to be James Rouncefield, soon to be known universally as "Jim" which, in itself, marked a significant break with tradition, as did his preference for the title of "Head Teacher" rather than "Headmaster."

A complete lack of pomposity and a straightforward, down to earth, friendly demeanour quickly communicated themselves to staff and pupils alike. "I think that the head of a school is no more important than anyone else," Jim Rouncefield declared in an early *Chronicle* interview. It was not a sentiment that Mc.Gregor Williams or Richard Pedley would necessarily have embraced, although the former would have enthusiastically endorsed the new Head's view of the Hurst Road buildings and his determination to change the décor, furniture and fittings as quickly as possible. Indeed, a hands-on sort of man, he set about doing so in the Summer holiday before taking up the post officially. Two young teachers, Tony

217

Tipping and Myrna Trigg, calling into School on separate occasions that August, found him on his knees or up a ladder and mistook him for a carpet-layer or a painter/decorator.

Jim Rouncefield was born at Redruth, Cornwall, in 1951. He attended the local primary school where his father taught before moving to the Humphry Davy Grammar School, Penzance, where, by his own admission, he went through "a bad patch" in his middle years, on one occasion being caned for truancy. "I was heavily into surfing," he told one interviewer. "I spent most of my youth on the beaches of Cornwall." At about this time he first met Andrea Davison, a pupil at the girls' grammar school in Penzance. They married in 1973. Five years later their first child, John, was born and, in 1981, their daughter, Ellen. The incoming Head was a keen mountaineer and had spent many holidays climbing in the U.K. and in Europe. Long-distance walking and cycling, particularly in lonely places, were other favourite pastimes though in later years, of course, he found few opportunities to indulge them.

Rouncefield spent four years at Goldsmiths' College, University of London, graduating with a B.Sc. in Geography to which he later added an M.A. in Education from the Institute. His first teaching post was at the Roan School, Blackheath, where he became Head of Geography at the early age of 24. On the Roan's amalgamation with two other schools some five years later he was offered the job of leading the enlarged Geography Department but chose, instead, a move to Sydenham Girls' School, a huge, fifteen-form-entry comprehensive. He served as Head of Geography for five years under the guidance of Headmistress Yvonne Zackerwich whom, to this day, he regards as the most important influence on his career. Then followed two years' secondment to the I.L.E.A. as an advisory teacher before he obtained the Deputy Headship of the Bennett Memorial Diocesan Girls' School in Tunbridge Wells.

In 1989, aged 37, Jim Rouncefield was appointed to the headship of Chatham Grammar School for Boys. Despite inheriting falling rolls and the threat of closure he worked unstintingly to raise standards. His success in enhancing the School's reputation and, subsequently, increasing the roll in difficult circumstances, doubtless weighed heavily with the selection committee when he applied for the post at Chis and Sid. During his tenure of the Chatham headship Jim was always conscious of labouring in the shadow of Rochester Maths, a neighbouring school with a stronger intake and greater resources. How ironic, then, that his main competitor for the Sidcup post should turn out to be none other than Keith Williams, his opposite number at the rival school.

Rouncefield was delighted at being selected, having long admired Chis and Sid which he regarded as "prestigious", even "renowned." He felt that coming to the post as an existing head with a strong track record gave him the necessary "credibility" to implement the changes that he believed to be necessary if the School was to move forward and not stagnate on its laurels.

The first hurdle to be surmounted was the OFSTED inspection scheduled for mid-October. This, of course, placed far more pressure on the rest of the Staff than it did on the new Head Teacher since he could hardly be held responsible, after just six weeks, for any shortcomings the inspectors identified, though doubtless any praise that might be forthcoming would not be rejected out of hand.

There was much gathering together of "documentation" as it had been made clear that departments must have "policies" on everything imaginable and meticulous records were to be offered up for the inspectorate's scrutiny, together with extensive samples of pupils' work. In the event the OFSTED team were astonished at the sheer quantity of the latter which they received, two or three dozen students contriving to fill an entire room with bulging folders to the discomfiture of those whose task it was to sift through them and form a judgement of the standards that had been achieved.

The School was probably never quieter than during the week of the Inspection since nobody knew exactly when a besuited figure would sidle, with chilly smile, round a classroom door and "observe" proceedings from a chair at the back before scurrying away with a sheaf of freshly scribbled notes which would later be adduced in evidence.

At the end of school on the Friday before Half-Term, with pupils and Inspectorate both safely off the premises, the Staff let its collective hair down in a noisy "F-Ofsted" party held in the Library. The week's pent-up tensions dissipated themselves in a series of satirical sketches and ribald songs which had been written hurriedly for the purpose the previous night and which provoked a hilarity quite disproportionate to any merit they possessed but entirely understandable as a response to what was felt to have amounted, in certain cases at least, to a "going over" which the Gestapo might have blenched to behold.

The Head described the Report, when it arrived a few weeks later, as "generally favourable" although criticisms were, of course, made. The fabric and condition of the buildings came in for particular censure and the Inspectorate were clear that additional savings would have to be made from within the staffing budget if much needed improvements were to be made in this area. In response the Head and his deputies drew up what they called a "shadow staffing structure" which identified cost-cutting opportunities that could be implemented as more senior colleagues made way, in the natural course of events, for younger (and cheaper) replacements who might be required to take on greater responsibilities to justify their salary or to run a department for somewhat less remuneration than their predecessor in the post had enjoyed.

In September 1994 the new standard intake into Year Seven had been set at 192 which meant 32 children in every form. Well over half of these students were from outside the Borough. In the Sixth Form, Business Studies and P.E. were now available as "A" Level subjects and proving very popular. Among the new staff that term was the young historian Richard Guy, who contributed greatly to School cricket over the next seven years.

During the course of his first year in charge, the energetic new Head set about the task of making significant improvements to the School environment. A new reception area was created in the Foyer, for example, and the fencing in of grassed areas greatly reduced wear and tear.

At the end of term the actors and musicians as usual came into their own. Three one-act plays – *Streuth, The Real Inspector Hound* and *After Magritte* – were performed by the Dramatic Society under the direction of Steve Anderson. The first of these was taken to the Tunbridge Wells One-Act Play Festival a few weeks later by Gary Janks, assisted by Sixth-former Katie Morgan. This was a new venture for the School and, at the prize-giving ceremony, Mark Williams was highly commended. The Christmas Concert featured Sibelius' Karelia Suite, played by David Grubb's Symphony Orchestra, together with pieces by the Madrigal and Jazz Groups. Jack Fitzgerald, Sally Spittles and Claire Troth made notable contributions to the evening's success.

In a new venture, a group of Sixth-formers, led by Janet Ainsworth and co-ordinated by the Geography Department's Brendan Murphy, set up their own business company under the "Young Enterprise" scheme, producing clocks and plates which sold extremely well in the lead up to Christmas. The project earned front-page coverage in the local press. Another "first" was the Dance Club production of *Grease* which took place in May '95 under the direction of Nicola Rigby.

The season's sporting honours went to the Under 12 Netball Team, captained by Katy Clement, which lost only 5 of 36 matches and, in the Kent Finals, finished 5th out of around 100 schools. Chris Moss and David Head-Rapson competed in the All-England Schools Championships in the 800m and the 400m hurdles respectively, the former winning the Final in the stunning time of 1-52.2. Two years later Chris ran in the World Junior Championships. The Boys' Athletics Team won the North-West Kent Championships held at Norman Park on a scorching day in May. In the Summer the Rugby Club toured Canada where they acquitted themselves with distinction against demanding opposition and proved excellent ambassadors for both School and country.

The end of term saw the departure of David Taylor who, after six years in charge of Religious Studies, left to train for the Baptist ministry. He was replaced by Joy Hadwin who, in her six years in charge of the Department, won universal acclaim for her energy, commitment and good humour. Another to leave was Anne White who retired after 27 years of part-time teaching in the English Department. In her *Chronicle* reminiscences she recalled her interview, lasting all of three minutes, with the Head of English, John Walsh, which he conducted on the bench in the Foyer during morning break. When she joined the School in 1968, Eva Jackson and Dorothy Stephenson ("Steve") were the only other women on the Staff.

Staff and pupils returning for the start of the school year were shocked to hear that Rebecca Philpott had been killed in a car accident in France a few days earlier, together with her mother and sister. Rebecca would have entered the Sixth Form at the start of term. The death of Beryl Freeman, widow of Bill and tireless Secretary of the Old Sedcopians' Association, was announced the following month. A third death in 1995 was that of Keith Jenkins, a pupil from 1957 to 1964 and then a member of the French Department from 1970 to 1993. He was only 49. That Autumn the number of Chis and Sid students entering university topped one hundred for the first time in the history of the School.

Amid considerable controversy it was suddenly decided to allow the girls to wear white shirts and School ties if they so wished, though "going the whole hog" and letting them wear trousers as well (thereby bringing the two uniforms fully into line) was deemed to be a leap too far. In the event, however, few girls availed themselves of the opportunity and, before long, the idea fell quietly into abeyance.

The musicians, as always, were busy during 1995, with performances from the various jazz groups, the Chamber Orchestra, the Choir, the Symphony Orchestra and the Grubbettes. Among the music performed one might single out Mozart's Flute and Horn Concertos in G and E flat, respectively; Brahms' Variations on a theme of Haydn and Haydn's own "London" symphony. Among the numerous performers involved, mention should be made of drummer David Pack, pianist David Eaton, violinist David Eades, vocalist Claire Troth and saxophonist Malcolm Paterson who would later join the band of the Coldstream Guards. The range and quality of the School's music at this period was a remarkable tribute to the skills of the three men who principally inspired it: David Grubb, Will Michael and Jeremy Laing. Very few schools can have boasted a stronger team.

A second dance production, *Cats*, again directed by Nicola Rigby, built on the success of the previous year and played to packed, enthusiastic audiences. The Autumn Term ended with the traditional School Play, the third staging of *A Midsummer Night's Dream* in twenty years and Steve Anderson's second full-scale Shakespeare production. An ambitious lighting plan by Paul Anning, making full use of the new, state-of-the-art lighting board, made a major contribution to the success of the three evenings, as did James Browne's portrayal of Bottom and Lisa Short's imperious Titania. Some seven years have now elapsed since this production which, at the time of writing, remains the last Shakespeare play to be performed at the School. It may be that it is no longer possible to mount productions on such a scale given the innumerable pressures upon the time of both staff and students, not least among them the public examinations which have proliferated in recent years, following each other thick and fast through the calendar. The fact remains, nevertheless, that seven years is by far the longest stretch without a Shakespeare play upon the Chis and Sid stage (if one excludes extracts and compilations) since that first production of *Henry V* back in 1943 and many hope that the next will be forthcoming before too long.

The 1996 edition of the *Chronicle*, edited by Danielle O'Connor, ran to 88 (heavily illustrated) A4 pages, making it the longest such publication to date. Unfortunately the practice of numbering each edition consecutively had fallen into abeyance some years earlier and, in consequence, it passed unnoticed that Amanda Darton-Bigg's issue for the following year was, in fact, the one hundredth which would surely have been a cause for celebration. Remarkably, in all that time, not a single edition failed to appear, even during the grimmest years of World War Two.

By the mid 1990s one highly significant trend had become steadily more apparent. In earlier decades a new member of the teaching staff would, in all probability, remain at the School for a considerable number of years. The two dozen or so who were appointed during the 1930s, for example, went on to average over 21 years of service each and only two of them stayed for fewer than eight. Of the 14 appointees who arrived in September 1997, however – the number being itself, probably, a record – only four of them (Claire Thomas, Christopher Wooll, John Greenwood and Carole Hazelgrove) still remained just five years later. The other ten averaged about 2½ years each before moving to posts elsewhere. Problems of recruitment and retention in the teaching profession are, of course, a modern phenomenon and the loss of continuity entailed is doubtless no worse at Chis and Sid than elsewhere. The cost of housing in the locality is a significant factor, particularly for those at the lower end of the salary scale. Even more worrying is the increasing tendency for young teachers to leave the profession altogether after a few years in the classroom. Paul Wilsdon, James Rees and Fiona Tucker are cases in point, all three switching careers in July 2000 and (one imagines) taking up work which is less stressful and better paid.

The second year of Jim Rouncefield's regime saw his determined onslaught upon the fabric of the School gather further momentum. The entire Hurst Road frontage of the main building was repainted, together with the staircases and corridors of the New Block. A third computer room was equipped which meant that the rooms formerly known as 22, 23 and 11 were now networked together. The large and airy Room 13, long a favourite, was colonised for the same purpose. By 1996 there were more than 150 computers in the School, a startling proliferation over just two decades. The Lecture Theatre – which had, in fact, been rarely used as such – was converted into a much needed Drama Studio in recognition of Drama's popularity as a G.C.S.E. subject along with Theatre Studies at "A" Level.

That Summer's G.C.S.E. results were the best ever, with 98% of candidates gaining five or more passes at grades A*-C. Kaj Rucinski passed all ten of his subjects with grades A* or A. Ben Burston, too, deserves mention for achieving A grades in all four of his "A" Level subjects. Two other Sixth-formers, Geoffrey Howie and Richard Lane, distinguished themselves by winning gold medals in the British Physics Olympiad, the former finishing ninth out of 700 entrants, one of only three students from state schools to reach the last 16. He went with Brian Burgess to a ceremony at the Royal Society where he received his prize from the Astronomer Royal.

Among the more unusual events of 1996 was a four day visit to the Lake District by a group of "A" Level English students studying the poetry of William Wordsworth. It was led by Gary Janks and Christine Head-Rapson who were, on the train back, mistaken for a married couple with nine rather large teenage children.

In September, for every new Year Seven pupil who duly appeared, resplendent in fresh purple blazer, another somewhere else was disappointed. There had, that Spring, been 382 first choice applicants for the 192 available places, a remarkable increase of 46% on the previous year's figures. To one of these nervous newcomers, Carly Smith, fell the distinction of being the School's 10,000th pupil, though, oddly, it seems that nobody thought to point this out to her and she left at the end of Year Eleven none the wiser, apparently. At the time of writing, the admissions register has reached 11,252. Miss Linda Lamthong and Mr Michael Carreck D.F.C. thus stand as book-ends to eleven and a quarter thousand assorted Sedcopians. The latter, of course, holds this role in perpetuity. The former, by the time these words are read, will already have passed hers on to the brief custodianship of someone else.

One of the first milestones of Jim Rouncefield's headship was the new Sixth Form Centre which opened in October 1996 at a cost of around £100,000. The Parents' Association raised £20,000 for the Centre's furniture and fittings. Situated adjacent to the Library Extension, the new building consisted of a study area, a social area and a teaching classroom together with a number of offices and interview rooms.

Another innovation during 1996 was the establishment of an "Explorers' Club" for the purpose of extending gifted students. Run, initially, by James Rees, the Club, in its early days, organised trips to the Tate Gallery, the Royal Institution, Guy's Hospital, Chislehurst Caves and the Natural History Museum as well as an "activities" weekend in Devon. The year also brought another staff marriage. Jeremy Laing and Louise Lee, after their wedding in Scotland, left for a new career in Qatar. Nicola Rigby also left for foreign adventures, Turkey and Indonesia holding for her, apparently, an allure with which Sidcup was no longer able to vie.

The Girls' P.E. Department passed to the incoming Donna Berry, assisted by another new teacher, the cricketing Kelly Mearns.

The School's talented musicians added Mendelssohn's "Italian" symphony, Ponchielli's "Dance of the Hours" and a Mozart "Divertimento", amongst much else, to their repertoire during the course of the year, the latter to the accompaniment of newcomer Christopher Wooll at the harpsichord. Daniel Eades led the Orchestra with his customary aplomb. A compilation of pieces exploring "the various colours, shades and moods of love", entitled *Love Is...* and played in front of an enormous pair of glowing red lips was the Dramatic Society's Christmas offering. Kaj Rucinski and James Browne led a strong cast and showed why they had both been selected for the prestigious National Youth Theatre.

The following year, 1997, was memorable for a number of major sporting achievements. A Chis and Sid ski-ing team competed in the Kent Schools' Championships at Chatham for the first time, Ben Clark winning the Under 14 slalom competition. The Under 19 team, consisting of Ben Clark, Sophie Clark, Peter Cruise and Catrin Alderman, then entered the English Schools' Championships in Derby and astonished everybody, not least themselves, by finishing in second place. Ski-ing holidays in Bulgaria and Canada completed an eventful year for those who preferred their descent of slippery slopes to be of the literal rather than the metaphorical kind. The Rugby 1st XV, superbly led by Fraser Hanks, enjoyed their best season for some years. Noel Horrobin hailed 1997–8 as a turning point in the fortunes of the Club which had been on the wane in recent times. The performance in the Rosslyn Park National VIIs, where the team reached the semi-final stage, was a particular cause for celebration. The hockey players, not to be outdone, also enjoyed a successful season. The Under 16 XI did especially well, finishing runners up in the Kent County Championships held at Canterbury, thanks in no small measure to a series of outstanding performances by the aptly named Dawn Shields in goal.

Will Michael's Jazz Concert was, as always, rapturously received. Malcolm Paterson, David Pack, Daniel Eades, Edward Dibble, Kate Trodd and William Johnson were all making their final appearances and determined to go out on a high note which they indeed contrived to do. The musical highlight of the year, however, was undoubtedly the performance, at Easter, of Beethoven's 5th Symphony, thus fulfilling one of David Grubb's lifetime ambitions.

Another landmark was reached with the 25th Junior Play Festival, instituted by Robert Solbé in 1972. Pride of place went to the hilarious Shakespeare parody *Julius and Cleopatra*,a collaboration between 9T and 9W directed by Grace Hosier. It was through this event that literally thousands of children had their first experience of "serious" acting on a "proper" stage and in front (very often) of a packed, enthusiastic house. For many it proved to be the gateway to a lifetime's enjoyment of live theatre as performers, as backstage technicians or simply as audience. In several instances it sowed the seeds of an entire career as, notably, in the case of Nick Starr, referred to later.

The programme of improvements to the School environment which characterised the new headship continued in 1997 with the installation of a steel perimeter fence from the West Field entrance to the cricket nets on the East Field. The Hall received a long overdue refurbishment and computers were installed in the Library for the first time, to the misgivings of the more luddite literati. The old Sixth Form Centre was redesignated the headquarters of the Economics and Business Studies Department.

The General Election of May 1st 1997 brought to an end eighteen years of Tory rule but the School's mock election was, as always, won by the Conservatives. Their majority of 113, however, was by far the lowest in the history of such events and, for the first time, the Labour Party pushed the Liberals/Liberal Democrats into third place. Even so, it is an interesting comment on attitudes in Hurst Road that, despite a Labour majority of 179 on the national stage, the Party could still not muster even a quarter of the votes from around the School. No hot bed of revolution, Chis and Sid, that much is for sure.

The Charity Committee, led by Mike Ashby and Gary Janks, was particularly active during 1997. Links were established with Imizamo Yethu Secondary School and Velaphi High School in South Africa and several thousand pounds raised to help them restore their damaged premises. Further sums were collected for Crisis, which helped to shelter the homeless in the U.K.; for the child victims of the Chernobyl nuclear disaster and for the Greater London Fund for the Blind. Over 300 shoe boxes full of gifts were sent to children's homes in Romania. Carol Geren's Sixth Form volunteers continued their excellent work with the children at nearby Marlborough Special School.

Again, as two years earlier, the start of the new academic year brought dreadful news. The School learnt that Matthew Bowden, who was to have entered the Sixth Form, had died in a railway line accident during August.

Martyn Berry retired in the Summer after 35 years at Chis and Sid. He was Head of Chemistry from 1967 to 1982 and joint Head of Sixth Form from 1976 to 1996. Only seven people have served the School for a longer time. To do justice to so illustrious a career would demand far more space than is available here. Martyn flung himself into everything he did with enormous enthusiasm and devoted a huge proportion of what would otherwise have been his spare time to the service of School sport, notably the Second XI Cricket Team which he ran for over thirty years. Table Tennis was another of his passions and also Rugby in his younger days. He was a keen walker and mountaineer and communicated his love of wide open spaces to many of those he taught. One of his publications was an anthology of mountain poems entitled *Speak to the Hills*. A favourite anecdote concerned an incident which occurred during his first term at the School. His Head of Department, the famous George Goddard, showed him the words "I hate Berry" which he had found scratched on a laboratory bench. Shocked, the young Chemist expected to be hauled over the

Martyn Berry in 1963.

coals but, to his astonishment, Goddard patted him on the back and said, "Well done!" Boys, to his mind, were best taught by a combination of what he termed "repression" and "repetition." Berry's encyclopaedic knowledge was legendary in the Staff Common Room and he was usually the first court of appeal when a dispute needed to be settled or a crossword clue went unsolved. After a year's part-time teaching, Martyn Berry turned his attentions to his numerous other interests, for example his work on the analysis of pigments at the National Gallery.

Another who finally retired after a lengthy career at the School was Ann Clifford who, as Ann Nex, joined the Mathematics Department in 1961. Further details about her appeared in Chapter Seven but one reminiscence from the *Sedcopian* is worth adding here. Referring to the early sixties Ann recalled: "The quality of Common Room life has lost much of its graciousness with the passing of time. We used to have coffee and tea served to us at Break from a trolley, tea in the Dining Hall after school each day and sustenance provided, when on detention duty, in the form of boiled egg and soldiers served on a tray laid with a cloth."

Others to leave at this point included Shirley Puxty, Myrna Trigg, Claire Jones and Samuel Pam. Linda Martin ended her second spell as a member of the Home Economics Department which she had first joined in 1975. Alastair Wilson's spell of part-time teaching came to an end and he finally severed, formally at least, a connection with the School that had lasted forty years. In October, Commander Paine resigned as Finance and Premises Manager, the post thereupon being divided in two. Anthony Sullivan arrived to take the role of Premises Manager and Maggie Lloyd was promoted to the new post of Finance Office Manager with responsibility for a budget in the region of £3.5m. Among new staff joining the School in September 1997 were two Mathematicians, Deborah Warren and Daniel Lee. Maggie Unwin became a full-time member of the German Department after seven years of part-time teaching during which she had introduced a highly popular and successful G.C.S.E. Italian course for Sixth-formers. Three years later she took over the Department on the resignation of Henning Fischer.

In the Summer examinations six students – Edward Dibble, Meeta Durve, Catherine Heyward, Geoffrey Howie, Qurban Khan and Richard Lane – performed the impressive feat of gaining four grade A passes at "A" Level. Almost 50% of passes at this level were at grades A or B. In the G.C.S.E. examination Catrin Alderman passed ten subjects with grade A* or A.

The following year was the most successful for a very long time on the sports field. Among the innovations was a mixed hockey team, led by the inspirational Karen Carr, which won three of the four matches played. The Senior Netball Team, captained by Amy Harrison, suffered only one defeat and the Cricket 1st XI, led by Rob Grummitt, lost only two of its twelve fixtures, Neil Dickerson contributing a magnificent 136 not out against the XL Club. At the Nationals the Senior Rugby VII recorded three victories and lost to the powerful Ampleforth by the narrowest of margins. The Girls' Rugby Team, fielded a side in the national VIIs for the first time. Led, again, by Amy Harrison they achieved a notable victory over Epsom College. In the Bexley Athletic Championships the School enjoyed its best ever performance, five of the six trophies being won. Kate Wright represented Kent at junior level in both Netball and Hockey.

Work began in October 1998 on the extension and redevelopment of the Music Block and a Tannoy system was installed in an effort to disseminate important information more efficiently across the scattered buildings that made up the School site. Although the pupils were unable to switch off the equipment they could, of course, switch themselves off and, once the novelty had subsided, contrived to ignore the word from on high as blithely as school children have always managed to do. Despite initial misgivings, interruptions to lessons themselves were pretty rare.

The Music Department's tour of Italy, led by David Grubb and Pauline Matkins, was greatly enjoyed. Amongst the highlights were a performance by the Grubbettes in St Mark's Cathedral, Venice and a memorable *Aida* in the famous Verona Amphitheatre. *Billy Liar*, the Christmas Play, directed by Steve Anderson, was, by common consent, the best for years. Alex Pudney, in the lead role, Jon Rowswell as Billy's father and Catrin Alderman as "Gran" were all outstanding. Helen Stawski, Sarah Flannery, Julia Smith, Lauren Stone and Ovishek Roy completed an exceptionally strong cast. Andrew Wilson directed his first dance production, *Rock Around the Clock*, with a cast of sixty girls chosen from over one hundred who auditioned.

In the Summer's G.C.S.E. examinations Deepak Kaur Hora passed all nine of her subjects with A* grades. She was the first Chis and Sid student to achieve such a feat and, given that only a tiny percentage of candidates are awarded a starred A, her performance ranks alongside any recorded during the so-called "golden years" of the sixties and seventies. Two years later Deepak achieved four grade A passes at "A" Level and went on to read Medicine at Imperial College. Eleven departments gained 100% pass-rates at "A" Level in 1998 and of the 35 successful candidates in Chemistry 20 passed at grade "A".

There was unhappy news too, however, since the deaths of Raymond Pope and Bill Hamblen were recorded, two men who, in their very different spheres, contributed greatly to the well-being of the School over many years, as detailed earlier in these pages.

Among the departures in July, pride of place must go to Garth Pinkney who retired after 32 years as Head of Economics. A native of Sunderland and a graduate of St John's College, Cambridge, Garth was in charge of Athletics for many years and was virtually synonymous with Cross-Country

Running throughout his time at Chis and Sid. He was also a keen skier and led many Winter trips abroad. In his valedictory reminiscences in the *Sedcopian* Garth took particular pleasure in recalling his most successful "A" Level student, Will Hutton, and the achievements of four notable middle-distance runners that he coached, all of whom became English (or British) Schools Champions: Paul Williams, John Sewell, Steve Garrett and Chris Moss.

Other members of staff to leave in 1998 included Naoufel Ben Fredj, Marilyn Stevens and Carol Geren. The latter gave an unusual reason for settling in England – her love of rain. "For someone born and raised in sunny California, who then spent much of her working life in the Sahara Desert, rain is very welcome."

In September the new staff arrivals included Diane Hill, returning for her second spell at Chis and Sid, this time as Head of Sixth Form. Katherine Fey, a graduate of Merton College, Oxford, took over Garth Pinkney's Economics Department (now expanded to include Business Studies) and Adrian Taurins arrived to assist her. Shelley Paterson, a former pupil of the School, joined to teach Modern Languages and Marelle Valentine, a Scot, came to teach Religious Studies. An important innovation was the appointment of the first full-time, non-teaching Librarian, Melanie Fisher.

Perhaps the key event of 1999 was the second OFSTED inspection which took place in February. In comparison with the experiences of four years previously, this was a slightly more relaxed affair although, naturally, everyone was on their best behaviour and a taut, edgy atmosphere prevailed. This time there was less emphasis on huge quantities of "documentation" (much of it pretty meaningless) and more concern with what was actually taking place in the classroom. The Inspectors' report was glowing. "C.S.G.S. is a very successful and high-achieving school with a great many strengths and few weaknesses." There was praise for the examination results and for pupils' positive attitudes towards their work. The report spoke of the "excellent range of extra-curricular activities" and the "high quality leadership provided by the Head." Of the lessons observed, 70% were adjudged "good, very good or outstanding" and the Inspectorate detected "noticeable improvements since 1994." The behaviour of pupils around the School was described as "outstanding", a considerable tribute when one bears in mind that some 1300 students were squeezing into corridors and staircases designed for half that number.

James Hanks won an England Under 16 Rugby cap, the first success at this level for the School since the 1980s. Peter Grayson was selected for Kent, for London and for S.E.England. Michael Pape was chosen as 1st XV Player of the Year. The Senior Hockey Team, led by county player Lucy Shepherd, lost only one of its six matches in season 1999/2000. The Netball teams did even better, the Under 14s, captained by Kate Wright, losing only two of twenty fixtures and Stephanie Ashwin's U13A team losing only one of fifteen and winning the Bexley Tournament with eight victories out of eight.

Andrew Wilson's dancers, led by Ursula Black, put on an exciting production entitled *Lost in Music*. Paul Anning's lighting crew again excelled themselves. In March twenty or so members of staff made fools of themselves on the stage in aid of African famine relief. This performance was called "Teachers' Karaoke", a not inappropriate title given that the latter word means "empty orchestra" in Japanese. One wonders what Cedric Morley would have made of it all.

Talk of orchestras leads naturally on to the Christmas Concert, 1999, at which the School Orchestra, led by Celal Kazim, performed part of Mozart's Symphony no. 38. The second half of the evening was given over to Will Michael and his jazz groups which, as usual, drew much foot-stamping and applause from a packed Hall. The re-built Music Block was formally opened on December 13th, the roof having finally, after initial reluctance, been made to fit the building on which it perched. The Mayor of Bexley unveiled a plaque, wine was drunk and the musicians themselves gave forth with solo performances from Sam Lathey and Simon Desbruslais (both trumpet), Kirsten Schulz (saxophone) and Rebecca Bright (flute).

To honour the nation's recently elected "Man of the Millennium" the Dramatic Society, directed by Steve Anderson, staged an entertainment entitled *Shakespeare's Dome*, the poster for which ingeniously linked the dramatist's famous high forehead and the notorious edifice recently erected in Greenwich, at great expense, a few miles up the road. Highlights included a witty sketch featuring Othello being interviewed by Oscar Wilde's Lady Bracknell masquerading as Desdemona's mother, "Lady Brabantia." "A sandbag?!" she cried, incredulously, when the General described what had gone into the fortifications he had hurriedly erected in the face of the Turkish threat. Ben Barclay looked extremely fetching as Thisby in a little black cocktail dress but the acknowledged star performer was Ovishek Roy.

In the Summer's G.C.S.E. examinations no fewer than 17 students obtained A* or A grades in each of their nine subjects and, at "A" Level, Robert Percival got A grades in all four of his.

On December 18th another staff marriage took place, the fifth such liaison between serving teachers at the School. Tony Tipping (P.E.) married Claire Thomas (Modern Languages) at All Saints Church, Footscray, Chris Wooll playing Widor's Toccata and Fugue in D minor as the bridal party processed up the aisle.

At the end of the Summer Term, 1999, Brian Burgess retired after 37 years at Chis and Sid, the last 22 of them as Head of Physics. In his valedictory piece in the *Chronicle* he wrote as follows: "Since 1962 the School has almost totally absorbed my every waking moment, and many of my sleeping ones as well." This is surely no exaggeration and it is hard to believe that any member of staff in the School's entire history showed more wholehearted commitment to its pupils than he did, or, for that matter, a more friendly and cheerful face to all he met. Much has been written about him already in these pages. He will be remembered for many things, most particularly, perhaps, for his huge engagement with cricket as player, as coach, as umpire, as organiser and as record-keeper par excellence. Brian's great gift for meticulous organisation underpinned everything he did, whether it was planning Physics syllabuses, stage sets, staff cricket tours of the West Country or holidays for the pupils in the U.S.A. For 35 years Burgess produced the School Timetable, a prodigious feat and one which grew more fiendishly difficult with every passing Summer. He was, for many years, a Governor and a key member of the P.A., taking particular pleasure in organising the Quiz Evenings that were always so much enjoyed. In earlier days he ran the Photographic and Philatelic Societies and once calculated that he had represented the Staff against the School at seven sports: cricket, badminton, squash, table tennis, chess, bridge and ten-pin bowling. The

Brian Burgess 1962–1999.

brother-in-law of another senior teacher, Bob Buxton, Head of Mathematics, Brian retired with a great stock of memories and anecdotes, particularly stories arising from his fifteen years working alongside Cedric Morley. He left, he said, with only two regrets: the poor state of the once near perfect cricket square and the great reduction in the number of those choosing to study "A" Level Physics.

Another long-serving member of staff to leave in 1999 was Stuart Cunningham who had joined the School as a young Scottish émigré in 1975. Although he came to teach Mathematics, he will be remembered, primarily, for establishing computing in the School and fostering its development from its inception at the start of the 1980s to its central position both as a teaching department and as an essential administrative tool by the time he left to become the Advisory Teacher for I.C.T. in the Borough. His prowess on the football pitch and the ski-slopes will be remembered too. The role of School I.C.T. Co-ordinator passed to Dominic Russan.

Head of Art Rachael Richardson left to teach in a school for autistic children and her departmental colleague, Andrea Lockheart, transferred to Judd. Christine Head-Rapson moved to Eltham College after twelve years teaching Physics (for many of them as a Governor, too) and Daniel Keep left after seven years in charge of Technology. Sarah Walsh – another in that long line of Chis and Sid Welsh, and a fluent speaker of the language – went to Bexley Grammar School to be Deputy Head of Mathematics.

Incoming staff in September included Sue Bishop as Head of Art and John Farrall, who assumed the somewhat odd title "Head of Resistant Materials and Graphics". No doubt many of his colleagues felt that "resistant material" was something that they encountered in their classrooms all too often. Eddie Powell arrived to teach Information Technology and Computing, Simon McNaught joined the Modern Linguists and Peter Bleach the Historians. Brian Burgess' longstanding role as Head of Physics passed to Vicky Parton who became only the third incumbent in almost seventy years. She moved on again, however, after just three more had elapsed.

The start of the following year occasioned great excitement since, to the mathematically challenged at least, it marked the beginning of a new millennium. What was undeniable was that it was the first year since 299 to begin with the figure two and, for most, that seemed reason enough for celebration. What was equally undeniable, if rather less widely remarked upon, was the fact that the 103rd edition of the *Chronicle* was the first since 1976 to carry the School colour on its cover.

The closure of the top floor of the New Block during the fitting of a new pitched roof to replace the worn-out flat one caused considerable difficulty. Classes were crammed into every available space around the remainder of the premises. The building had been fraught with problems ever since its erection, on the cheap, in 1975 and some claimed to have heard the rattle of skeletons flying home to roost. Two further improvements to the site saw the removal of the last "mobile" classrooms (huts) from the West Field and the completion of the steel perimeter fence, with the virtual elimination, as a consequence, of the trespass and vandalism that had been prevalent for so long. Thanks to the munificence of the Parents' Association the School Library was endowed with twenty P.C.s. Librarian Melanie Fisher left in July. Though in post for less than two years she brought about, during that time, a major overhaul of the stock. Her successor was Sharon Bradford who continued the process of modernisation and renewal.

There were many other changes of personnel during the year 2000. Charles Wells (the present writer) retired after a quarter of a century as Head of English. In his valedictory remarks he took particular satisfaction in the reflection that he had made over 250 appearances for the Staff Cricket XI, most of them as wicket-keeper – the fourth in an unbroken line of succession back through Bob Buxton, Bill Hamblen and Cedric Morley to the Second World War. He recalled with pleasure the Shakespeare Marathon of 1983, his production of *Romeo and Juliet* nine years later and an entirely unexpected invitation to meet the Queen at Buckingham Palace in his final term. The next two years he devoted largely to the writing of the book which you are (presumably) holding now. The English Department passed into the safe hands of John Hazelgrove who had joined the Staff in 1981 as its second-in-command, though latterly he had been a Head of Year. Another to leave the School in 2000 was Henning Fischer, who had been Head of German since 1984. Eluned (Lynne) Hughes retired after 15 years of dedicated service to the French Department and to the youngest pupils in her Head of Year role. Steve Gooden left the Chemistry Department unexpectedly after 28 years during which he had made a major impact not only in his laboratory but also on the sports field, in Christian circles and in charitable undertakings. Andrew Wilson (P.E.) and Jo Petley (Biology) gained promotions and moved on. Donna

Berry moved to a post at a special school in Maidstone and the Girls' P.E. Department was taken over by Emma Reynolds, the seventh holder of that office since Joyce Crust relinquished it in 1987. Assistant secretary Mavis Beedle left the School after 25 years of cheerful and dedicated service, almost certainly the longest career of any member of the non-teaching staff.

Among the newcomers in September 2000 were Jean Hitchcock as Second in the English Department, Martin Davey as History teacher and Head of Year Eight, and Richard Wallbridge who, fresh from three years' teaching in Japan, joined the P.E. Department and took charge of cricket. Clive Madel, an Old Sedcopian, joined the Classicists. Mike Rushton was promoted to Assistant Head Teacher with particular responsibility for staff development, training and performance management.

A major change to the Sixth Form curriculum was introduced in September when preparations began for the new A.S. examinations. Students chose five subjects on which they would be examined a year later after which they would pursue three of them for a further year when they would sit yet more exams, to be known as "A2s". Whatever the merits of this new system – and it was heavily criticised by staff and students alike – one thing was certain. The scope for extra-curricular activities was still further constrained. Jim Rouncefield observed: "What is clear is that we are rapidly moving towards a situation within the English education system where we are testing to oblivion and increasing the pressure on staff and pupils constantly to perform, often to the detriment of wider educational opportunities."

In that Summer's G.C.S.E. examinations Amy Oliver achieved ten passes (twelve if one includes two so-called "short courses") all at grade A* or A. Disappointingly, however, for the first time in fifty years, no Chis and Sid candidate gained admission to either Oxford or Cambridge Universities. This dip, however, was temporary since, the following year, three such places were gained. Christopher Bunce went up to Trinity College, Cambridge to read Theology; Glyn Salton-Cox to King's College, Cambridge to read English and Fatima Maktari to Somerville College, Oxford to read Chemistry, bringing the total of such "Oxbridge" places to 370 since Walter Smith took up the first of them, at Pembroke College, Cambridge in 1945. For the benefit of anyone interested in this matter, but not possessed of a calculator, this averages out at nearly seven such admissions per year since the first at the end of the War.

The year's major sporting honours fell largely to the girls. Jo O'Sullivan gained an international Rugby cap at Under 18 level – a memorable "first" in School history, of course. The girls' Under 18 team which she led reached the semi-finals of the National Sevens at Rosslyn Park. Sharon Oakes became national Senior Girls champion in the Triple Jump and was selected for Northern Ireland. The girls' Under 14 and Under 15 Rounders teams both won both the Bexley and the Bromley tournaments. In what must surely rank as the most stunning spell of bowling in School 1st XI history, leg-spinner Mark Willoughby took six wickets in eight balls, conceding not a single run in the process. BETHS, who must have wondered what had hit them, went suddenly from 148 for 4 to 148 all out. In that year's Winter Olympics, Old Sedcopian Steve Harrison represented New Zealand in the four-man bob-sleigh event. They crashed, admittedly, but it was another "first" for Chis and Sid.

The year's musical highlights included Glyn Salton-Cox's playing of the second movement of Mozart's Piano Concerto No.20 and Chris Wooll's production of Purcell's *Dido and Aeneas*, the lead roles being sung by Nicola Moore and Simon Desbruslais.

The actual first year of the new millennium, 2001, was notable for more outstanding sporting achievements. Peter Grayson, one of the best 1st XV Rugby captains in recent times, was an England trialist for his age-group and, apparently, unlucky not to be selected for the squad. The first official Chis and Sid Soccer Team for almost fifty years was formed from an enthusiastic group of Under 13 girls by new P.E. teacher Naomi Connor, herself a player with Charlton Ladies. The new team, captained by Hannah Riddock, competed in the London Schools Coca-Cola Cup and won their group. They also reached the semi-final of the Charlton Athletic girls' six-a-side tournament. The Senior Netball Team, captained by the engaging Emma Howes, had a successful season, finishing mid-table in the Whiteoak Women's Netball League – a considerable achievement given that they were competing against adult sides. Ben Clark became the World Junior Dry Slope Slalom Champion and a member of the Great Britain Junior Team, setting, in the process, another precedent for the School.

The longest serving member of staff to leave in 2001 was David Chandler who retired at Christmas after almost 27 years at Chis and Sid as Head of Classics. Under his leadership the Department taught not only Latin but also Greek and Classical Civilisation, achieving outstanding

Under 13 Girls' Soccer Squad, 2001, with coach Naomi Connor.

results in all three. Additionally, David devoted much of his free time to teaching Archaeology. There was student involvement in digs and many went on trips to archaeological sites in England and abroad. One of the true scholars on the Staff, David Chandler devoted himself, uncompromisingly, to the maintenance of the highest standards and the fact that so many of his former students kept in touch in later years was testimony to the respect in which he was held. His replacement as Head of Classics was Joanne Gray.

Valerie George, the Physicist, retired after 15 years of sterling service, her blunt, common sense approach and concern for her pupils winning her many friends who were sad to see her go. Pauline Matkins (Maths and Physics), one of the first girls to join the School in 1973, left teaching altogether after 14 years on the Staff, making 21 years in total at Chis and Sid. Another to leave the profession was Joy Hadwin after six years as Head of R.S. – a great loss to teaching as a whole as well as to the School. Marelle Valentine was promoted to her position. David Grubb, Head of Music, was another former pupil to leave the staff in 2001, moving on to a similar role at Blackheath High. He had been a byword for enthusiasm and commitment during his twelve years in post and the quality of the music produced under his leadership has rarely, if ever, been surpassed at the School. Richard Guy gained a well-merited promotion to be Head of History at Judd and moved on after seven years. Dan Lee (Mathematics) and Shelley Paterson (Modern Languages) – the latter the third Old Sedcopian to leave the Staff that year – married and went to teach in Tanzania. Dominic Russan moved to a school in the Potteries after nine years at Chis and Sid during which time he made a valuable contribution in such areas as D.T., computing and sport. Eddie Powell took over as Head of I.C.T. and Simon McNaught became the Head of Year Ten.

Following the success of *Dido and Aeneas*, Chris Wooll and the Music Department staged John Blow's early opera *Venus and Adonis*. The leading roles were sung by Claire Troth (making a welcome return after taking her degree at the Northern College of Music) and Tom Stoddart whose versatility was becoming something of a legend. The Madrigal Group sang a double choir piece by J.C.Bach at the National Music Festival and the three Music teachers led a tour of Italy which included a performance in no less a venue than St Peter's, Rome.

"Dance Odyssey 2001" was directed by Emma Reynolds with assistance from Richard Wallbridge and Paul Anning, who produced the spectacular light show that had come to be expected of him. Ursula Black and Debbie Mullooly led the dancers, who included several boys for the first time.

The year's saddest event was undoubtedly the death of Richard Atkinson in March. A moving celebration of his life was held in the School Hall following his funeral in Eltham during which his coffin was carried by close friends from Year Eleven.

The Summer's examination results brought cause for considerable satisfaction in both Years Eleven and Thirteen. No fewer than 11% of G.C.S.E. passes were achieved at A*, by far the highest proportion obtained by the School to date and, at "A" Level, half of all passes were at grades A or B, a remarkable achievement when one bears in mind that the pass grades range from A to E.

In February 2002 Tony Arlidge Q.C., a pupil at the School from 1948 to 1956, organised a 400th anniversary performance of *Twelfth Night* in the Middle Temple Hall. In the audience were Prince Charles, Camilla Parker-Bowles and Bill Bray, editor of the *Sedcopian*. Forty-nine years prev-

Performing a madrigal, 2001 (L to R: Stephen Wickenden, Bradley Collins, Chris Wooll).

iously, Arlidge had played the title role in the School's production of *Henry Vth*, as mentioned in Chapter Six. He had, for some years, been Master of Entertainments in the Middle Temple and recently wrote a book entitled *Shakespeare and the Prince of Love*.

After a quiet spell, actors returned to the School stage in April with Maya Tse's *An Evening of Drama* which, perhaps uniquely, included pupils from all seven years. Among the highlights were extracts from *The Real Inspector Hound* and *The Crucible*. Another terpsichorean production – "Addicted to Dance" – again featuring several boys among the hordes of girls, took place in the Spring and, at Easter, Clive Madel led a Classics Department trip to Pompeii and Herculaneum, the first such visit for a number of years.

Anther memorable happening during the early months of 2002 was the achievement of two Chis and Sid students, Seemin Morshed and Adam Holbrook, in winning awards in a prestigious competition, "Working with Resources", run by the Tate Modern and the Clore Foundation. Each received a signed, limited edition print by Anish Kapoor worth about £2,000. The School, in fact, took two of the fifteen awards on offer, a success all the more remarkable given that there were

55,000 entries in all. The prizes were presented in a ceremony at the Tate Modern in June, the two sculptures concerned – "Junk Metal" and "Bulb Man" – then going on display at the Gallery over the Summer months before touring the country. Sue Bishop's Art Department had cause to feel very proud.

More pride was felt, particularly by older members of staff, when news came through that Nick Starr, a pupil from 1969 to 1976, had been appointed Executive Director of the National Theatre, a position he took up in June 2002.

At Easter, Barbara Brown retired after some sixteen years of teaching English. Her professionalism and her devotion to her charges were unsurpassed and she was held in respect and affection by colleagues and pupils alike. Unusually in mixed schools, English at Chis and Sid has tended to be a male-dominated department. Barbara did much to redress this balance and her going left a gap which is difficult to fill.

In July, Dennis Charman became Chairman of the Governors in succession to Graham Holland. He had become a Parent Governor in 1990 and, over the next decade or so, his three daughters, Helen, Sarah and Alice, all attended the School.

July's departures included that of David Bartlett who, like Mrs Brown, had joined the Staff in 1986. Like his Head of Department for many years, Brian Burgess, David was a graduate of Imperial College. He subsequently read Theology at Oxford and became a nonconformist minister before arriving in Hurst Road to teach Physics. His unconventional outlook on life and quirky sense of humour made a striking impact and he will not be forgotten by those who knew him. Coincidentally yet another of the 1986 intake left the School that Summer. Tony Tipping, the tall, athletic P.E. teacher, moved on after a prolonged period of ill health. An outstanding sportsman himself, Tony made a huge contribution both to the physical education of numerous students during his sixteen years at the School and also on the pastoral side as a Head of Year. Deborah Warren (Mathematics) left after five years at Chis and Sid and Vicky Parton, the Head of Physics, moved on to become Head of Science at Bexley Grammar School after three. Barbara Durkin was appointed to take her place.

By the end of the academic year 2001/2002 the situation was rather mixed for Chis and Sid. On the bright side the Bexley 'eleven plus' passmark was being moved in an upward direction, which would ensure an improvement in the academic quality of the School's intake. There were

380 students in the Sixth Form, a record number. Business Studies was a popular choice of A. level subject and Psychology was about to come on stream. These innovations, together with a freeing up of courses available to those in the Sixth Form, ensured a pleasing vibrancy at Key Stage 5. The extra curricular activities on offer were still of a very high quality. Arts and sport seemed to have a promising future at the School, a future that would be enhanced if Gordon Brown's promise of fifteen billion pounds of extra funding for education was to be fulfilled. There were exciting plans afoot for a series of major building projects and improvements to the fabric of the School.

On the rather gloomier side, however, recruitment of staff was something of a problem in the somewhat stark economic conditions. Teachers were feeling, quite acutely, the pressures of league tables, the proliferation of examinations, testing and constant control from above. These fears and worries were often, understandably, transmitted to the students. The interference by central government was a problem that was not going to go away.

CHAPTER THIRTEEN
The Interregnum

AND SO, THE ACADEMIC YEAR 2002/2003 opened in a maelstrom of educational change and uncertainty. The clouds over the school were not, however, all stormy; there were glimpses of a silver lining. Certainly a series of gloomy issues needed to be confronted. All teachers, those at Chis and Sid included, had, of necessity, to come to terms with a world dominated by accountability. OFSTED was becoming a fearful institution that governed most precisely what should be taught and, most worryingly, how it should be taught. For a school that had prided itself on the quality and creativity of its staff and pupils this was a bitter pill to swallow. To many the burden of rapid change, the constant flow of government designed initiatives, the tyranny of the league tables, the proliferation of centrally generated data, that on the surface looked valueless, was almost too much to bear. All of this may account for the difficulties the school was experiencing in recruiting and retaining suitable colleagues; house prices were, of course, another element that did not help the situation.

Yet there were moments of light in the darkness. Chis and Sid had much to look forward to and feel confident and excited about. On July 15th 2002 the Chancellor of the Exchequer, Gordon Brown, announced fifteen billion pounds of additional funding for schools: heady days. How would Chis and Sid use its share of the honey pot?

'To stand still is to go backwards' declared Jim Rouncefield in an article in the *Chronicle* published at this time. It would of course be churlish to point out that, logically therefore, to go forward is to stand still. However, the vision for the future, as outlined in 2002, was radical. Plans for a major premises refurbishment were at the gestation stage as was the exciting prospect of the School obtaining, with local authority support, Sports College status that would enable it to become a local centre of sporting excellence. Collaboration with Hurstmere for a ground-breaking joint application for specialist status was being considered. There was talk of a shared floodlit Astroturf pitch, a new state of the art sports pavilion, the development of a Sidcup Community Sports Centre on the Golf Club site with a grand sports hall that would be for the exclusive use of the students during school hours; the future in September suddenly looked brighter than many might have predicted not long before.

So as staff and students came to terms with the rigours of Curriculum 2000, the most significant change to sixth form teaching for decades, as the SAT examinations began to look slightly less threatening the School was blessed with an influx of talented teaching and support staff.

Alex Becky, a young and very talented sportsman - middle distance running and rugby were his strengths - arrived and immediately impressed with his enthusiasm and easy manner with the students. Dibran Zeqiri brought his own brand of wit to the History and Politics departments (in 2002 the School still taught in departments, faculties were to arrive with Dr. Vitagliano). Some years later Dibran was to become a very successful Head of the Government and Politics Department, achieving some excellent results with his students and delighting many of them with his knowledge and dry sense of humour. History was lucky to secure the services of Susan Shires, an old girl of the School, who later was to become an innovating and popular head of the Sixth Form. Other notable appointees included Hayley Briggs to Geography, a return as a part timer by Katherine Fey, who had previously led the Economics Department, and the arrival in the spring of 2003 of the flamboyant and charismatic American Steve Mckiel. Steve, who brought rock and roll to Chis and Sid, took over from Christopher Wool whose musical tastes had been rooted in the world of the classics and whose madrigal groups had drawn much praise. Following Steve's appointment pop concerts, school rock bands, rock competitions became the order of the day and aptly supported the outstanding tradition of jazz music that Will Michael had built up. Steve Mckiel was eclectic in his tastes however, and his choirs achieved much success in both national and international competitions. Aline Marshall arrived in the summer of 2002 to set up the Psychology Department. This was a vital move in the expansion of the curriculum at Key Stage 5. The Department was what might be called an overnight success and did much to increase numbers in the Sixth Form.

As was the case for many schools, OFSTED had highlighted a need at Chis and Sid for a rapid and radical improvement in Information Technology facilities. The appointment of Parm Thind as an assistant head teacher was the School's response to the technology revolution in education. Parm was educated at Essex University where his degree was in Information Management. He brought a variety of expertise to the School, including Mathematics, Accountancy, Economics, but most significantly Information Technology. His I.T. skills had been honed while working at a number of schools and now he had to take Chis and Sid that had five P.Cs, a few early version Interactive Whiteboards and no budget for Information Technology and turn it into a dynamic centre of education driven by the computer. As this book goes to print Chis and Sid has its own sophisticated website, each member of staff has a laptop, the budget for this kind of technology hovers around £100,000 a year, there is a whiteboard in every teaching room and the system is controlled by an external company, Class Technology, who provide twenty four hour support via three technicians. Reporting, tracking, registration of students as well as discipline of pupils are all aided by computer. Much of the communication among groups and individuals is carried out by email. Nearly all communication with parents is by computer, no more scruffy notes delivered to parents three months late. 'It's on SIMS' or 'You will find it on Fusion '(the School's Managed Learning Environment) are, in 2011, common currency at Chis and Sid. This truly is a brave new world and all created within a little less than a decade, with no sign that the revolution is over.

The importance of Parm's role was flagged up by the fact that he was appointed as an assistant head teacher. The early years of the century saw a burgeoning of management posts in schools; gone were the days of a head teacher, a deputy head for boys and a deputy head for girls. The assistant head layer of management, which was subsequently redefined as "leadership", seemed to be in response to the proliferation of initiatives hailing down from the government. Mike Rushton was already in post as an assistant head when Parm arrived. When Mike's responsibilities are reviewed we see how the turn of the century was changing education as a whole as well as changing the style of education at Chis and Sid. He was the overseer of staff professional development (CPD), the mentor for newly qualified teachers (NQTs), the member of staff charged with the introduction of tracking and target setting, but, most significantly, it was his duty to drive forward the move to specialist status at the School, probably the most important event for Chis and Sid during the first decade of the 21st century. By the time Mike Rushton left in 2005 the School had been designated as a sports college jointly with Hurstmere. This was a unique relationship nationally and it was the first and last joint designation for sports college status involving a grammar school and a non-selective school; it laid the foundation for a highly fruitful and mutually beneficial relationship between these two schools, which were geographically so very close.

The whole move towards specialism probably came when Chis and Sid was approached by Hurstmere with a request in early 2002 for support for its bid for Sports College status. Hurstmere had difficulties in submitting a request because it had no sixth form and was a single sex institution; this apparently presented almost insurmountable difficulties. On consideration Jim Rouncefield began to see the benefits that would accrue to the School if the bid were to be made jointly. The grounds on which the two schools stood were perfect for a sports college. The funding available was irresistible. It was an obvious choice because of the sporting tradition of the School and it would generate the least political tension among academic departments, as P.E. was a subject that included all students. And so Mike Rushton was deputed to write the bid with Andrew Stringer, then the Head Elect at Hurstmere.

The bid was deemed successful in 2004 and a very promising marriage between the two schools was solemnised; the inevitable, but amicable, divorce came in 2007 when both schools had to apply for re-designation only to find that government policy had changed and joint status was no longer viable.

There was a series of convenient and helpful coincidences that eased the passage of the bid for Sports College status. At the time the London Borough of Bexley was seeking a site in the south of the Borough to locate a floodlit Astroturf pitch to counterbalance what had already been provided at Erith School for the north. The land striding the two schools was perfect. The desire to create a leisure centre to replace the Lamorbey swimming pool was also fortuitous. A sizeable portion of the School's West Field, together with the land upon which the Sidcup Golf Club pavilion was standing, was deemed ideal for the project. How could a bid which offered these excellent facilities on-site possibly fail? Of course, it did not!

In September 2010 Richard Wallbridge, the Director of Sport and Performance, reflecting on the coming Olympics, waxed lyrical about the benefits, opportunities, responsibilities and changes that Sports College status had brought to Chis and Sid. While still a rugby school with an outstanding tradition and fixture list in that sport, Richard noted that, as he spoke, there were over forty sporting activities available to students at the School. What would old boys and girls from any previous decade make of yoga, lacrosse, archery, sailing, mountain biking, all being available; a rich diet indeed. He spoke warmly of the notion of inclusion. He commented on the fact, however, that Chis and Sid was still competing in any number of cups and tournaments. The fine tradition of teams touring had been maintained and expanded, but now everybody 'gets a go.' The P.E. Department had doubled in size in terms of staffing, an army of coaches was being brought in to man the Enrichment Programme, Sports Day had become a festival of activities open to all, and furthermore the local community and, most importantly, local primary schools were encouraged to use the facilities. Richard was proud that Dance, Drama and Music had all developed under the umbrella of Sports College status.

2002/2003 was not just about sport. March 2003 saw the dance production *Groov Jet*. Directed by Yvette Lee and Rachel Keeler, this show was noted for its energy and the presence of some talented male dancers; Matt Harris, a promising amateur ballroom dancer was one who took the eye. The sporting theme was, however, continued with Steve Anderson's production of the comedy classic *Outside Edge* that took place in February 2003. Steve praised Steven Wickenden, who played the lead, calling him a 'classy actor'. This was not the first of Steven's shining performances at Chis and Sid. Yet again the Charity Committee worked hard and the Old People's Christmas Party provided much pleasure to the senior citizens attending. Young Enterprise, Chess Club, Christian Union and the War –Gaming Society enjoyed successful years, as did many other clubs and societies in 2002/2003. The well-travelled students of Chis and Sid enjoyed trips to Ardeche, Berlin, Paris, Saumur, Le Touquet and less distant locations such as a geography field trip to Preston Montford in Shropshire.

It was in this academic year that the first edition of *Past Purple* was published.

Chis and Sid, like all schools, has experienced sadness and tragedy over the years and 2003 brought both. A headline in the *Chronicle* for 2002/2003 reads, 'It is with regret that the editorial staff of the *Chronicle* announce the death of Mr. Brian Burgess, a highly valued member of staff at Chis and Sid.' The last part of this sentence is somewhat of an understatement. The fact that Brian is mentioned in seven chapters of this book is testament to his 'value' to the school. Martyn Berry movingly commented in his address at Brian's funeral, 'So many young-and not-so-young- lives were bettered and brightened by Brian's work and play during his four decades linked with Chis and Sid. He was a truly good man, whose life we can genuinely celebrate and thank God for.' Let us hope these comments will encourage readers to search the index of this book for references to Brian in order to reflect on the detail of what he did for the School. How sad that he died so relatively soon into his much-deserved retirement.

The tragic circumstances of Dominic Russan's death in a terrible glider accident were hard to come to terms with for staff and students alike. Student Stephen English, a self-confessed Russan fan, made it his task to gather a series of staff reminiscences of Mr. Russan for the *Chronicle*. Stephen was impressed, but not surprised, by the warmth and affection for 'Dom' expressed in these memories.

This section of *Past Purple* is entitled *The Interregnum*, so called because of the events that began to unfold at the end of 2003. Graham Lightwood, then a deputy head, recalls one late autumn day in that year when Jim Rouncefield 'casually popped' into his office and said, 'The Local Education Authority have asked me if I would like to be seconded to Hill View for a few weeks. How would you feel about being Acting Head while I'm away?' And Graham said, 'Yes.' So the interregnum started. The 'few weeks' became sixteen months. These sixteen months, it could be argued, were as packed with incident as any that the School had experienced hitherto. Two major building projects, the bedding in of the new specialism, a full OFSTED inspection, a quite radical change to the school day, the remodelling of the Senior Leadership Team were just some of the issues which characterised the controlled turmoil and upheaval of this period. It has been said though that given this innovation, change and, in a sense, uncertainty, there was a 'relatively seamless transition from one Head Teacher to another.'

Inevitably as one academic year succeeds another there will be changes and with September came the familiar replacement of leaving staff with new colleagues. Carole Tipper, a stalwart of the Chemistry Department, respected by her students for her expertise, moved on after seventeen years at the School. Sidikar Bayar, an excellent scientist, replaced her. Andrew Hutton joined the Art Department and it was not long before his I.T. skills were put to good use in the School. Readers who visit the school website can see for themselves his talent for graphic design. He was joined by Mercedes Phillips in that department. Alicia Nongbri also arrived; another good graduate, with a fine background in the classics. As this edition goes to print Alicia leads a well-qualified and popular Classics Department.

However, some staff, it might be said, are almost impossible to replace. One such was Mr. Robert Buxton who celebrated his retirement on Friday 14th November with friends, colleagues and a whole bevy of students who were clearly going to miss him. Bob had been at the School for thirty six years. He was remarkable in as much as he entered the profession at Chis and Sid (he undertook his training at the School) and left all those years later as Head of Mathematics, having, like his brother-in-law, Brian Burgess, devoted his life to the School. All reports confirm that Bob was a great classroom teacher; at the party one of his students told the author that he 'really made maths fun, you just wouldn't believe that was possible.' A fine mathematician, Bob was not always happy with modern developments in Maths and when his outstanding results are reviewed, it might be that he had a point. A strong character, with firm opinions, as befits a northerner, Bob could be incredibly kind and sympathetic to colleagues. He was an

Bob Buxton (1966-2003).

248

enthusiastic sportsman and had a devilish sense of humour. It surprised few that his retirement saw him devoting time to his family, to travel and to his local church. Towards the end of his career Bob had been plagued with poor health, but he had been lucky to secure the services of Cecilia Connor who moved easily up from Deputy Head of Maths to the position of Acting Head of Mathematics for 2003/2004. Cecilia joined the School in January 1985 and, like Bob, very quickly gave much of her time to Chis and Sid, becoming a governor by September 1985 and working assiduously on that body, with a particular talent for finance, for some nineteen years before retiring in late 2005.

But what of the two major building projects that had been conceived, planned and completed in the first decade of the 20th Century? The Jubilee Pavilion was very much the brainchild of Jim Rouncefield. He had undertaken an enormous amount of planning work and had striven, almost desperately at times, to secure the funding from within the School's resources. By September 2004, using a design by Shane Jell, a local architect, building could begin. The logistics of such an operation, particularly with students on the site, are complicated, to say the least. Anthony Sullivan, Premises Manager, who had cut his teeth, so to speak, on the Music Block, was highly instrumental in ensuring that any disruption was kept to a minimum. Anthony had been a significant appointment for Chis and Sid. No longer was it possible to employ a caretaker and a couple of cleaners to service the premises needs of what was now a large institution. Anthony by this time had built a sophisticated team of site assistants, cleaners and contractors and consequently the build went well and provided an excellent precedent for the rather bigger project which was the Arts Block. The Jubilee Pavilion, so named to celebrate the School's 50th anniversary on the Hurst Road site, was opened on Thursday 19th May 2005. By early September 2004 the formative discussions for a new art block, which would subsequently become The Quentin Blake Building, were underway.

Let me entertain you, was the apt title for the 2004 dance production, directed jointly by Sophia Port and Faye Sheehan. Dance was, at this time, becoming a real strength in the school. *Sins and Lovers*, a review based loosely on the idea of The Seven Deadly Sins proved an entertaining melange of sketches, songs and poems and saw the emergence of some promising youngsters who were to provide the foundation for drama for some years to come; Matt Harris, Emma Richardson, Alice Boynes and Simon

Ellis were names that would appear on billboards around the school for some years. As usual the Summer Jazz Concert of 2003 further established the tradition for this genre of music at Chis and Sid. Singing was a particular strength at the concert with Eleanor Martin, Katie Martin and Alice Boynes showing great maturity and sensitivity on such classics as *Blame it On My Youth*. Most pleasingly the guest soloist was the outstanding tenor player, Paul Wheeler, who was an old boy of the school. Paul was one of many professional musicians who had emerged from the Music Department over the years. Let us not forget that The Christmas and Easter concerts of the academic year 2003/2004, provided suitable platforms for students like Bryony Mycroft, James O'Doherty and the members of the Senior Choir, Brass Group, Chamber and Full Orchestra to confront the sophistication of the likes of Mozart, Bizet and Delibes.

We might want to call this academic year *The Year of the Trip*. The range and variety of places visited and events attended was stunning. There were of course some old favourites. Saumur in July, Berlin in February, Le Touquet, Canterbury, The Tower of London were all exciting return visits. However, the first visit to Russia, taking in Moscow and St. Petersburg and led by Susan Shires was certainly a remarkable experience for the students. The mounting of such an excursion with all the problems associated with flights, visas, accommodation, temperatures as low as minus 18 degrees is a mammoth undertaking, but for students of History, Politics, Art and Languages an invaluable experience. The First Challenge Expedition to Spain, a demanding cross between a holiday and an outward-bound course, was designed to test the leadership skills of the students, as well as their fitness, initiative and endurance.

Those readers who are not in the business of education, either as a provider or a consumer, will have no idea what happens to individuals and institutions when OFSTED is mentioned. Those whose business is education are all too aware of the tension, nerves, disruption and often downright terror that even the thought of OFSTED, let alone an actual visit from the inspectorate, can cause. In 2004 the OFSTED regime, it could be argued, was even more invasive and aggressive than it is in 2011. Seventeen inspectors spent a total of sixty seven inspector days in September 2004 conducting a full OFSTED inspection. Jim Rouncefield, who had been seconded back to Chis and Sid for two days a week to deal with matters arising with finance and premises, was now in school full time to take staff and students through the inspection. As many schools find with these experiences, all that is discovered is what is already known; it just costs so much in terms of money and stress to find this out. As Graham Lightwood commented, 'As our examination results spoke for themselves, and as 98% of all lessons observed were rated satisfactory or better, it is not surprising that we were found to be "a very good school."' A perusal of the Summary Report by those who have nothing better to do will reveal that Graham's analysis was pretty much spot on. The School was praised for its strong ethos, the good attitudes, behaviour and attendance of the pupils, some excellent teaching was observed, the Senior Management was found to be strong, extra-curricular activities were thriving and the academic achievements of the pupils in all years was good; as Graham said, the results spoke for themselves. A government cannot spend thousands of pounds on such an exercise without discovering some weaknesses, but quite whether such expenditure was necessary to find out that the School's resources and accommodation were not up to scratch and that Chis and Sid was not always teaching and organising the curriculum in the way that the mandarins in the Ministry deemed they should is a debating point.

So OFSTED came and thankfully went and when it was all over Jim Rouncefield returned to the Local Authority and soon after decided that he would take up a full time post with the London Borough of Bexley as Deputy Director of Schools and Quality Assurance. The Interregnum was thus nearly at an end by January 2005 when Jim finally left the school. He had been the Head Teacher for almost eleven years. At a time when many on the shop floor were suspicious of the management, Jim had bucked the trend by being appreciated, respected, and, most importantly, liked, by all who worked with him. The Interregnum had been a time of upheaval and uncertainty, yes, but the School had survived, and, as OFSTED had confirmed, it was in good shape. Whoever was to take it on would inherit a strong and stable institution that was officially, 'A very good school.'

The Second Doctor

Dr. Joe Vitagliano (2005-2008).

THE SECOND DOCTOR

ON 17TH SEPTEMBER 2004, and again on 24th September, an advertisement appeared in the *Times Educational Supplement* for a new head teacher for Chislehurst and Sidcup Grammar School. October of that year saw an almost constant stream of prospective head teachers undertaking the guided tour of the school accompanied by students who were no doubt laying bets with each other as to which of these visitors was to take over the School from Mr. Rouncefield, who had been very popular with the student body. The interviews took place over two days in early November and, at the end of what had been a gruelling process, it was decided to offer the Headship of Chis and Sid to Dr. Joseph Vitagliano and he was happy to accept.

As the name suggests, the new Head Teacher was of Italian stock. His parents had arrived from Italy with little English, so it is a great testament to Dr. Vitagliano's upbringing, diligence and intelligence that he went to York University where he took a first in English and Philosophy. He explains what was something of a dazzling academic career with reference to his parents' enthusiasm for education. He is proud that he grew up in a household that truly valued learning. A surprise to no one then, that Dr. V. (this was the nickname used by both staff and students for the Head) should choose teaching as his profession. His first appointment was at a boys' catholic school as a teacher of English. This was in 1986 and was quickly followed by a move to a school in Barking and Dagenham that was undergoing a major reorganization. The experience at this institution might explain his readiness to take on his duties at Midhurst Rother Academy when he left Chis and Sid. It was while teaching at Barking that Dr. V decided to read for an MA in Contemporary Literature at Birkbeck College: a tough assignment while holding down a teaching job. Success at Birkbeck brought about a move to Cambridge University where, with a British Academy Studentship, he studied for his doctorate. In 1994 Doctor, as he now was, Vitagliano left Corpus Christi College and returned to the classroom, taking up a post as Head of English at Coopers Company and Coburn School in Essex. Here he stayed until 2001 when he was appointed as Deputy Head at Robertsbridge Community College. He returned to Coopers Company and Coburn in 2003 and then, of course, on to Chis and Sid as Head in April 2005.

Dr. Vitagliano took over a very healthy institution, but he was aware that change was needed. The world of education evolves so rapidly, often driven by political whim, but Dr. V realised that the School would have to swim with the tide of educational innovation if it was to be deemed an 'outstanding school', to use the OFSTED jargon. 'Teaching and Learning' was the buzz phrase and 'Accountability' was the watchword. Besides all this it was all too clear to the new Head Teacher that the local area was changing and hence the intake would be different from that of the nineties, to say nothing of the sixties! He detected that the popularity of Chis and Sid was somewhat on the wane and he felt that his first task was to address this issue. It is for the reader who knew the School under Dr. V's headship to make the judgement as to whether he addressed these concerns successfully.

Although, of course, the arrival of a new head teacher is very significant for any school, and particularly one that had been through as much as Chis and Sid had in the months of the Interregnum, there were other very important comings and goings in 2004/2005. Barbara Durkin, the Head of Physics, left to take up a post at local rivals Colfe's in 2004. Emma Reynolds, the popular Head of Girls' P.E., went on maternity leave never to return in a full time capacity. Giles Phillips, Biology teacher and Head of Year, who had made a name for himself as a fine rugby coach was off to St. Dunstan's College. His departure was something of a disappointment as under the talented and committed leadership of Phil Ubee, the recently appointed master with overall responsibility for rugby and 1st XV coach, rugby was enjoying a certain renaissance. Simon McNaught, the charismatic Head of Sixth Form, also moved on to pastures new. There were some impressive colleagues joining the Staff Common Room during this academic year. Brad Visser, hailing from South Africa, himself a talented hockey coach, took over as Head of Science, ably assisted by Keith Aspin, who saw out the few years before his retirement as Head of Physics at the School. Doris Evans, a colleague of German extraction, provided the Mathematics Department with some much needed stability and continuity as Head of Department. The Sixth Form found a new supremo in the form of Yvette Bellis who quickly established the tone of her regime by organising a mammoth cultural visit to New York for her charges and then reorganising the responsibilities and roles of the prefect body. Lizzie Lymer, a flamboyant geographer, joined, as did Jenni Rowe whose skills as a P.E. teacher were soon transferred to the pastoral system. Elizabeth Bonnaud née Johnson, a keen linguist, arrived and the School quickly benefitted from her knowledge of the Duke of Edinburgh Award Scheme and her talents as a teacher of languages.

While many schools at this time were having to abandon much of their extra-curricular provision in the appalling scramble for examination passes (a disturbing consequence of the tyranny of the government inspired league tables), Chis and Sid seemed to be expanding the diet of out of hours activities available to its students. Graham Lightwood in his *Chronicle* feature, *View from the Top*, commented glowingly on the very ambitious Senior Drama performance of *Oedipus Rex*. Clive Madel, an old boy of the school and member of the Classics Department, not only directed the piece, but also produced a refreshingly modern translation of the play for his actors. Daniel Kelly's portrayal of Oedipus received much well-deserved praise. The Junior School continued the tradition of drama across all years at Chis and Sid with the Year 7 and 8 Drama Club under the expert guidance of Maya Tse producing a lively review *That's Life*. English teacher Graham Best wrote both the Prologue and Epilogue for this energetic romp. The music groups, as celebrated in the *Chronicle* for the academic year 2004/2005, were a remarkable eight in number. Jazz again was thriving with Olaf Vas, a prestigious and talented multi instrumentalist and local professional, joining the students on stage for the Summer Concert. Some stunning musicianship was heard from the likes of Liam O'Brien, Katharine Vincent, Joe Stoddart, Jon French, James Dempsey and the enthralling trio of leavers, John Clemenson, Tim Newis and Andy Corrigan who performed a captivating rendition of the Billy Strayhorn classic, *Lush Life*. As has been said, at this stage music in the school was not just confined to the jazz genre and rock. Madrigals, brass music, choral music, as well as orchestral work, were all afforded public performances. Dance too swung into action with the 2005 production, *Disco Inferno*. Again a series of exotic trips and excursions found Chis and Sid students in South Africa, Chelsea Harbour, The Tower of London, Le Touquet, Berlin, Athens, New York, and, interestingly, the battlefields of the Somme. This trip, a joint project between the History and English Departments, was to become a regular event for students in Year 9 for some time to come.

Artistically, culturally and academically, this gives the reader a flavour of the Chis and Sid that Dr. Vitagliano was to lead into the second half of the first decade of the 21st Century. He had arrived in time to witness something of a renaissance on the playing fields of the School, no doubt driven by the recently acquired Sports College status. Apart from the very early years of the School when the boys played football, Chis and Sid had been considered a rugby school. Previous chapters detail highlights on the rugby pitch and celebrate star players and coaches, but the 2004/2005 season was particularly fruitful in a providing a platform upon which the successes of the following years could be built. Noel Horrobin, with the assistance of recently appointed coach, Phil Ubee, re-established the tradition of senior squads touring and accordingly a junior and a senior side entered the Limerick Rugby Festival. The Rugby Club has toured on a biannual basis ever since this enjoyable trip and possibly this success has lead to the School's cricketers attempting some equally impressive tours to glamorous locations like St. Lucia and St. Kitts. The Irish adventure turned out to be more than just preparation for the coming season as the boys were lucky enough to find themselves billeted with the Newcastle Falcons premiership rugby team on the Limerick University campus, but were also able to tell friends and family that they had been training on the same pitch as the great Jonny Wilkinson. It was no surprise that this team, led by the admirable Matthew Walters and well supported by the talents of James Ahlers, Jolyon Bond and Rhys Boxall, soon to play for England, achieved the best playing record for many years. Some very promising young players, Adam Hunt, Jamie Cutler and child star Jack Berry won their spurs in Ireland.

Three highly significant departures took place in the summer of 2005. As has been mentioned, Mike Rushton moved across the East Field to take up a senior post at Hurstmere School. Ian Page, one time Head of Sixth Form, temporary Deputy Head and long term Head of History, something of an eccentric, but a remarkably inspirational sixth form teacher, left to devote more time to his union activities and his work in the realm of adult education. Paul Avery, who had led the Geography Department since 1983, moved to Woldingham Independent School. It was, one supposes, a sign of the times that soon after Paul's departure Geography was to be subsumed into the Humanities Faculty. *What's in a name*, but the new century saw faculties replacing departments.

Jo Gray left to run the Classics Department at Chelmsford County High School and Cecilia Connor was at last able to retire. Derwyn Williams, a robust Welshman, who was, predictably, a rugby aficionado, took over from Ian Page as leader of the History Department. Emma Rayner took on the Geography Department, while Leila Ward, a gifted cellist, came as a junior member to the Music Department. David Evans, another rugby player with a Welsh background, was appointed as the Number Two in Mathematics.

Christmas 2005 saw the departures of Assistant Head, Diane Hill, and

Head of Information Technology and self-confessed Dartford Warbler fancier, Eddie Powell. It was however this Yuletide that brought the appoint-

ment of a new deputy head for Chis and Sid. The arrival of Brian Simber was, in a sense, the breaking of a mould at the School. The leadership group of Rouncefield, Ford and Lightwood, so long the senior staff, made way for a new leadership team and, the tone and style of the School would inevitably change. It is interesting to note that this history is testament to the fact that, within the world of edu-

Brian Simber, Deputy Head since 2006

cation, no matter how much there is a need for stability and continuity, change is inevitable. For those who labour in the classroom, all things must pass. Another fascinating strand in this book seems to be that however flexible and adaptable Chis and Sid is forced to be, there is a set of core values that has never been lost.

Brian Simber took up his appointment before Graham Lightwood retired and for a while they investigated the technicalities of the timetable and the curriculum together. Brian hailed from Liverpool and, as the posters in his office testified, he was definitely from the red side of that historic city. He studied Architectural Engineering at Leeds University. Although he had intended to train as an architect, on completing his PGCE at Leeds, and not having enjoyed his experiences in the architect's studio, he found his vocation in the world of education. There followed a series of posts in Leeds, but the wanderlust was too much for Brian and he took up an appointment in Bogata. This was certainly an exotic location and, although some might consider Colombia a rather dangerous place in which to settle, Brian remained for five very happy years, becoming Head of Maths and Head of Secondary Section in his school before returning to the UK. Coincidentally, Brian Seve, a flamboyant and popular teacher of Physics at Chis and Sid in the nineties, arrived to teach at the same school in Colombia while Brian Simber was in post, a truly small world. Once settled back in England Brian had a range of teaching experiences at Hurstmere, Abbey Wood School, Tunbridge Wells High School, all in senior posts, until he made his move to Chis and Sid from Kidbroke School where he had been a deputy head. His mark was made very quickly at the School with a simplification of the timetable. Almost immediately he ensured that the students at Key Stages 4 and 5 were given greater freedom in their choice of subjects. Like the new Head Teacher, he was concerned to realise the tremendous potential of the students that he had noted within the first weeks of his appointment.

One of the problems for the author of a book like this is the difficulty of ensuring the accuracy of dates and times, but the following catalogue of changes and innovations within the school is not altogether fictional. It was in 2005/2006 that the Senior Management Team became the Senior Leadership Team, Heads of Year became Heads of Learning, the Caretaker's House became the School House, paper registers became electronic, Homecall (the telephone system for monitoring attendance) started, Sports Day was revamped, Line Management, Assessment For Learning (a comprehensive review of how work is assessed by teachers), Raiseonline (a government mode of ensuring students achieved high grades by means of pretty colour codes), Performance Management, Fusion (Managed Learning Environment, i.e. the use of computers and the internet) all arrived, or were overhauled; the Student Voice was heard loud and clear as groups of children became part of the interviewing process for new staff. And so much more. Such change and reincarnation that some of the older members of staff hardly knew which universe they now inhabited.

Certain features of the School, thank goodness, remained constant. The Drama Department was now in the experienced and professional hands of Linda Woodacre. She had no intention of changing the age-old tradition of public performance at Chis and Sid. Steve Anderson had had to take a back seat due to ill health and Lin started her regime with the blockbuster *The Frogs* by Aristophanes. She was as well versed in the backstage arts as any previous drama teacher at the School and this production was characterised by the expertise and size of the backstage crew. Many of the participating students went on to enter the world of theatre as technicians; Sally Roy found a niche in stage management, Kieran O' Brien trained as a lighting designer and others have found employment on the technical side of theatre. Matthew Harris, one of the leads, went to study Drama at Exeter University and Matthew Hutchinson, another lead, became a name in the world of puppetry.

Chis and Sid, following the days of football in the thirties, has been seen as a rugby school. Certainly the powerful and single-minded influence of Noel Horrobin in the eighties and nineties secured the School a prestigious fixture list and established a solid reputation for Chis and Sid as one of the premier state schools for rugby. The 2005/2006 season was, it could be argued, the highpoint in the history of that sport at the School. Led by their talented captain, Adam Hunt, this outstanding team was packed with great players, Jamie Cutler, Jon West, international Rhys Boxall, Bert McDonald, Ross Westwood, Jolyon Bond, who also played cricket for England schoolboys, Alex Pillow, to name but a few. This side, who had been together since Year 7, achieved the best playing record ever. The *Chronicle* celebrated this feat quite simply with the following caption: 'Played – 20, Won – 19, Lost – 1. Much of this success was due to the professionalism of coach Ubee and the persistence of Head of P.E. Horrobin, but those who played in that side agree that the pervading sense of loyalty generated by Adam was the key.

Dr. Vitagliano was certainly keen to promote the cultural and social side of the School and a series of concerts and small scale musical events, combined with a number of studio style drama productions, (*Grimm Tales* springs to mind), ensured that Chis and Sid had so much more to offer than just an academic diet. And speaking of diets, a very interesting trip to Venice was undertaken by the Home Economics Department in October to sample the delights of Italian cuisine, but more importantly to unpack some of the culinary secrets of the Veneto.

Dr. Vitagliano in his headline article in the *Chronicle* for that year spoke of it being one of, 'many highs and some lows.' And the 'low', certainly was just that. In the same article the Doctor caught the mood of the School in the middle of the Christmas Term when he wrote of 'the great sadness that the School felt when it received the news of the death of Mr. Noel Horrobin.' There are some teachers who are 'unforgettable' and there can be few students who came under the tutelage of Mr. Horrobin, who would ever forget him. It is a sad, but almost predictable, irony that the cancer that struck Noel first emerged at a Parents' Evening in May

Noel Horrobin 1976-2006.

of the previous year. He was in the process of organising a ground-breaking rugby tour to Romania, a tour that he sadly was unable to participate in and was looking forward to a retirement during which he believed he would turn Chis and Sid into a centre of rugby excellence. Most disappointingly this would not come to pass, but the legacy of this larger than life character and great supporter of all things Chis and Sid is still clear to see. This 'devoted servant of the School for 30 years' had laid the groundwork for Sports College status, built a thriving Physical Education Department, produced a group of rugby players of the highest calibre, a number of whom had become internationals, and inculcated a lasting sense of the value of loyalty, determination and discipline in all those he had taught. Many a young Year 7 student who quaked at the sight of this giant of a man would leave Chis and Sid having benefitted from his advice, his kindness and his avuncular care. The author would like to commend to the reader the tribute paid to Noel in the 110th issue of the *Chronicle* by Phil Ubee.

Other than this very sad farewell, the School also said goodbye to a long serving senior member of staff. Graham Lightwood, who had spent nearly two years as Acting Head, took retirement at the end of the Spring Term. This was not the only departure as moving on was very much in the air in July 2006. Steve Anderson took early retirement, on the grounds of ill health, after more than two decades of strong and selfless commitment to the creative life of the school. Head of Lower School, Martin Davey, took up a senior post at Langley Park School for Girls. Derwyn Williams went on to develop his career, achieving promotion to Assistant Headship in Dagenham. Geoffrey Rishman left the Chemistry Department to teach at the highly prestigious independent school, Bedales. French teacher Marissa Morland became a Head of Foreign Languages in Chigwell, while Maya Tse, an outstanding English teacher, left to teach at Dartford Girls' Grammar, much to the disappointment of her students and her colleagues, but it was time for Maya to move on. Alex Becky was sorely missed by the P.E. Department, but he had decided to ply his trade in Italy. He was replaced by the multi-talented Stuart Bromley. This was not the only new face in P.E. as Sports College status necessitated an expansion in staff numbers. Daniel Gower, another fine sportsman, who knew the school well having played rugby against Chis and Sid as a student at Dartford, arrived in the Summer of 2006 and his qualities as a teacher were quickly spotted as only some three years later he was promoted to Head of Boys' P.E.. Joanne Rycroft also arrived to strengthen the Department and she too found herself leading the girls' section of the Department soon after; she also found herself with a husband four years later, marrying Daniel Gower in 2010. Gary Panton came from local rivals Bexley Grammar School to take up the post of Director of Key Stages 3 and 4. As a practising P.E. teacher, he also added to the growing Sports Faculty. Lindsey Delve arrived in the Science Faculty with John Sheehan. Tim Perry was taken on to teach Geography and soon became a Head of Learning. Doug Wise, who had made a significant mark during his PGCE training within the English Department, was snapped up as a full time teacher on Maya Tse's departure and he too soon found himself promoted to Head of Learning. Caroline Parrott and Christopher Ruth were two more of this young and happy breed that joined in the summer of 2006 and within a few years were appointed to positions of responsibility within the middle management ranks.

If one reads the earlier chapters of this history carefully, it becomes clear that certain years are characterised by a sense of sadness and loss. Schools are remarkable institutions in terms of regeneration and recovery, so even the bleakest of years will inevitably have bright sides and moments to savour and enjoy. Although the academic year 2006/2007 could be described as an anus horribilis, there were many events to enjoy and celebrate.

On the academic front there was good news. A sound crop of Arts students gained Oxbridge places, John Hildred and Vicky Greenhalgh at Cambridge, Rose Manley at Oxford. For many teachers the SATs exams were part of what was seen as a particularly sinister and tyrannical government move to control teaching and teachers from the centre (luckily these exams, that proved almost impossible to run successfully, have disappeared from secondary schools). Nevertheless, for Chis and Sid the 1st March 2007 brought the news that the School had achieved the accolade of 'top London School' in the *The Evening Standard* KS3 League Table. The cynical response to such a gong is that league tables are fine if you find yourself at the top of them. Academic success is not always measured in terms of examination grades, thank goodness, and for a lively group of Year 11 students prompted by Dorothée Lorsery of the French Department the Tidemill Primary School experiment was an enriching experience both academically and personally; they discovered in a highly interactive and investigative way that facilitating (teaching) the development of foreign language skills for ten year-olds is no easy business.

Sport and the Arts were again areas worthy of celebration. Lin Woodacre showed once more the potential for musical drama within the School with her mammoth production of *Jesus Christ Superstar*. Traditionally the main school production had been the preserve of the Upper School, but Lin was initiating a new tradition that tapped into talent right across Chis and Sid. This production involved over 200 students and continued the healthy and relaxed liaison between the Drama and Music departments. The production was the perfect showcase for a crop of fine actors including Aaron Heinemann, Kirsty Oswald and Emma Richardson, whose abilities had been nurtured by Lin Woodacre for some time. Music was moving in all sorts of strange directions at the School. The 25th of January 2007 saw the second visit of native African drummers, while the two senior rock bands, Six Foot Sir and Celibate Monks entered the XFM radio's Rock School Competition. There were also huge turnouts for the more traditional Easter and Christmas concerts and the well-established Jazz on a Summer's Day Concert. Debating and public speaking were highlights of this year as the School team of Joe Williams, Lawrence Easterbrook and Anna-Marie Treloar coasted to victory with their topic, 'Political apathy among younger voters today' in the Bexley Borough Public Speaking Competition. How interesting too that the 2nd XV Rugby Team, under the watchful and professional eye of Mr. Ian Johns, should top their national league when they clinched victory over local adversaries St. Olave's Grammar School on the last day of the season. This illustrated the strength in

School's most successful 1st XV Rugby Team (2005-2006). Captain Adam Hunt centre with ball. Coach Noel Horrobin standing left. Coach Phil Ubee standing right.

depth of rugby in the school when seen alongside the award of London Borough Of Bexley Sports Team of the Year presented to the 2005/2006 1st XV Rugby Squad. The girls were not to be outdone as Jenni Rowe took her netball team to the Sports' Colleges National Netball Finals where they performed with great spirit.

With the sad and premature death of Noel Horrobin, the retirement Graham Lightwood and the approaching exeat of Sheila Ford, the School was in need of a major event to raise spirits and this came after a long two year wait. At the end of the Spring Term 2007 the new £3.3 million Art and Technology Block was officially opened by Quentin Blake, after whom it was named, at a delightfully informal and relaxed ceremony. How fitting that this remarkable building should be named after the famous illustrator whose career at the school is charted in this history. How pleasing too that Quentin should provide the characteristically spirited cover design for this second edition of *Past Purple*. Mr. Blake in a gently witty and nostalgic

speech stood up for art and technology as central to a well-rounded education. That balmy evening seemed to make those two long years, in which the School seemed more like a building site than an institution for education, fade into insignificance.

Quentin Blake

Quentin Blake Art and Technology Building

If 2006/2007 had not been difficult enough, the start of the following academic year seemed to compound the emotional strains the school community had been experiencing. The beginning of 2007/2008 brought the very sad news that Adam Hunt, the charismatic captain of the School's most successful rugby team, had drowned in a tragic episode while on a working holiday in Greece. The sense of shock was palpable in the School for some months. Fittingly the planting of a tree just outside the cricket pavilion celebrated Adam's contribution to the School. Adam's memorial was appropriately sited close to the tree that was planted for Noel Horrobin. How sad, in a way, that the team that Adam had done so much to nurture should, in 2010/2011, have found itself reformed, so to speak, at Sidcup Rugby Club, where, under the managerial care of Phil Ubee, many played for the 1st XV. Alas, Adam did not join them.

July 2007 saw a significant tranche of staff move on from Chis and Sid. One of the most significant departures was that of Sheila Ford, Deputy Head. With the going of Sheila the Rouncefield senior leadership regime that had guided the ship through the tricky waters of the 1990s and the early 2000s finally came to an end. Sheila, who had always been a great traveller, set out on further adventures to many far-flung places during the summer in which she retired and is still visiting areas far from the more routine tourist destinations as this book goes to print. She was replaced by

Joanne King, almost a local lass, who came to the School from Hall Mead, where she had been Head of Humanities. Ms King started something of a trend at Chis and Sid, being the offspring of a vicar; Nigel Walker, the seventh Head of the School, also came from a clerical background. Joanne was raised in Lewisham and Gravesend, attending St. George's school in Gravesend before winning a place at Mansfield College Oxford where she read Modern History. Having thoroughly enjoyed her time at school it was no surprise that she should choose teaching as a profession and so she moved from Oxford to Birmingham to study for the P.G.C.E. qualification. Then followed a move back to the South to take up a History

Joanne King, Deputy Head since 2007

post at Campion School in Essex. Campion, of course, is well known to Chis and Sid, being longstanding opponents on the rugby field. Joanne came to Senior Management at Chis and Sid through the academic department route, rather than the more common assistant head pathway. She was appointed as Deputy Head at the School in September 2007. She, like her colleagues on the very new leadership team, was impressed by the sense of tradition and community at Chis and Sid. However, in her role as Deputy Head responsible for Assessment, Recording and Reporting, she felt the need for the traditions to be nuanced to take into consideration the changing clientele.

A late arrival in 2006/2007, but a very significant one, was Nigel Walker. He was appointed as Deputy Head for Specialisms: more of Mr. Walker later in this history.

It was not just 'all change ' within management in terms of staffing in that summer. There was a significant amount of movement at all levels. Amanda Smart resigned her post as Assistant Head to move to Hillview where she joined Jim Rouncefield in the world of education administration. Doris Evans who had been Head of Mathematics in turn replaced her; Doris remained with a watching brief for the Mathematics Faculty until a newcomer, Lucy Rose, took the Faculty in 2008. Yvette Bellis, who had introduced some popular initiatives in her capacity as Key Stage 5 Coordinator, moved on to Buller's Wood School. Susan Shires, an old girl of the School, was subsequently appointed to run the Sixth Form, but remained part of the History Department, which found itself with a new leader in the guise of Hayley Saunt née Allen. Clive Madel, Classics, another former pupil, moved on. John Greenwood, highly successful Head of the Business Studies Department, went to local grammar school, St. Olave's. Sidikar Bayar was another who took the short walk across the East Field, in her case to run the Science Department at Hurstmere. Emma Reynolds, who had led the Girls' side of P. E. with notable professionalism and enthusiasm, left to devote time to her expanding family. Keith Aspin retired from the profession having stayed on beyond his allotted time to help the School out in a period when good science teachers were at a premium.

However, the summer of 2007 saw the departure of one of the School's genuine *characters*. Michael Ashby, linguist extraordinaire, staffroom comedian and film buff, took his well-earned retirement after thirty seven years at Chis and Sid. In typically surreal style, Mike, a notorious campaigner against all things sporty, devoted himself to rowing on leaving the profession and became a highly successful oarsman.

The School was lucky to welcome a promising group of colleagues in September of that year. Harry Acton, a proven academic, added his intellectual weight to the English Faculty and Philippa Snell brought her talents to Drama. Matthew Thomas abandoned the world of opera to strengthen the Religious Studies Department. In the January of 2008 Chis and Sid secured the services of Helen Everett, who made an immediate impact on morale in Business Studies and Economics. There were also some well-deserved internal promotions as Jenni Rowe and Tim Perry became Heads of Learning. What in July had looked like an uncontrollable upheaval had settled and the School moved on.

Although the motto of the School, *Abeunt Studia in Mores*, remained enshrined over the stage in the Main Hall, under the influence of Dr. Vitagliano a new informal motto was to be adopted: *Helping the learners of today become the leaders of tomorrow*. Besides a certain balance and catchiness, the motto captured a new concern within Chis and Sid. 'Leadership' became the buzzword. This was reflected within the curriculum. Sports Leadership Awards for the Sixth Form were on offer. The School Council and Year Councils achieved much higher profiles than hitherto. The Charity Committee and the Duke of Edinburgh Award were important to students, as they were encouraged to gather portfolios of achievement as well as examination grades. Other initiatives reinforced the notion of leadership. A series of International Days was inaugurated, the first being a whole school investigation, across departments, of all things Chinese. The School was presented with an Intermediate International School Award as a result of this and subsequently efforts were made to achieve the full award. It was no doubt pleasing to many parents to know that in 2008 the School was officially designated a Healthy School, but whether the average student celebrated the removal of chips with everything from the dinner menu is a point to debate.

It was around this time that those with a very observant eye noticed that a horse had disappeared from the school badge.

Culturally things were also on the move. Dance was developing as a key area in terms of examinations and also in the extra-curricular sphere. There had been a number of dynamic dance shows at Chis and Sid, but February 2008 saw the dance troupe attend the prestigious World of Hip Hop lead by the Robert Hylton Urban Classicism Group. March 2008 saw the same troupe attend a series of dance workshops in the delightful setting of Lake Garda. Besides the routine number of high quality concerts, there were some innovative musical events in 2007/2008. Professor James Sclater, Professor of Music at Mississippi College, worked in the School for a week as Musician in Residence. The Senior Choir travelled to Morley College to represent Chis and Sid in the Music for Youth Regional Music Festival. This was followed by an exciting journey to Ireland to perform at a number of venues. Other elements of the cultural life of the School included the Speak Out public speaking workshop, a visit to the Roman Villa at Fishbourne, a debate organised by Mr. Ziqiri, Head of Government and Politics, between Nigel Farage, MEP and Leader of UKIP, and Dr. Alan Bullion, a pro-European, on the topic of a possible referendum on the Lisbon Treaty and another World Challenge expedition, this time to Malaysia. Miriam Adisa, one of the School's most talented Year 12 students, was pronounced Young Business Writer of the Year 2008 and her prize was to read her competition entry at a prestigious business conference at Kent University.

The sporting life of the School was feted by the award of a Sportsmark in November 2008 and the sporting facilities on offer to students were greatly enhanced when the local authority sports centre opened on the old Sidcup Golf Clubhouse site in April 2008. While the School has always taken pride in the strength of its sports teams 2007/2008 was in some ways the era of the individual. Rebecca Smith, through her club, represented Great Britain in the 800 metres at the European Junior Athletics Championships in Brno in September 2007. Catherine Stent captained Kent Under 13 Ladies' Cricket Team. Jack Taylor played for Kent at football, Jack Stemp won the London Youth Games Judo competition and Chad Knapman became a county water polo player. Cosmo Elms became one of the first Young Ambassadors for Sport in Bexley. There were, of course, some exceptional team performances. The girls Under 14 Netball Team came third in the National Sports College Tournament. The Under 14 Rugby Team hosted a touring side from Romania. There was a remarkably successful joint cricket and netball tour to St. Lucia. Boys' hockey flourished and the School produced one of its most successful swimming teams. However, it could be said that the sporting laurels for this academic year should go to Mrs. Sharon Breen, for it was she who brought Goalball to the School. This is a Paralympic sport. It is played by teams of three with a football filled with ball bearings. The players try to score and defend in a similar way to football, using their whole body, while blindfolded. What a bonus for the few students at Chis and Sid at this time who suffered from quite severe visual impairment. And if this was not enough, guided by the administrative expertise of Mrs. Mandy McWhinnie, the School was fulfilling its responsibilities as a sports college by organising community and primary school sports events.

Sadly though, among all the enthusiastic hustle and bustle that characterised this lively institution, tragedy struck again. Once more the staff, students and friends of the School had to draw upon their emotional reserves when they heard of the death of Mr. Will Michael who had been Head of

Will Michael (1990-2008).

Music for some years. Will had been ill for a little while, but the news in May 2008 came as a terrible shock. Dr. Vitagliano wrote movingly of Will in the summer newsletter: 'It is our sad task to announce the death of Mr. Will Michael, who passed away on Friday 16th May 2008. Will joined Chislehurst and Sidcup Grammar School in September 1990 and soon established himself as an outstanding and inspirational educator . He created a wonderful tradition of music at this school, both in terms of performance as well as the teaching of the subject.' The

word 'inspirational' is overused in the teaching profession, but the memorial concert for Will illustrated that in his case the term was entirely apt. The number of old boys and girls who are now professional musicians who played at that concert was stunning. Will had himself been an outstanding jazz piano player. The Will Michael Trio created a name for itself as a backing band for the very best in British jazz and Will worked with many of the greats in the world of jazz. The Trio's residences at Lazers and The Green Man were well known on the jazz scene. How sad that Will, who had seen his son play at Ronnie Scott's club (the leading European jazz venue) with the National Youth Jazz Orchestra, should miss his own gig at this Mecca of his beloved music (he had won a date at Ronnie's as his prize for an outstanding performance at a national piano competition).

Thus an academic year so full of energy and activity was sadly framed by two tragic events, one at its start and the second at its close.

Walker Steps In

Nigel Walker.

EARLY SEPTEMBER 2008 was a time tense with gossip at the School. It was interesting to note how the proliferation of what is known as *social networking* had created a sophisticated rumour mill at Chis and Sid. Strangely, on this occasion rumour, usually so unreliable, proved to contain more than a nugget of truth. It really was the case that Dr. Vitagliano was leaving. The second interregnum period in only a few years was about to commence.

This interregnum was, however, a short-lived affair. Dr. V had been offered a post as principal of Midhurst Rother College, a newly created academy in the attractive Sussex town of Midhurst. Dr. Vitagliano was to return to the school of which he was a former pupil and oversee a massive amalgamation of three institutions. The Chis and Sid governors acted rapidly and Nigel Walker was appointed as Acting Head in January 2009 following Dr. Vitagliano's departure in December 2008. With almost unheard of speed in education circles, by the end of the Spring Term and after an arduous round of interviews and 'in tray' tasks, Nigel Walker had taken up the post of Head Teacher; he was the seventh holder of the position and the fourth from the West Country – Plymouth, Bristol, Cornwall and Dorset (the fifth if you care to include Wales!).

Mr. Walker, the son of an Anglican priest, had been brought up in Bristol and Swindon. His first degree was in Economics, but on deciding that education was the career path for him, he read for an MA in Curriculum Management in the early nineties. Nigel's professional development before Chis and Sid had taken place in a series of challenging institutions. In this respect he had much in common with the Senior Leadership Team that Dr. Vitagliano had assembled. Interestingly he was the first internal appointment to headship in the School's history. So the man who had had such a strange start at the School (Nigel was convinced that some elaborate practical joke was being played on him when he came for interview, as the purple uniform was identical to the uniform of The Bexley Academy, the school in which he was teaching at the time) was the new Head Teacher. A detached retina delayed his arrival at the School; this incident occurred on Nigel's garden trampoline following a long and stridently delivered sermon to his children on the safe use of sporting equipment. However, given this less than auspicious start, and given the eyesight problems, that were quickly cured, there was no doubt that Nigel's vision for the School was crystal clear. A proven fundraiser, Mr. Walker wished to continue and accelerate the improvement of the fabric of the school. One central concern was to inculcate the highest expectations into all pupils, from the highflying Oxbridge candidate, to those who might struggle to achieve five A-C grades at GCSE. Pleasingly, he saw care of the teaching and administrative staff as the key to a thriving school. His philosophy concerning headship was both simple and, paradoxically, challenging: a head teacher must strive to create a school that he or she would be proud and excited to have their own children attend.

And, as was the case with a former head teacher, Jim Rouncefield, no sooner had he closed his office door and settled into the Head's Chair but OFSTED came knocking in July 2009. It felt, however, that this visit that had been anticipated for several years was much less invasive and bullying, at least for the ordinary teacher, if not the Senior Leaders. Dr. Vitagliano had done much of the groundwork for this inspection, but, nevertheless, Nigel's highly tuned diplomatic and negotiation skills were required to deliver the very positive outcome of the short inspection. Forty three summative judgements were made about the School. Eight of those judgements found the School to be good and a staggering thirty five found it to be outstanding. The Sixth Form in particular emerged from the process with flying colours. The post sixteen students were found to be exemplary. Sixth Form provision was judged outstanding in every respect. It is a sad irony that many of these students, so rightly praised by Her Majesty's education watchdog, should, only a year or so later, consider turning down the opportunity to move on to higher education as a result of Her Majesty's government increasing university fees to extraordinary levels.

Mr. Walker was not the only internal promotion for that academic year. Ebenezer Oniasanmi became Head of Physics, Leila Ward Head of Music, Doug Wise Head of Learning for Year 11, Lizzie Lymer filled the vacant post of Head of Citizenship and Coordinator of the School Council, and Peter Leaton took over as Deputy Head of Maths. After thirty four years at the School Clive Wederell, who had been a stalwart of the History Department and leader of the Politics Department, took retirement, to be replaced by Dibran Zeqiri. Andy Fraser, a talented and creative woodworker and technologist also retired in July 2008. Linda Woodacre moved on, as did Lyn Connell, who had taught Biology at Chis and Sid for nearly two decades. Brenda Allen who had run the School Office with outstanding professionalism for some twenty years retired and was, thankfully, immediately re-employed on a part time basis, so Nicola Sayell, the new incumbent, could draw on Brenda's expertise. Maggie Lloyd retired from the Finance Office and her brusque but caring manner was certainly missed. Diane Ames took over a rapidly expanding Finance Department. The arrivals that July all very quickly made their mark on the School. Claire Alexander, a proud Geordie, brought studio theatre to Chis and Sid and continued the strong tradition of drama in the School. Ed Bretherton, with his dry sense of humour and natural rapport with senior students, was a perfect choice to move into the Deputy Head of Sixth Form role a year or so after

271

his appointment to the History Department in July 2008. Claire Cameron and Christina Robinson were two very strong appointments at that time as were Natasha Porter and Natalie Harding who added some much needed life and verve to an English Faculty that was becoming rather dull under a crusty and ageing Head of Department.

By 2008/2009 the relationship between Chis and Sid and Marlborough Special School was certainly thriving. For years sixth form students had visited and assisted at Marlborough, but in 2007, under the guidance of Mr. Walker a classroom was converted to house a few Marlborough sixth form students for one day a week. By 2009 some eighteen students, effectively the entire Marlborough Sixth Form, were on the Chis and Sid site five days a week and were sharing many of the School facilities with their Chis and Sid friends. The liaison between the schools blessed Chis and Sid students with the opportunity to involve themselves with an educational environment very different from that which pertains at most schools. One such involvement was the Orchid House and Five-a-Day garden, a project whose funding by Bexley Council was secured by a bid prepared by Post 16 pupils at the School. By 2009, after a grand opening by environmentalist Tom Hart Dyke, the garden was being enthusiastically cultivated by both sets of students.

Cheers were heard throughout the land in 2008 when the announcement to abandon SATs for Key Stage 3 was made; how had they lasted so long? However, Chis and Sid examination grades were continuing to impress with 100% of students achieving at least five A- C grades at GCSE in 2008. The decision was taken at this time to start teaching the International Baccalaureate as from September 2009, an exciting, if unpredictable innovation. On 8th October 2009 Doris Evans accepted an International School Award on behalf of Chis and Sid from newsreader and journalist George Aligiah. London Mayor, Boris Johnson, opened the newly built Sidcup Leisure Centre, a facility, the proximity of which, allowed for an expansion of the Physical Education curriculum. The tradition of taking Year 11 students to the Wrotham Study Centre was developed as the opportunity to enjoy the outdoor activities on offer there was extended to Year 7 pupils. By the end of 2008/2009 every teaching area (classroom) was equipped with an interactive whiteboard (IWB): the brave new digital world had not passed Chis and Sid by.

Culturally the School was thriving. Dance was again to the fore with *On The Radio* conceived, directed and produced by Matthew Rowlands

272

and Grace Bowyer under the artistic control of Miss Rycroft. The Music Department entered new territory with The Battle of The Bands, the aptly named Celibate Monks taking on Six Foot Sir and Jeremy By Hands in an exciting, if noisy, competition. The more classically inclined musicians performed in the Black Forest, the Festival Hall and the rather less glamorous Bluewater Shopping Centre. There were cultural outings to The London Design Museum, The Globe Theatre and to see *The Lion King*. Studio Drama kicked off with a series of well-received sixth form performances including the enigmatic piece *A Trip To The Stars*. Probably the most interesting venture in terms of culture was the planning and development of the Communal Amphitheatre by Year 12 Art students in collaboration with Tim Norris, a member of The Royal Society of Sculptors.

A thoroughly enjoyable pre-season rugby tour to the Basque region of France got sport off to a flying start. This acted as a powerful stimulus to a sporting year full of success. Joe Appiah and Courtney Ubank competed in the National Youth Athletic League in Manchester. The Under 14 cricketers lifted the North West Kent Championships. What a boost for girls' cricket at the School that Catherine Stent's inclusion in this victorious side made it effectively a mixed team. Sarah Wray, a Year 8 student, was establishing herself as a Kent tennis star. Perhaps most notable was the progress of Harry Allen. A truly dynamic and fearless rugby player, Harry had worked his way to England honours and as this history goes to print, he is a professional contracted to Saracens Rugby Club.

The notion of change has been something of a leitmotif in the last three chapters of this work. By July 2010 there was a sense that administration, staffing and management structure changes were almost complete. From the early days of the decade when leadership was still only management and three managers effectively ran the School the leadership team, in response to government initiatives, had burgeoned to six with the arrival in April 2010 of Linsey Hand who was taken on as Assistant Head for Learning. This team was occasionally supplemented with three or so colleagues from middle management when the perceived need arose. Not only had the entire management group of early 2000 moved on, but also the Heads of the bigger departments had been replaced by the end of the academic year 2009/2010. Chis and Sid was a very different place from ten years before. Reading this history, however, shows it was ever thus. Jim Rouncefield's comment, used earlier in this book, which suggests that standing still is akin to going backwards, describes this phenomenon in education most accurately. As the School moves ineluctably forward to its eightieth birthday celebrations, with the possibility of a radical change of status on the horizon (by the time this book goes to print Chis and Sid may well be on its way to being a Govean academy), change is still item one on the agenda.

The departure of Mrs. Valerie Perryman in July 2009 flagged up in a very graphic way the changes afoot at middle management level. Val, Head of Modern Foreign Languages, who had devoted herself to her students and the School for over thirty years, said farewell at a delightful, if somewhat emotional, gathering. For some present at Val's leaving function it felt as if an era was passing. This feeling was reinforced in July 2010 with the departure of two other long serving members of staff; John Hazelgrove, Head of English took retirement and Linda Williams left the classroom, but was too valuable to the School to sever all connections and was rapidly re-employed to run the Examinations Office. Whether these departures really did see the school turning its back on the eighties and nineties is debatable, because John and Val were both replaced internally, Jean Hitchcock took over the English Department and Elizabeth Bonnaud née Johnson, stepped up to run M.F.L.. Maybe the reader can spot some sense of continuity here. Even Marelle Valentine, Head of Humanities, who left in 2010 to take up a post as Assistant Head, was replaced from within the existing staff by Hayley Saunt née Allen. Aline Marshall, who had almost single-handedly set up and developed the very popular Psychology A. level course, left after some years of poor health. Some other notable characters, who had made themselves very much part of the Chis and Sid fabric, left in July 2009. The flamboyant and unpredictable American import, Steve Mckiel moved to Christchurch Canterbury University to study for a postgraduate qualification in conducting. A much respected and highly valued antipodean colleague, Rob Kearney, returned home after several spells at Chis and Sid. His sporting prowess was missed, as was his sharp sense of humour and fun. Stuart Bromley, another P.E. specialist left to go abroad and at Easter 2010 Lucy Rose, Head of Mathematics left. She was replaced by Lisa Allen. Daniel Stackhouse joined the English Faculty following the departure of Harry Acton and Peter Dunn took over from Hilary Hildred as master statistician.

As preparations went ahead for the eightieth birthday celebrations, this second edition of *Past Purple* being part of these festivities, the School wended its way to the end of the first decade of the 21st century and looked towards the second. Quentin Blake opened the Amphitheatre on a cold, but entertaining, November evening. The World Challenge Expedition took on Malaysia in this year. The *Chronicle*, which had changed its format somewhat, becoming rather more journalistic, was supplemented by a series of comprehensive newsletters. The website and the communications protocol, paperless communications with parent via the Internet, were experiments that were now standard elements of school administration. Young Enterprise was a consistent feature in the Sixth Form and The Charity Committee enjoyed a very high profile, as did the House Competition that had undergone a refurbishment in the previous two years. The Sixth Form Ball, which was now very much part of Chis and Sid tradition had a rival as the Year 11s celebrated the completion of their examinations with the very successful River Boat trips. In August 2010 the Head Teacher was almost too excited to announce that, for the first time, the School had achieved a 100% A-C pass rate at GCSE that included Maths and English, the new government benchmark. Maybe the Year 11s of 2010 deserved their jaunt up the Thames. The Sports Dinner Awards reflected another pleasing year on the sports field. Bringing the community in to use the facilities on offer at the School was now very much a central characteristic of how sports specialism worked at Chis and Sid. Girls' rugby, girls', cricket, Sport Relief, rugby festivals, revamped sports days were all indicative of how the sporting makeup of the School had changed over ten years. The Dance Department trip to New York and the very polished musical *Bugsy Malone*, starring Chris Flynn, Jamie Lott and Daniel Hey, were all part of the energy created by Sports College status; interestingly, even though Drama was now part of the P.E. Faculty, it had lost none of its artistic dynamism. Music continued to thrive as the arrival of a drumming group from South Africa to run a workshop illustrated. As a result of the efforts of student Daisy Meager, Amnesty International found a voice at the School.

So there would be much to celebrate on 16th June 2011. But what of the medium and long term future for Chis and Sid? The first edition of this history concluded with a sense of uncertainty. The author pondered a future that looked financially secure with the then Chancellor, Gordon Brown, promising significant funds for education. Tony Blair's maxim, 'Education, Education, Education', suggested good times ahead. League tables, exam overload, teacher shortages, changing patterns of pupil behaviour all seemed to counter any truly rosy outlook for education. What then is seen in the crystal ball in 2011? 'The web of our life is of a mingled yarn, good and ill together,' remarks an anonymous lord, wisely, in *All's Well That Ends Well*. One is all too well aware how true his words are when one comes to attempt a summing up of the situation in which the School finds itself in 2011 as its eightieth birthday approaches. It is at this point that the second edition of *Past Purple* must close. Others may wish to add further chapters in the years ahead. It can be stated with some certainty that Academy status is the dominating issue for the School at this time. However, 2010/ 2011 is a time of great austerity and the current coalition government only has cutbacks and financial pain on offer for public institutions. How well will the School cope with this fiscal hardship? Time will tell.

In 2002 Jim Rouncefield and Graham Lightwood detailed much of the ' ill' element of the fabric that constitutes Chis and Sid. Jim saw the School plagued by the tyranny of targets and statistics, graphs and diagrams. He was concerned about the prevailing social conditions in the suburbs, violence, drugs, lack of discipline. Graham too was worried about the proliferation of modular examinations and the effect this would have on the rich diet of extra curricular activities that the School enjoyed. Maybe, at the time of writing, even given financial constraints, it is more appropriate to emphasise the 'good' elements of this 'mingled yarn'. SATs have gone. Targets are still with us, but the word from the coalition is that they will be used less aggressively. League tables are progressively being phased out. A. Levels are to be rationalised and the amount of coursework in GCSE syllabuses is to be reduced. The building programmes at the School, the new Sixth Form Centre excluded, have been completed. Numbers remain secure. The Sixth Form, as evidenced by the OFSTED Report is flourishing. The cultural and sporting life of the School is vibrant and looks to be expanding. The extra curricular opportunities for students have never been so plentiful. There is an entirely warranted pride in Chis and Sid's examination results.

Shadows may be lengthening in some directions, but, as Arthur Clough memorably put it, 'Westward, look, the land is bright!' As the institution approaches the ripe old age of eighty, its constitution is strong and it is enjoying good health. The School seems to take the whirlwind of educational innovation in its stride, teasing out and running with the best and quietly abandoning the weak, the laughable and the frivolous. It was ever thus at Chis and Sid. There will be much to celebrate at the eightieth birthday party!

Index of Names

Abbott, Jane 149, 157
Ackland, Ben 190, 193
Ackland, Rebecca 205
Acton, Harry 266, 274
Adams, Margaret 209
Adisa, Miriam 267
Ahlers, James 256
Ainsworth, Janet 220
Alderman, Catrin 225, 228, 229
Alexander, Claire 271
Alford, Andrew 171, 197
Aligiah, George 272
Allen, Brenda 209, 271
Allen, Harry 273
Allen, Lisa 274
Ames, Dianne 271
Anderson, H.J. 63
Anderson, Jean 54
Anderson, Stephen 165, 175, 194, 199, 204, 205, 220, 222, 229, 246, 258, 260
Anning, Paul 209, 222, 231, 238
Ansell, Matthew 187
Appiah, Joe 273
Appleby, Enid 71, 100
Arlidge, Anthony 90, 239
Ashby, Michael 130, 150, 157, 226, 265-266
Ashwin, Stephanie 231
Aspin, Keith 254, 265
Atkinson, Richard 238
Aubel, Felix 199
Aughterlony, Derrick 100
Avery, Paul 75, 184, 256

Backhouse, Robert 139
Baker, Andrew 195, 201
Baker, Kenneth 184, 188, 171
Baker, Michael 114, 142, 192
Baker, Neil 195
Banfield, James 5, 6, 7, 23, 25, 27, 28, 33, 35, 38, 45, 82, 196
Barber, Norman ("Toddy") 6, 28, 29, 30, 33, 51, 63
Barclay, Ben 232
Barker, Anthony 173
Barker, W.A. 111
Barnard, Clifford 75
Barrett, Alison 142, 149, 156-7, 165
Barrow, L.R. 41
Bartlett, David 189, 240
Basri, Naim 55, 62, 73
Batchelor, Gordon 29
Bayar, Sidikar 247, 265

Baynham, Anne 148
Baynham, R.G. 63
Bechervaise, J.R. 44
Becky, Alex 243, 260
Beedle, Mavis 235
Beeton, Thomas 4, 34
Beetschen, Matthew 172, 190
Bell, Elizabeth 193
Bellis, Yvette 254, 265
Ben Fredj, Naoufel 200, 203
Bennett, Mark 185
Bennett, William 75
Beresford, Judith 152, 153-4, 157, 168, 173
Berry, Donna 225, 235
Berry, Jack 256
Berry, Martyn 107, 109, 112, 113, 121, 143, 160, 191, 194, 227, 247
Berry, Susanna 171
Berry, Tim 266
Best, Graham 255
Bewsey, Carole 149
Birchall, Ian 173
Birchenough, Edwyn 32, 35, 36, 49, 54, 77
Bishop, Sue 233, 240
Bizet 250
Black, Dr 161
Black, Ursula 231, 238
Blair, Tony 275
Blake, Quentin 13, 74, 75, 81, 87, 124, 213, 214, 263, 275
Blatch, Corinne 175, 185, 186
Bleach, Peter 233
Blunkett, David 161
Blyghton, Richard 199
Bond, Jolyon 256, 259
Bonnaud, Elizabeth 254
Bowden, Malcolm 54
Bowden, Matthew 227
Bowyer, Grace 273
Boxall, Rhys 256, 259
Boxwell, Gerald 29, 32, 33, 35
Boynes, Alice 249-250
Brackpool, Lorraine 195
Bradford, Sharon 234
Bradley, John 75
Bramwell, Frank 43, 47, 53, 78
Brand, Alec 201
Brand, David 107, 125
Bratcher, Robert 107, 121
Bray, William 12, 14, 83, 239
Breen, Jennifer 167, 202, 209

Breen, Sharon 267
Bretherton, Ed 271
Brierly, Ronald 111, 135
Briggs, Hayley 243
Bright, Rebecca 231
Brimson, Matthew 189, 195
Bromley, Stuart 260, 274
Bronks, Jeffrey 173
Brook, D.G. 121
Brooke, Harold 64, 79
Brown, Gordon 242, 275
Brown, Barbara 189, 240
Brown, L. 81
Brown, Michael 117-9, 121, 123, 126, 128, 131-2, 134-5, 141-2, 144-5, 147, 149-51, 159-60, 166, 190, 192, 210, 214, 215
Brown, Rosemary 118, 145
Browne, James 222, 225
Browning, Irving 66, 74, 75, 76
Brunning, Fergus 170
Buckingham, Dorothy 162, 167
Buckingham, Mark 165
Bullion, Alan 267
Bunce, Christopher 235
Bundell, Katherine 172, 187, 191
Burgess, Brian 94, 107, 121, 152, 153, 160, 168, 172, 186, 187, 200, 224, 232-3, 240, 246-248
Burnell, Mary 39, 97, 100, 209
Burnip, Jack 79-80, 90, 127, 129, 140
Burston, Ben 223
Burton, Helen 185
Butler, Eileen 104-5, 162, 167, 209
Butterworth, John 168
Buxton, Robert 121, 157, 160, 168, 192, 233, 234, 248-248

Cade, Leonard 6, 29, 33
Callow, Michael 131, 159, 199
Cameron, Claire 272
Cannon, Elizabeth 196, 199, 204
Carey, Rosemary 171, 195
Carlysle, Robert 167, 189
Carr, Karen 228
Carreck, Michael 5, 67-9, 157, 224
Carter, Derek 41
Carter, Sharon 173
Chadbourne (the Misses) 3
Chandler, David 142, 237
Chapman, Gwen 97, 104
Chappell, David 187

INDEX OF NAMES

Charman, Alice 240
Charman, Dennis 240
Charman, Helen 240
Charman, Sarah 240
Chavasse, Christopher 89, 101
Christian, Sally 125
Churchill, John 171
Churchill, Winston 18, 52, 71
Claggett, Robert 193
Clark, Ben 225, 236
Clark, Sophie 225
Clarke, Andrew 190
Clarke, Dennis 40, 52, 53, 79, 113, 196
Clarke, Kenneth 184
Cleghorn, Neil 175
Clement, Katy 221
Clemenson, John 255
Clifford, Ann 106, 148, 227-8
Clinton, Graham 129, 201
Clough, Arthur 276
Clowry, Matthew 185
Cole, Bob 83, 105, 107
Cole, David 121
Collet, Mark 3
Collins, Bradley 239
Collins, Jenny 167
Collins, Peter 63
Colwell, Kevin 174, 189
Connell, Lynn 204, 271
Connor, Cecilia 249, 256
Connor, Naomi 236-7
Cook, Geoffrey 5-7, 21-2, 24-5, 28, 30, 34-5, 39, 49, 53, 63, 74
Cooling, Cyril 59, 75-6
Cooney, Michelle 153, 188
Cornish, Peter 75
Cornwallis, Lord 101, 102
Corrigan, Adam 187
Corrigan, Andy 255
Corrigan, Dominic 205, 209
Cottee, Penny 152
Court, Maurice 100
Coutts, Sharon 168
Cowmeadow, Bill 170, 201
Craven, Robert 61
Crittenden, Henry 33
Cronin, John 112, 121, 124
Crook, Roger 157
Crook, Sue 149
Crosland, Anthony 101, 108, 110, 161
Crossley, Timothy 164, 169, 170
Croxson, Derek 43
Cruise, Peter 225
Crust, Anthony 138-9
Crust, Jane 165
Crust, Joyce 138, 149, 151-3, 192, 194, 211, 235
Crust, Nancy 113, 125, 134-5

Cruttenden, Henry 6
Cullingworth, Victor 54, 107
Cumbers, Brian 107, 114
Cunningham, Lily 54, 148
Cunningham, Stuart 141, 201-2, 233
Cutler, Jamie 256, 259
Dale, Gerald 58
Dale, Richard 22, 29, 30, 33-4
Darke, Stanley 104, 112
Darton-Bigg, Amanda 222
Davey, Martin 235, 260
Davies, I.C. 125
Davies, Meredith 187
Davies, Michael 189
Davies, Nia1 53
Davies, Richard 107
De Lury, Nola 167
Dean, Audrey 168, 172
Dean, Colin 165
Delibes 250
Dellar, E.J. 43, 53, 55, 74
Delve, Lindsey 261
Dempsey, James 255
Desbruslais, Simon 231, 236
Detnon, Mark 169
Dibble, Edward 225, 228
Dibble, Tom 209
Dickerson, Neil 228
Dimbleby, David 139
Doxey, Stuart 189
Doyle, Maureen 167
Dracup, Roger 18, 54, 82, 148
Duck, William 28
Duggal, Rohit 208
Dunball, Steve 103, 113, 114
Dunn, Peter 274
Dunn, Tony 128, 132
Durban, David 130, 144, 195
Durkin, Barbara 240, 254
Durve, Meeta 228
Dutton, F.W. 43, 49, 78

Eades, Daniel 225
Easterbrook, Lawrence 262
Eaton, David 222
Edlmann, Francis 3, 4, 12, 30, 34, 37, 38, 43, 74, 83, 197
Edwards, Anthony 75
Ellis, David 171
Ellis, Simon 249-250
Elms, Cosmo 267
Empson, Jackie 153-4, 196
English, Stephen 247
Ernsting, J. 41, 75
Evans, David 256
Evans, Doris 254, 265, 272
Evans, Robert 101
Everett, Helen 266

Fairweather, Colin 199, 204
Farage, Nigel 267
Farrall, John 233
Farrant, Rosemary 184
Fentiman, Julie 199
Ferguson, Julie 167
Fey, Katherine 230, 243
Fielding, Douglas 124, 131
Finch, Samantha 153, 196
Fischer, Henning 186, 196, 202, 228, 234
Fisher, Melanie 230, 234
Fitzgerald, Jack 220
Flannery, Sarah 229
Flaxman, Stanley 58
Flindall, Douglas 31, 51
Flint, Peggy 170
Flower, John 101
Flynn, Chris 275
Foot, Henry 125
Ford, Geoffrey 43
Ford, Sheila 198, 199, 257, 263-4
Forsdick, Nicholas 166, 204
Fowler, David 139
Fox, Joe 54, 58, 61
Franklin, Martin 208
Fraser, Andrew 204, 271
Freeman, Beryl 40, 145, 171, 221
Freeman, Bill 16, 23, 40, 53-4, 78, 82, 89, 105, 117, 120-1, 127, 132, 143-4, 159, 166, 170, 172, 210, 213
French, John 163
French, Jon 255
French, Nancy 172
Frost, Allan 199, 205, 206, 211
Froud (Biology) 54
Fuller, Anne 140, 167

Gallop, William 187
Gardner, Alan 63
Garrett, Ian 185, 186
Garrett, Steven 184, 230
Geen, Philip 103-4, 141
Geiringer, Erich 15, 55
George, Valerie 189, 202, 237
Geren, Carol 204, 226, 230
Gibbs, G.R. 39, 53
Gibson, Jane 209
Giles, Alex 199, 205
Gill, D. 88
Gladwell, Scott 191
Goddard, George 17, 23, 79, 107, 111-2, 121, 166, 227
Godfrey, Zoe 204-5, 209
Goldby, John 67
Goldstein, Cyril 20
Gooden, Stephen 130, 175-6, 182, 234
Goodman, Maggie 159, 171

INDEX OF NAMES

Gordon, A.S. 75
Gower, Daniel 260-1
Grassby, Ben 40, 90
Grassby, C.F.B. 124
Gray, Joanne 237, 256
Grayson, Peter 231, 236
Green, E.R. 41
Green, M.A. 131
Green, Raymond 182, 187
Green, Robert 165, 195, 199
Greenhalgh, Vicky 261
Greenway, K. 56
Greenway, R. 37, 42
Greenwood, John 223, 265
Greer, Germaine 171
Gridley, Maurice 32, 34-5, 53, 74
Grindrod, Sydney 81, 114
Gross, P. 56
Grubb, Andrew 188
Grubb, David 197, 199, 200,
    220, 222, 226-7, 238
Grummitt, Rob 228
Gunner, William 31
Guy, Richard 220, 238
Guyatt, Derek 56

Hadwin, Joy 221, 238
Hahn, Douglas 137-8, 155,159,
    162, 176, 177, 188, 190-1, 193
Hahn, Janice 190
Hales, Bryan 162, 209
Halford, Ronald 114
Hall, J.H. 47
Hall, Peter 6
Hamblen, Barbara 188
Hamblen, Bill 100, 109,
    167-8, 188, 229, 234
Hand, Linsey 273
Handa, Mohindra 165, 214
Handy, Elgar 111, 113, 126, 133-4
Hankinson, Michael 128, 197
Hanks, Fraser 225
Hanks, James 231
Hansen, I.V. 119
Hanson, Alan 55
Harding, Natalie 272
Hardyman, Michael 195, 214
Harris, Margaret 137-8, 147,
    149, 150-1, 155, 197, 198
Harris, Matt 246, 249, 258
Harrison, Amy 228-9
Harrison, Steve 236
Harrison, Tara 187, 188
Hart Dyke, Tom 272
Hartley, Jonathan 138-9
Harvey, Eddie 200
Harwood, Alistair 186
Harwood, Diane 149, 153, 157, 172
Hawkins, Maureen 167
Hawkins, Rita 167

Haye-Forbes, E. 100, 109
Hayter, Lord 31
Hazelgrove, Carole 223
Hazelgrove, John 171, 173-4,
    185, 187, 190, 193, 234, 274
Head-Rapson, Christine 192,
    224, 233
Head-Rapson, David 221
Heath, Edward 114, 123, 128,
    133, 135, 139, 142, 169,
    173-4, 204, 212
Heinemann, Aaron 262
Hellyer, Brian 167, 173, 189
Hennessy, Louise 191
Hester, Alec 75
Hey, Daniel 275
Heyward, Catherine 228
Hickey, Lawrence 140
Higgins, Alec 124, 141, 173, 195
Hildred, Hilary 274
Hildred, John 261
Hill, Diane 195, 202, 208, 230, 256
Hill, Steve 169
Hitchcock, Jean 235
Hoare, Jeff 103
Holbrook, Adam 239
Holland, Graham 199, 240
Holt, Janice 149, 152-3
Homewood, Robert 70
Honour, Beryl 174
Hora, Deepak Kaur 229
Hornsby-Smith, Patricia 18,
    84, 86, 103
Horrobin, Noel 157, 159, 195, 209,
    225, 256, 259-260, 262-264
Horsbrugh, Florence 84-6,100
Hosier, Grace 226
Howard, Barry 168
Howes, Emma 236
Howie, Geoffrey 223, 228
Hughes, Eluned (Lynne)188, 195,
    202, 234
Huke, David 114
Hunt, Adam 256, 259, 262, 264
Hunt, Geoffrey 52
Husband, William 171, 196, 199
Hutchinson, Matthew 258
Hutton, Andrew 247
Hutton, Will 124, 214, 230

Ims, Robert 42, 114-5, 132, 171,
    175, 184
Ives, Susan 149, 157, 169, 185

Jackson, Eva 54-5, 79, 104, 113, 231
James, Bertha 19, 91, 125, 131
Jamieson, Edna 140, 184, 195
Janks, Gary 211, 220, 224, 226
Jell, Shane 249
Jenkins, Carol 204

Jenkins, Edward 34, 90, 105, 117,
    119, 129, 136-7, 199, 201, 210
Jenkins, Keith 129, 187, 221
Jewson, Geoffrey 107, 129
Johns, Ian 262
Johnson, Boris 272
Johnson, Paul 157
Johnson, William 225
Jones, Claire 228
Jones, Debbie 190
Jones, R. 123
Jones, Teresa 186
Joseph, Keith 183, 188
Judd, Richard 209

Kamen, Henry 101
Kazim, Celal 231
Keard, J. 36
Kearny, Rob 274
Kearney, David 174
Keeler, Rachel 246
Keep, Daniel 208, 233
Kelly, Daniel 255
Kemnal, Lady 37
Kemsley, P.A. 131
Kennedy, David 199
Khan, Qurban 228
Kidd, Jane 170
Kidney, Donald 75
Kimber, J.D. 97
King, Joanne 264-5
King, John 107, 124-5
King, Martin 185
Knapman, Chad 267
Knight, Martin 175
Kuruppu, Rohan 208
Kuypers, Birgit 184, 204

Laing, Jeremy 222, 224
Lamthong, Linda 224
Lane, Richard 223-4, 228
Larkins, Sarah 188
Lathey, Sam 231
Leaning, John 45
Leaton, Peter 271
Lee, Daniel 228, 238
Lee, G.J. 191
Lee, Louise 224
Lee, Yvette 246
Lester, Alex 187
Lester, Harry 83, 101, 103, 111,
    131, 196
Levey, Fiona 164, 169
Lewis, Gerwyn 97, 105, 121, 138,
    174, 212
Lewis, Jestyn 123, 208, 211
Lidiard, David 168
Lightwood, Graham 193-4, 202,
    214-5, 247, 251, 255, 257, 260,
    263, 276

INDEX OF NAMES

Lilly, Terry 107
Linton, Stanley 174
Lloyd, Maggie 212, 228, 271
Loakes, Brian 88
Lobb, Howard 96, 98
Lockheart, Andrea 233
Lorsery, Dorothee 261
Lott, Jamie 275
Loweth, S. H. 96
Lymer, Lizzie 254, 271
Lynch, Ian 140, 142, 162, 164-5

MacDonald, Wendy 153, 201, 207
Mace, Andrew 205
Madel, Clive 235, 239, 255, 265
Madgett, Hedley 43, 63
Maktari, Fatima 235
Manley, Rose 261
Mann, H. 62, 101
Marchant, Peter 52
Marriner, Richard 205, 209
Marshal, Aline 243, 274
Marsham-Townshend, Hugh 29, 30
Martin, A. 41
Martin, Audrey 111, 124, 131,133, 135, 141
Martin, Edgar 77, 103, 121, 163
Martin, Eleanor 250
Martin, Geoffrey 6, 36, 42
Martin, H.J. 42
Martin, Katie 250
Martin, Linda (English) 138, 171
Martin, Linda (H.E.) 142, 199, 228
Martin, Sidney 38, 63
Martin, W. 97
Marvell, P. 88
Mason, Keith 173
Mason, Richard 121, 124, 192
Matkins, Pauline 151, 155, 192, 229, 237
Maxfield, Suzanne 149
Maylam, Terry 107, 166, 168, 172, 187, 192
McCulloch, Ernest 33
McDonald, Bert 259
McDonnell, Maureen 172
McDonough, Julian 172
McElroy, Bill 105, 107-8
McJames, D. 36
McKenna, Peter 111
McKiel, Steve 243, 274
McNaught, Simon 233, 238, 254
McWhinne, Mandy 268
Meager, Daisy 275
Mearns, Kelly 225
Meehan, Brian 187
Mennie, Miss 61
Meredith, Roger 173
Michael, Will 200, 222, 225, 231, 243, 268

Miller, Sian 172
Mills, E.V. 71-2
Mills, Jenny 140
Mitchell, Charles 30, 32, 34-6, 41
Mitchell, P.C. 41, 76, 102
Mitchell, W.J. 90
Moat, Walter 83, 96, 109, 132
Mobey, Elizabeth 196
Mobey, Neil 201
Monk, Trevor 165
Monks, Mary 173, 201
Monks, Ted 201
Moody, Kevin 197, 212
Moore, Nicola 236
Morgan, David 200
Morgan, Katie 220
Morland, Marissa 260
Morley, Cedric 17, 23, 54, 79, 88-9, 105, 107, 113, 117, 120, 121, 143-5, 156, 160, 163, 166, 201, 210, 231, 233-4
Morley, Colin 145
Morley, Hilda 145
Morris, H. 79
Morris, P. 124
Morshed, Seemin 239, 240
Mortimore, K. 38, 54, 74
Moss, Christopher 221, 230
Moulinie, Heidi 187-8, 191
Mozart 250
Mulberry, Ted 113
Mullooly, Debbie 238
Murphy, Brendan 197, 220
Murray, Alan 6, 23, 29, 33, 36
Murray, Anthony 196, 199, 205
Murray, James 46
Mycroft, Bryony 250

Nathan, Alan 190, 193, 195
Naylor, Amanda 195, 205
Newell, Samantha 195
Newis, Tim 255
Nex, Ann (see "Clifford")
Nongbri, Alicia 248
Norris, Craig 140
Norris, Frank 31
Norris, P.R. 48
Norris, Tim 273

Oakes, Sharon 236
O'Brien, Kieran 258
O'Brien, Liam 255
O'Connell, Donald 75
O'Connor, Danielle 222
O'Doherty, James 250
Oddie, Hugh 53, 64
Oesterreicher, T. 65
Oliver, Amy 235
Oniasanmi, Ebenezer 271
O'Rourke, Angela 199, 207, 214

Osbiston, Barbara 148
Ost, Peter 5, 6, 29, 33
O'Sullivan, Jo 236
Oswald, Kirsty 262
Owen, Cyril 6, 30, 58

Pack, David 204, 222, 225
Paddon, Don 164
Page, Ian 129, 157, 184, 191, 256
Page, Lindsey 132
Page, Tim 194
Paine, Roger 211-2, 228
Palin, Michael 121
Palmer, E.T. 5-7, 24-5, 27-8, 31-2, 35-6, 41, 46, 54, 76, 79, 87, 104-5, 114, 117, 126, 128, 136-7, 146, 175, 189, 210
Palmer, Enid 41, 54, 137
Palmer, Robert 6
Pam, Samuel 192, 228
Pannell, N.M. 123, 160
Panton, Gary 261
Pape, Michael 231
Parker, Colin 186
Parrott, Caroline 261
Parsons, Arthur 5-7, 14, 23-5, 35, 38-9, 53, 65, 71, 79, 87, 104, 121, 136, 200
Parsons, Constance 14
Parton, Vicky 233, 240
Partridge, Joan 60, 148
Pascoe, Lionel 82, 105
Paterson, Malcolm 222, 225
Paterson, Shelley 193, 230, 238
Patrick, Jackie1 53
Patten, John 184, 212
Payne, Raymond 105, 113
Peacock, Martin 215
Pead, John (Pead Major) 32
Pead, Stuart (Pead Minor) 32, 43
Pearson, Les 215
Pedley, Jean 115
Pedley, Richard 19, 91-6, 99, 100-1, 103-14, 122, 135-6, 159-61, 166, 186, 192, 194, 210, 212, 214, 217
Pedley, Robin 95
Pedley, Susan 115
Pedley, Timothy 115
Peirse, Jenny 194
Pendrich, Susan 206
Pennycuick, David 114, 127, 142
Percival, Robert 232
Perry, Tim 261, 266
Perry, Tony 109
Perryman, Valerie 166, 192, 202, 274
Petley, Jo 235
Pettet, E.C. 39, 57, 61, 63
Phillips, Giles 254

INDEX OF NAMES

Phillips, L.H. 24, 32, 41
Pillow, Alex 259
Philpott, Rebecca 221
Pickard, Alfred 107
Pinkney, Garth 114, 124, 229-30
Pinnell, W. 83
Pitts, Adrian 171, 185, 187-8, 190-1, 197
Poltock, John 45, 72, 84
Pope, David 168, 172
Pope, Raymond 125, 135, 160, 173-4, 178, 181. 190, 199, 229
Port, Sophia 249
Porter, Natasha 272
Potrac, Lisa 207
Potter, Alderman 135
Powell, David 58, 59
Powell, Eddie 233, 238, 257
Preston, Jim 113
Prew, Juliet 187
Price, Kathryn 148
Pudney, Alex 229
Pullum, Geoffrey 174
Purkiss, Deborah 149, 153
Puxty, Shirley (formerly Beck) 184, 228

Quinnell, Shirley ("Bill") 77, 105

Radelat, Adele 171, 204
Rahtz, Roland 74, 81, 83-4, 108, 124, 133, 140
Railton, Sarah 191
Rand, Roy 75
Rayner, Emma 256
Raynham, Edward 34
Reddaway, E.J.F. 130, 171
Redman, Alderman 101
Rees, James 211, 223-4, 235
Rees, Malcolm 138, 204, 208
Reeve, Andrew 173
Rehling, Nicola 187, 190
Reynolds, Emma 235, 238, 254, 265
Reza, Ali 200
Richardson, Dennis 17
Richardson, Emma 249, 262
Richardson, Rachael 233
Riddle, C. 109
Riddock, Hannah 236
Rigby, Nicola 220, 222, 224
Rimmer, Diana 188
Rishman, Geoffrey 211, 260
Roberts, Tony 107
Robertson, Charles 48
Robinson, Christina 272
Robinson, W.H. 45
Robshaw, A.P. 110
Roche, F.L. 45
Rose, Lucy 265, 274

Rose, Michael 168
Ross, D.J. 108
Rouncefield, Andrea 218
Rouncefield, Ellen 218
Rouncefield, James 216-9, 220, 223-4, 226, 230, 235, 242, 245, 247, 249, 250-1, 253, 257, 264-5, 271, 273, 276
Rouncefield, John 218
Rowe, Jenni 254, 263, 266
Rowland, Jim 164
Rowlands, Matthew 272
Rowswell, Jonathan 229
Roy, Ovishek 229, 232
Roy, Sally 258
Rucinski, Kajtan 223, 225
Ruffer-Turner, Marianne 208
Rushton, Michael 197-8, 235, 244-245, 256
Russan, Dominic 208, 233, 238, 247
Rust, Pippa 192
Ruth, Christopher 261
Ryan, Mary 149
Rycroft, Joanne 260-261, 273

Sale, Mike 138, 148
Salton-Cox, Glyn 235, 236
Sams, Brian 160-1, 170, 206, 208
Sander, Kenneth 43, 46, 59
Sandercock, W.J. 90
Sargent, Daniel 195
Saunt, Hayley 265, 274
Sayell, Nicola 271
Schulz, Kirsten 231
Sclater, James 267
Scott, Will 130, 204, 208
Selvey, E. 87
Semple, S. 118, 122, 127-8, 147
Sennett, Alice 162
Sennett, John 158-9, 161-4, 166-7, 170, 173, 176-8, 180-4, 186, 188, 190-1, 203-4, 209, 212-5
Sennett, Karen 162
Sennett, Paul 162
Seve, Brian 189, 199, 257
Sewell, John 132, 230
Sexton, Richard 193
Shaw, Ruth 149
Shaw, Susan 149
Sheehan, Faye 249
Sheehan, John 261
Shepherd, Lucy 231
Shields, Dawn 225
Shires, Susan 243, 250, 265
Short, Lisa 222
Side, Eric 83, 107-8, 121
Simber, Brian 257-258
Simmonds, Stanley 79, 96, 114, 140, 167

Simmons, Brian 172, 190
Simmons, Gary 188
Simms, Valerie 125
Simons, "Bud" 54
Simpson, Colin 204, 208-9
Sked, Julia 174
Slater, David 131
Smart, Amanda 265
Smith, Carly 224
Smith, Cynthia 141, 167, 199, 214
Smith, E.T. Ashley 96
Smith, Glynis 199, 211, 215
Smith, Hayley 207
Smith, Julia 229
Smith, Julie 125
Smith, Mark 169
Smith, P.J. 81
Smith, Rebecca 267
Smith, T.M.C. 172
Smith, Walter 66, 236
Smith, William 33
Smithers, Waldron 18, 26, 84-6
Snell, Philippa 266
Solbé, Robert 130, 141, 226
Southgate, Diane 138, 159
Spicer, Arthur 43, 48
Spinks, Angela 190-1
Spinks, Michelle 172
Spittles, Sally 220
Spurgin, Basil 7
Stacey (caretaker) 60, 63
Stackhouse, Daniel 274
Stafford, Andrew 141-2, 164, 168, 171
Standidge, Eric 132, 148
Stanyon, Arthur 6, 28, 31, 41, 51, 76
Starr, Nicholas 142, 226, 240
Statham, P. 123
Stawski, Helen 229
Stead, Barrington 75, 88
Steele, William 99
Stemp, Jack 267
Stent, Catherine 267, 273
Stephenson, Dorothy ("Steve") 113, 150, 155, 165, 214, 221
Stevens, Marilyn 204, 230
Stoddart, Joe 255
Stoddart, Tom 238
Stone, Lauren 229
Stonham, Douglas 30, 33, 60
Strange, Nicola 193
Strayhorn, Billy 255
Stringer, Andrew 245
Stringer, Leslie 52, 79, 125, 186
Stuart, Kenneth 6, 28, 29, 31-2, 34
Stubberfield, Gareth 172
Stubberfield, Mark 165
Stubbs, H.G. 33, 37

INDEX OF NAMES

Suddards, Colin 59
Sullivan, Anthony 228, 249
Sutherland, Gordon 129
Sutton, J. 123
Sweet, B. 81
Swift, John 75
Syms, J. 58

Tabert, J.K. 104
Taggart, Hilary 165, 189
Talbot (caretaker) 66
Talbot, Anne 66
Talbot, P.K. 124
Taurins, Adrian 230
Taylor, David 197, 221
Taylor, Helen 140, 157
Taylor, P.H. 42, 53
Taylor, Patrick 164, 167
Taylor, Jack 267
Temple, John 160, 195
Thatcher, Margaret 18, 123, 126-8, 142, 161, 169, 185, 191, 202
Thomas, Claire 223, 232
Thomas, Eric 151
Thomas, J.H. 9
Thomas, Matthew 266
Thompson, Pat 130, 150
Thomson, K. 41
Thornton, Patricia 159
Tiarks sisters, the 15
Tipper, Carol 189, 249
Tipping, Claire (see "Thomas")
Tipping, Tony 189, 218, 232, 240
Tolliday, Richard 140
Tomlin, Cyril 23, 32, 76
Tomlinson, Frank 79, 80, 88, 100, 140
Tomlinson, George 75
Treloar, Anna-Marie 262
Tricker, Kenneth 164, 171, 196, 214
Trigg, Myrna 218, 228
Trodd, Kate 154, 225
Troth, Claire 223, 232
Trotz, Clarence 200
Tse, Maya 239, 255, 260-261
Tucker, Fiona 223, 232
Tuppen, Peter 168
Turner, David 121, 131
Turvill, Ian 185, 187

Ubank, Courtney 273
Ubee, Phil 254, 256, 259-60, 262-64
Unwin, Maggie 228

Valentine, Marelle 230, 238, 274
Vass, Olaf 255

Veness, Peter 61
Vignaux George 75
Vincent, Katherine 255
Visser, Brad 254
Vitagliano, Joe 243, 252-255, 259, 268-71

Wakeford, A.H. 96
Walker, Nigel 264-265, 270, 272
Wallbridge, Richard 235, 238, 245-6
Walledge, Christopher 187
Wallis, Cheryl 157
Walsh, John 34, 40, 63-4, 74, 80-1, 88-9, 97, 107, 117, 124, 129-30, 140-1, 210, 221
Walsh, Sarah 233
Walters, Matthew 256
Ward, Leila 256, 271
Warren, David 174
Warren, Deborah 228, 240
Warwick, David 199, 200
Warwick, Geoffrey 196, 199, 200, 204
Waters, Alan 29, 33
Waters, Arthur 130, 160
Watkins, Jack 64
Watkins, Jane 156
Watson, Nigel 115
Watson, Rex 65, 75
Watts, J 123
Weatherly, Philip 130, 171
Webb, Canon 48, 89
Wederell, Clive 140, 195, 271
Welbourne, G.V. 100
Wells, Charles 141, 168, 189, 209, 215, 234
Wessels, Ian 199, 214
West, Jon 259
Westgate, Ruth 170
Westwood, Ross 259
Weston, John 97, 186
Wheeler, Louise 175, 186-7
Wheeler, Paul 250
Wheeler, Sarah 205, 209
Whitbread, John 6, 29, 31
White, Anne 124, 150, 155, 221
White, Barrington 75
White, Morag 164
White, P.G. 75
Whitehorn, Francis 6, 52
Wickenden, Stephen 239, 246
Wickes, Richard 193, 199
Wild, Lorraine 173, 190
Wiles, Peter 159, 174
Wilkinson, Ellen 75
Wilkinson, Jonny 256
Williams, Andrew 130-1, 160

Williams, C.R. McGregor 5-14, 21-3, 26, 28, 31-6, 38-45, 50, 52-5, 58, 63, 65-7, 71-7, 81, 83-8, 90-1, 100, 103, 110, 113, 143, 148, 169, 171, 199, 207, 217
Williams, Charles 17
Williams, Derwyn 256, 260
Williams, F.A. 73
Williams, Janet (Marshall) 131, 153
Williams, Joe 262
Williams, Keith 219
Williams, Kenneth 139
Williams, Linda 159-60, 195, 274
Williams, Mark 205, 220
Williams, Milton 12, 73, 81, 102, 112, 151, 159, 171, 209
Williams, Norah McGregor 16, 19, 63, 125
Williams, Paul 139, 230
Williams, Roger McGregor 11, 12, 15, 19, 207
Williams, Shirley 160
Williams, Susan McGregor 10, 16-7, 103, 141
Willingham, Keith 107
Willis, Steven 189
Willoughby, Mark 236
Wilsdon, Paul 204, 223, 235
Wilson, Alastair 103-4, 124, 138, 145, 167, 209-11, 228
Wilson, Alexa 172-3, 188-90, 210
Wilson, Alistair 67
Wilson, Andrew 229, 231, 235
Wilson, Harold 110, 112, 122, 135
Wilson, JoAnna 152
Windeatt, Ian 160, 189
Wise, Doug 261, 271
Wittgenstein, Ludwig 55
Wood, Godfrey 52
Wood, J.B. 96
Woodacre, Linda 258, 261-262, 271
Woodall, Sharon 142
Wooll, Christopher 223, 225, 232, 236, 238-9
Woollard, K.G. 97
Wray, Sarah 272
Wright, Bernard 63
Wright, Edward 75
Wright, Kate 229, 231

Yeoman, J.B. 75, 81
Young, Catherine 156

Zackerwich, Yvonne 218
Ziqiri, Dibran 243, 267, 271